FIRE & LIGHT

an off-road search for the spirit of god

FIRE & LIGHT

an off-road search for the spirit of god

JON ROBERTSON

CELESTIAL ARTS
Berkeley | Toronto

This book is dedicated to the Fire and Light that lives
in all of us—the Spirit of God that makes us one.

Celestial Arts
an imprint of Ten Speed Press
PO Box 7123 • Berkeley, California 94707
www.tenspeed.com

Distributed in Australia by Simon and Schuster Australia, in Canada by Ten Speed Press Canada, in New Zealand by Southern Publishers Group, in South Africa by Real Books, and in the United Kingdom and Europe by Publishers Group UK.

Cover and text design by Katy Brown

Library of Congress Cataloging-in-Publication Data
Robertson, Jon.
  Fire and light : an off-road search for the spirit of God / Jon Robertson.
    p. cm.
  Summary: "A nondenominational search for the Spirit of God that surveys scriptural, historical, and philosophical traditions; psychological and scientific theories; and personal anecdotes to discover a means of tapping the power of the Spirit"--Provided by publisher.
  Includes bibliographical references and index.
  ISBN-13: 978-1-58761-266-4
  ISBN-10: 1-58761-266-6
  1. Spirituality. I. Title.

  BL624.R6219 2006
  204--dc22

2006018283
Printed in the United States of America
First printing, 2006

1 2 3 4 5 6 7 8 9 10 — 10 09 08 07 06

contents

Acknowledgments

This book would not have been possible without the generosity of a number of wonderful people. Foremost among them is Robin Robertson for her dauntless assistance with transcription, proofreading, advice, guidance, and patience throughout the year it took to write it.

Grateful appreciation also goes to the many people who granted interviews, for the theme of the Spirit is so vibrantly alive in their experiences, expertise, and comments. They are Joan Borysenko, Ph.D.; Larry Dossey, M.D.; Richard Henry Drummond, Ph.D.; Charles T. Tart, Ph.D.; Rev. R. Scott Walker, Ed.D.; Fred Alan Wolf, Ph.D.; Santi Meunier, Ph.D.; Connie Faivre; David Gordon, Ph.D.; Dani Vedros, LCSW; Carol Sue Janes, J.D.; Adam Ward; Franklin Takei, Ph.D.; Tish Kronen-Gluck; Sangeeta Kumar; Herbert "Avrum" Levine; Nelson Linaburg; John Mein, Ph.D.; Carole Lazur; Rev. Kieth VonderOhe; Rev. Albert Wingate; Kay Sturgis; Rabbi Israel Zoberman; Yug Purush Swami Paramananji; Elaine Hruska; Frank Dolan; and Richard Stoddart.

Also deserving a mountain of gratitude are several readers and advisors, including Rev. Thomas Ehrhardt; Wendell C. Beane, Ph.D.; and Douglas Richards, Ph.D. I also thank Charles T. Tart, Ph.D., for permission to quote from his TASTE online journal; BeliefNet.com, for use of a portion of Laura Sheahen's interview with Susan Sarandon; and Kevin J. Todeschi, for permission to quote from his interview with Deepak Chopra in *Venture Inward* magazine.

Many other kind people lent their inspiration, encouragement, and spiritual support; they include Sensei Shigeru Kanai, religion columnist Betsy Wright Rhodes, B. J. Atkinson, Larry Van Hoose, A. Robert Smith, Peter Schoeb, D.C., Pema Chödrön, and Eithne Ní Bhraonáin.

I also thank my editor, Julie Bennett, for her wise guidance, as well as the entire Celestial Arts/Ten Speed Press team, and my agent, Stacey Glick, of Dystel & Goderich Literary Management.

Preface

The best part of writing the preface is that I know what's coming. As the author, I've had the privilege of writing *Fire and Light*, choosing its content, and plotting a most unusual journey that I hope will intrigue you and perhaps lead you to think about God and yourself in a fresh new way.

My challenge was to write a book that could help people of any belief system discover a deeper understanding of the Spirit of God—the Original Creative Intelligence known the world over by a variety of names. To most people, the Spirit is mysterious and downright confusing. We find passages in the Bible describing actions that the Spirit performed—how it created the world and made it beautiful, turned Saul into another man, and appeared as "tongues of fire" over the heads of the messengers—however, these passages don't really define the Spirit in an understandable way. Ask for a clear definition of the Spirit, and a pat answer often follows: "It is a mystery that we cannot know."

I hope to change all that. I've never had the sense to turn down an opportunity to attempt the impossible, so in 1998, when ideas, people, and resources appeared that an average kid from the Pocono Mountains of Pennsylvania would never have ordinarily encountered, I couldn't resist the urge to try.

My heart pounded with the possibilities of *Fire and Light*—what if I could find a new paradigm for understanding the Spirit of God that could unify people of all faiths in a direct experience with the Divine without all the fine print? Such a book would lay out a common ground for Christians, Jews, Muslims,

Buddhists, Hindus, Orthodox Catholics, evangelicals, and even for scientists, the nonreligious, the agnostics, and the atheists. If successful, such a book would provide an open door to the Spirit for the walking wounded of every faith who not only are spiritually starving, but who also have been mortally wounded by inadequate, enslaving, misleading, or downright hurtful theologies.

Why should it be so difficult to experience and know the Creator—God? If we can't, or aren't supposed to, then it's all a cosmic joke, and I now know that is not the case. In this book, I set out to find a way to convey to the reader a new, unvarnished understanding of the Spirit.

When I first started speaking with experts on this subject, however, I was greeted with stunning pessimism.

"You mean you've got enough on the Holy Spirit to write a whole book?" one Christian minister laughed. "Heck, we only had one unit on it in seminary."

A theology professor with a major American university asked, "How are you going to do that? You mean you actually convinced a publisher that this was a good idea?"

Another said, "Are you sure you want to wade into this dangerous territory?"

I didn't understand their negativity at first, but I do now. Writing about the Spirit of God would be a big job for any scholar, but it was especially tough for a mere philosopher journalist such as me. The arguments go back centuries. Think of the prejudices that come bundled with that word, *spirit*. If someone says "Holy Spirit," you know it's a Christian talking. But what type of Christian? A kid receiving his confirmation at St. Patrick's? A Pentecostal speaking in tongues on Saturday night? If you say "I was guided by Spirit," someone might sneer "Roast in hell, New Ager." The fact is, certain quotations from Scripture have become a threatening litmus test: "Are you saved?" "Are you born again?" Jews would be offended. Buddhists wouldn't know what you're talking about. Such verbal challenges may strike the unsuspecting heart with annoyance or even anger. They can be offensive, used as weapons—as though the Spirit of God would ever need a weapon.

That's why this investigation into the Spirit had to be nontraditional, nondenominational, and unorthodox—that's why I call it an off-road search. I sought to discover the Spirit as the Spirit really is, unadorned, free from prejudice, free from interpretation, and free from jargon and dogma. It had to be an off-road search to determine if the Spirit really exists, how it operates, how living people experience it today, and how we can experience it more. It was ultimately a search that would open my eyes to more startling discoveries about the Spirit than I ever dreamed possible. Throughout the research and writing, I felt that I received progressive levels of understanding, as though revealed by some unseen hand that, one by one, lifted the veils of misunderstanding. It was an adventure that I herein pass on to you.

I started my off-road search with the second line of Genesis, "The earth was without form and void, and darkness was upon the face of the deep; and the Spirit of God was moving over the face of the waters." I then moved through the time of the prophets, to the time of Jesus, and explored the Spirit in various religions—after all, if the Spirit existed before there were any religions, then the Spirit is surely apparent in the scriptures of all people.

It was also important to consider the stories of individuals who have experienced the Spirit of God directly—the mystics and saints—and also a roster of fascinating contemporary people—scientists, psychologists, ministers, and everyday people whose stories weave a picture of the Spirit as the Grand Divine Force that apparently operates without regard to churches, doctrines, or politics, yet empowers any willing heart that inches toward becoming like the Spirit. It's important to note that the people who participated in the interviews for this book used a variety of ways to describe their experiences, of which "Spirit" was only one. Yet the similarities of their experiences, both to each other and to the prophets and mystics, are remarkable and also unexpectedly, or perhaps predictably, comforting.

I wanted to search between the doctrines and around the assumptions for an understanding of the Spirit, naked, as it were, and free of any particular human stamp, while still respecting the potential validity of all views. For this reason, I took the bold step of dropping the use of "He" to refer to the Spirit, using "it" instead. Even though certain Biblical writers used the pronoun, the Spirit is unquestionably not some type of man—man, as these chapters show, is actually some type of spirit! In this effort, I have sincerely tried not to take a side and to let the Spirit speak for itself, as clearly as it could, through my imperfect journalistic lens.

This book answers, at least to my satisfaction, a number of questions that have bugged me for years:

How does the Spirit operate in people?

Does everyone have access to it?

Is the experience the same for everyone?

Why can't more people experience it?

Why don't we experience the Spirit whenever we want?

How did it happen that people, even experts, can't explain the Spirit?

Were there times in history in which people experienced the Spirit every day like the sunshine? Did historical events cause the fading of our experience and understanding?

Does the Spirit only come to us from outside or does it also operate inside us?

How can we best understand the Spirit and experience it more in our lives?

To reach those answers, part of my job was to explore how our experience of the Spirit has been manipulated over the centuries and how we became so far removed from the essence of all that's real and eternal. Because the Christian churches have handed the Spirit off like the puck in a hockey game, and because the historical Roman Church in particular stood guilty of deliberately distancing people from a direct experience with God, certain chapters trace that process; others track the persistent reemergence of the Spirit wherever it could find an open door in the human psyche.

I respectfully draw on the scriptures of many lands and on history, the writings of the prophets and the mystics, and the first-person experiences of people like you and me. For those who care, all Bible quotes are from the Revised Standard Version except where otherwise specified. Endnotes show where I found the quotes I used, and a glossary and index are provided to help you navigate. The bibliography lists my sources and also provides a peek at my personal library and some of the books I love—books that helped me find the Spirit in the years of study, research, and writing that led to this book.

Fire and Light is for anyone who wants to understand God, the Spirit of God, and the meaning of the Divine Image within. The book may turn off those who believe the Bible can only be understood one way or who cannot allow that God speaks to humankind through all the scriptures of the world. But I hope the book will stimulate open-minded thinking in individuals and spur group discussions. I hope it can kindle a fresh new understanding in the hearts of readers who choose to follow the progressive understanding as I discovered it on my off-road search.

This is the journal of how I arrived at the fresh new understanding that *the Spirit seeks that which is like itself.* Conceptually, it's that simple. In practice, however, knowing the Spirit directly is quite another matter. Research shows that there is no single definition of the Spirit of God, yet in people's experiences of the Spirit, I found an amazing "oneness," alive within all of us, that transcends the boundaries of religion.

Introduction

Santi Meunier knows the Spirit of God. The Rhode Island psychologist relates one event in particular that occurred many years ago after a series of crushing disappointments.

Santi grew up in a household devastated by alcoholism, and a lot of guilt had settled on her shoulders. In her mid-twenties she was married and attempting with her husband to get pregnant and start a family. But seven years of trying had produced no results, and the guilt of her childhood bristled. Around the same time, she had been diagnosed with severe endometriosis, had endured two surgeries, and was dreading another. But there was one more disappointment to come.

"That's when I found out that my husband had been seeing my girlfriend up the street. He had gotten her pregnant and told me he wanted to leave me for her. I felt so violated on so many levels."

One Saturday afternoon Santi was lying on the couch in front of the wood stove feeling so much pain she could barely get off the couch.

I wasn't praying, but just being with my pain. I wasn't trying to fix it or exaggerate it, but just being with the grief of what was happening in my life. And I felt this spirit come. As I'm lying flat on the couch, I felt this spirit touch my shoulder and say to me—and I heard very clearly "It's going to be all right."

When he or it touched my shoulder, there was this energy field, and I could see that it was just like light, and it touched my shoulder, and when it touched my shoulder there was this bolt of energy in my body. I remember thinking at the time that this is beyond what a human being can feel, this is a spiritual feeling. It was such bliss. I had such ecstasy. And I knew in that sense not only was the situation okay, but that everything in the world was okay, and that all human experiences were okay. It wasn't just a personal message.

Santi's experience lasted about five seconds, and then it vanished.

Now, whenever I'm afraid or whenever I feel like something's hard or I have doubt, I think of that moment. It wipes out whatever concern I have because in that moment I think I was given a glimpse of what we experience after we die, when we're just spirit.

Years later, Santi is now remarried, but her experience with the Spirit helped pave the way for a new life. It actually turned her life around in a most unexpected way.

Through that experience, I was actually able to forgive my husband and my girlfriend and be happy for them. And I have remained that way. They now have three children, and they're happily married. I came to realize that they were meant to be together, and meant to have those children. Because of that experience, I was able to get past it. Not instantly. It was a process, but I knew that it was meant to be, and that I had to work through my hurt and grief about not having children and not having that marriage. I was eventually able to celebrate what they had found with each other and their children.

One can call Santi's story a divine blessing, a transcendent experience, synchronicity, intervention by the Lord, cosmic consciousness, an experience of unity, inner knowing, or a trick of the subconscious mind, but her description bears remarkable similarities to a whole range of experiences with the Spirit of

God described in the world's scriptures and historical documents, and by people living today.

So what is this Spirit? Is it a being or a divine force? Is it separate from God or another name for God? Is it the sole property of Christians, as many claim—the third member of a divine trinity, even though no such trinity is named in the Bible? Does the Spirit belong to everyone or only to people who practice a religion? Or does everyone actually belong to the Spirit? Does one need a mosque, church, or synagogue in order to experience it?

As a student of philosophy and religion, I've always been intrigued by the most difficult questions. In 1998, it struck me that the concept of a unifying, divine, spiritual intelligence was the toughest question of all to grasp, and I wondered if it would be possible to investigate the Spirit in an objective, journalistic, and nondenominational way. Such an investigation could potentially provide a fresh perspective that anyone could understand. It would have to untangle centuries of theological debate and a centuries-old fog of mystery: Some believe in the Spirit fervently with no understanding; others relegate the whole idea to the province of the Holy Rollers or just plain wishful thinking. Still others get so touchy at even the mention of the word, they're willing to fight about it, either for or against.

Despite the debates, however, millions of people around the world experience unexplained spiritual interventions—last-minute changes that belay some personal disaster or provide an unexpected opportunity. We all have surprise revelations that bloom in the mind or sudden understanding, independent of rational thought, that changes everything at just the right moment. Some people attribute such experiences to serendipity, intuition, or simple coincidence. Others call it the Spirit, grace, Jesus, the Holy Spirit, angels, or the Spirit of God.

THE SPIRIT DEFINED

Throughout the world's religious texts, the Spirit is known by many definitions: it is the "blazing fire" and the "rushing wind" of the Old Testament, the Ruach Elohim that moved over the waters, created the world, and breathed the breath of life into nostrils of humankind. In the New Testament, it's the "light in every man," the "Holy Spirit," the "Spirit of Wisdom," the "Spirit of Truth," the "Spirit of Christ," and others. The Bible also describes a long list of "gifts" that the Spirit gives. The Spirit was the numinous reality of awareness known by the prophets. It was the voice that led Moses through the desert, "clothed" itself with Gideon, and gave Jesus of Nazareth the power for all he did—he even said so. It was also the "comforter" Jesus promised to everyone who observed his simple rules. It is the "fire and light" mentioned in the Midrash, the source from which I have borrowed the title for this book. This is the Spirit that showed on the face of Moses, brought Buddha to enlightenment, and enabled Muhammad to receive the Qur'an. The Spirit became a political pawn in the early Christian churches that separated the East from the West, eventually demanding a reformation.

Yes, the Spirit of God was central to all that.

The Spirit has left its imprint on every page of human history. Browse a little, and you find that the Spirit brushes the lives of people around the world, even now, in mysterious, unpredictable ways. It turns out that nearly every belief system acknowledges such a Spirit, known by various names, that not only activates and unifies the universe, but is also alive inside us.

If that's not intriguing enough for you, the Spirit has been at the center of many bloody battles, reaching back four thousand years, that divided nations and churches and caused the deaths of thousands. The disputes divided the Roman Church from the Eastern; inspired Martin Luther and his followers to separate from Rome; and continues to splinter the Protestant churches today. All this for a two-word phrase—*Holy Spirit*—

that was used only twice in the Torah and uttered by Jesus merely five times.

Did you know that entire communities formed around the Spirit? Or that bands of traveling musician prophets were identified in the Book of Samuel? There were also the second-century Enthusiasts, huge communities in Asia Minor, the twelfth-century Cathars, and the fourteenth-century Beguines who lived in direct, uninterrupted contact with the Spirit of God. And there were many others. The spiritual "elite" thrived in their communities, and the Spirit operated freely among them. Even after spiritual experiences were outlawed by the Roman Church, the Spirit never stopped prodding new prophets and mystics to awaken to the pure and simple, ultimate and eternal, indivisible and knowable Truth.

EXPERIENCING THE DIVINE

For many years I have observed the misery of the spiritually disenfranchised who just don't find God in organized religion, yet who intrinsically feel they know the Divine. I, too, have felt cut off by teachings that insist on some innate human sinfulness and unbridgeable separation from God that can only be transcended after we die, if we have somehow pleased God along the way. I wondered for years if there were some universal solution by which we could unite with God as people once did—in essence, an all-purpose theology.

Most writers who attempt this topic tend to adhere to the Biblical stories, minutely analyzing the spiritual "gifts" described in the Book of Acts and Paul's letters. Little wonder. Describing the Spirit is daunting. Tell it wrong, and you might tiptoe into the swamp of blasphemy, tease the serpent of sacrilege, or even tick off the Spirit—how would you know? We need a new paradigm of understanding and experience with the Spirit that can ratchet us up closer to a direct experience with the Divine. This may be why you are reading this book today.

To achieve a fresh paradigm, I wanted to pursue it without the deadening effect of evangelical buzzwords and intimidating phrases. I also wanted to avoid the New Age habit of referring to everything as the ambiguous "spirit"—spirit did this and spirit did that—and the ubiquitous, but equally vague "connection to spirit." Theologians on all sides rarely agree on a concise definition of the Spirit, against which Jesus said no blasphemy would be forgiven. For me, it's the most important, least understood, most neglected concept in all theology, philosophy, and daily living.

I scrupulously tried to avoid religious lingo and pandering to any particular church or religion. I started by talking to friends and acquaintances to see if I could establish a context for just what the Spirit is and how it operates. My hope was that the Spirit would lead me to an understanding that could unite people instead of divide them. I wanted to discover the Spirit of God— as it was in the beginning, without the prejudices of the ages.

My off-road search honors a broad range of world religious traditions in the hope of discovering the real Spirit, to be able to recognize when the Spirit has touched our lives; the various ways in which the Spirit is known throughout the world; and how one can feel closer to God. I also wanted to find out what went wrong in the religions that keeps the Spirit so remote from real people living real lives. I collected personal stories of the Spirit from a wide variety of people in various traditions, as well as people who live outside any formal belief system.

Writing *Fire and Light* has kicked me upstairs more than I ever thought possible, and I hope it does the same for you. During my interview with biologist and psychologist Joan Borysenko, she used the word *transparent* to describe her state of mind when occasions of contact with the Spirit of God came best. In reading this book, I hope you find your own transparency—a receptivity of heart and mind to the influence, the healing, the wisdom, and the truth that the Spirit of God imparts ceaselessly to anyone who openly, lovingly "has the ears to hear."

Let the off-road search begin.

chapter 1

HIDDEN
in
PLAIN SIGHT

The American philosopher and psychologist William James once said that if you want to understand religion in America, avoid the churches; go directly to the people and listen to their stories, epiphanies, and visions. I found this to be true right off. Although most people you ask haven't a clue what the Spirit is, they can tell you about the day something wonderful happened that changed their lives.

When I began writing this book, I didn't know where to start looking for people who just simply "know" the Spirit, but I didn't have far to look. I have a very interesting collection of friends and acquaintances, so I started with them. For instance, take my friend Nelson Linaburg, a Suffolk, Virginia, organist, composer, and music director, who has had many experiences with the Spirit.

"In my time, I have had what I considered visitations, an aura, or presence, palpably felt," he confided. "And especially on occasions of great need."

Nelson has worked in an astonishing variety of institutions, both Christian and Jewish; this has given him a unique perspective on how the Spirit works. He believes that the Spirit has often influenced his life; for example, when he had been deeply hurt, an event that is still difficult for him to talk about.

> I found myself at home alone, collapsed, desperate to leave this, to sleep, to escape. My body lay quiet, but my mind was restless. Within that state there came silence, and a glow appeared by the door. It was a luminous white light, but I didn't look there. There was no need, because it filled the entire space. There was no sound, just light.
>
> I can't say when it left, but leaving, it left its presence. Though I felt it intensely then, I no longer had any stress. It was as though it had said, "Now all is well." And I knew a peace. I believe there was a visitation. Someone was sent to right things for me. And it was so. This form without being, left its memory. As I have read, "The spirit also helpeth us."

Nelson said that some part of the Spirit has stayed with him ever since, returning like a periodic visitor.

"Great comfort came instantly," he said, "and it's occurred to me that the Spirit is really a personal thing. You have to have 'been there' to understand it. You can hardly even write or talk about it, but you can know it."

Nelson also said he feels the Spirit when he is composing music or playing the organ. He said it's not like a "burning bush" experience, "but perhaps at times there's a certain fervor or heat that may be the nearness of God."

> For me it's certainly something that comes and goes. There can be, indeed, an ecstasy—is that God? And in playing, yes, but more rarely. In my second year in college, I might have been possessed in one afternoon piano class program. The teacher was thoroughly convinced that my playing was exceptional—and good, exceptional things have to come from a divine source.

Nelson also said,

Creations and re-creations have to have the Godhead somewhere just behind them. Sometimes, and often in these later years, I have things revealed in dreams. Solutions to problems appear, like filling in missing or unfinished parts. I like to think that this is the Spirit at work. Comfort and serenity come to the whole being, and one can walk with a calmness and assurance.

Both Nelson and Santi described a visitation by some entity or force that conveyed instant reassurance and comfort. They also explained that their experiences with the Spirit come and go— the influence of the Spirit has remained with them. For Nelson, revelations now come in dreams, and solutions to problems can appear. Their stories encouraged me in my off-road search, so I asked around. It wasn't long before I met up with eighty-year-old Frank Dolan of Los Angeles.

TIME VANISHED

Frank Dolan travels the country in a motor home. At eighty, the retired career Navy man was mysteriously guided back into the arms of a love that he had lost during World War II. His story begins in April of 1944.

"I was in a Navy school in Boston," he explained, "when I first met and fell in love with Marie Ferguson."

Then twenty-four, Marie had gone to Boston from her home near Townsend, Massachusetts, just south of the New Hampshire border, seeking a secretarial job in the war industries there. Four years earlier, Marie had lost her husband, Raymond, to a car accident. She had a five-year-old son named Ray, Jr.

"Marie and I fell in love almost right away," he told me, "and we wanted to get engaged."

But during wartime, people's lives take sudden, unpredictable turns. Marie found a better-paying job in the War Department in Washington, D.C., so she was moving again. The plan was that Frank, then nineteen, would finish school in Boston and then catch up with Marie and her son while on leave.

"We wanted to get married," he said, "but with the war, I didn't want Marie to find herself widowed again, so we decided to get engaged and wait."

In the summer of 1944, Frank drew fifteen days leave. The plan was that he'd take Marie across the country by train to meet his parents. They'd pick out rings and make the engagement official. The war, however, had other plans for them.

"Instead of my leave," he continued, "I got an immediate transfer to the Pacific."

In the process, Frank lost his sea bag, and with it Marie's address and phone number. "I had no way to reach her or explain what happened. I couldn't remember where she worked or even the name of the town where she was from. I had said goodbye to Marie in the summer of '44 and never saw her again."

After the war, millions of prewar love affairs faded as peacetime led the war's survivors along different paths. Without another word between them, Frank and Marie moved on, eventually marrying others and bearing the unhealed wounds that the fates of war had dealt them. Frank continued his Navy career and had three children with his wife of fifty years, who died in 2004.

Then one day in the spring of 2005, Frank found himself driving his motor home down through New Hampshire. When he crossed the Massachusetts line, the name of a town jumped out at him.

"Townsend!" he said aloud. "I couldn't get the name out of my mind. I drove on past it, but this strong feeling kept bothering me about it, urging me to go back. It was then that I remembered—that was the town Marie was from."

He decided to see if there were any relatives still around, and amazingly ran into some cousins of Marie's first husband. They not only remembered Marie, but they knew where her now-grown son Ray was living, near Santa Fe, New Mexico. Not only that, they told him that Marie was living there with him.

Frank immediately jumped back into the RV and drove practically nonstop to New Mexico.

"I was overcome with the need to find her," he explained. "As nervous as could be, I knocked on Ray's door, and there she was—Marie. And we fell in love all over again. We picked up right where we left off."

Frank was overjoyed to finally be able to explain why he had disappeared, and Marie finally understood what went wrong so many years ago.

"Sixty-one years was like sixty-one seconds," they agreed. They got married that June. Frank credits the Spirit of God for bringing him back to Townsend and guiding him to his lost love from a lifetime ago.

Santi, Nelson, and Frank were individuals from diverse backgrounds who made contact with—or were contacted by—some loving intelligence that changed their lives. This unseen contact intervened in their perceptions, altered their thinking, or brought blissful comfort in the face of certain disaster, and, in a small but indisputable way, altered the course of history. They all believed they had contact with the Spirit of God, and I found dozens of others with revealing stories to tell. Their stories remind me of my own experiences with the Spirit, which began at age thirteen, when I was first inspired to contemplate all things divine—a pursuit that remains with me to this day.

CHANGED FOREVER

When I was a child, I was filled with something powerful and free. I felt like I was a part of some invisible loving energy that charged my days and nights. It was in the clouds, the sun, the stones, and the living things. The feeling was in the background as I played kickball, explored the woods, or walked to school. It fueled my fascination with a mud puddle or the movements of a strange new bug. It supercharged my innocence as I ventured from my neighborhood for the first time or hid behind the hedges with my platoon of eight-year-olds.

As I grew up, however, early training kicked in, and I gradually lost touch with that happy feeling. By the time I reached junior high school, I had forgotten about it completely, until one night when I experienced what I now understand to have been the Spirit of God.

At thirteen, I was already a fugitive from Catholicism, having attended Catholic school only through the fifth grade. I'm not sure how much of that training stuck, but I was certainly afraid of committing sins. I always prayed when I was afraid, though I hadn't seen much proof that prayer worked.

THE PURLOINED MONOGRAPH

When I was in the eighth grade, my mother, worrying for my soul, enrolled me in religion classes at the local rectory on Tuesday nights, where Monsignor Logan coaxed me and my fellow public school reprobates through a study book. (We were actually more interested in the beer we had stashed for later.)

During that class in the winter of 1963, I wrote down my first theory about the nature of God. This shouldn't be construed as the work of a child preoccupied with religion, or that I was the star student of those weekly classes. At thirteen, I was a rebel without a cause, a freethinker who always thought he could find a better way to say things, express some concept, or ask a question that could stump the teacher. Father Logan didn't realize it, but he was the cause of my curiosity. He had not been able to answer to my satisfaction what God was.

"Well, of course, God is the Supreme Being," he said. "Beyond that, he is too great for us to comprehend."

"You mean, God made us so we can't understand him?"

I wasn't going to take no for an answer. If he couldn't answer it, I was determined to dazzle him with my penetrating insight. And then one night, I was contemplating the starry winter sky on a promontory overlooking the Pocono Mountains in Pennsylvania where I lived. In school, we had been studying atomic theory, so as I gazed at the planets and stars, I was seized by a powerful vision. Under the sparkling canopy of the heavens, I was overwhelmed by a profound expansion of my understanding. Suddenly, I perceived the stars and planets as the atoms of some grander universe, and our atoms as the stars and planets of some smaller universe. I was possessed with the instantaneous perception of the infinite—a worlds-within-worlds universe that never ends. It was a warm joyful feeling that seemed to come from outside of me, yet also within me. It poured down through me and then bubbled up like fizz. It filled my sails with a wind of new awareness.

The realization vividly revived that old background happiness I had known as a little boy. It was that feeling again. My childhood power and freedom. That night, I suddenly beheld the universe in its simplest essence. I perceived how God permeates everything: outer and inner space, planets and molecules, nature, matter, and the mind—all alike in a unified substance of common light. I knew God was everywhere. Everything was connected to everything, and God was the force that held it all together. It was thrilling, like at age five when I visited the beach and saw the bright sun and the crashing waves for the first time. In that moment, I knew that everything in my life, in the world, would be all right. All creation—everything—was in the mind, I thought. It was all one, and not separate in any way. My mind was part of the backdrop of the universe—God's mind encompassed human mind. To God, there was no difference between mind and substance. All was one, as air knows air. And the divine Spirit was there for us to unify with any time we wished.

At thirteen, of course, I didn't have the vocabulary to express all this, but this was how it felt. I excitedly wrote down my experience in pencil on loose-leaf paper, like a young Galileo (or Martin Luther) bursting with discovery. The following Wednesday I presented my monograph—my first rebellious religious writing—to Monsignor Logan, who mumbled that he would read it when he had time.

But the next two classes were mysteriously canceled, and it was nearly a month before I saw him again. When the day finally arrived, I asked him about my paper, and he impatiently said that he hadn't read it yet. I was deeply disappointed. I asked for two more weeks, and after that, I stopped asking and eventually forgot about it. I moved on into the emotional labyrinth of my teens, and my memory of the spiritual event winked out until many years later.

Then one day in 2001, while I was researching this book, the memory of that early experience returned. I remembered both the experience and how Monsignor Logan put me off. That day, I realized how hard I'd have to work in order for this book to be taken seriously by clergy members across the board.

I didn't know it then, but I now believe that what happened to me at thirteen was my first intervention by the Spirit of God. Unlike Santi and Nelson, I wasn't in the throes of a crisis—yet, like them, I experienced physical and emotional sensations while perceiving the profound unity of life. The Spirit didn't clue me in to some existential need, as with Frank Dolan, but the knowledge that everything in my life—everything in the whole world—was going to be okay. In common with all of them, my understanding expanded, and I was changed forever.

IN THE BRIGHTEST OF LIGHT

My first experience with the Spirit had not been planned. I hadn't asked for it, nor had I earned it by "being good." It was never in my mind to set forth a personal cosmology—I didn't even know what it meant. The experience just happened. One thing was certain: I would look at the universe through new eyes forevermore. I'd never go back to a way of thinking that excluded the beauty of the all-pervading oneness. I've forgotten the specifics of that event many times, but the added awareness has always been with me. In the 1980s, it returned again and saved my life.

In 1987, my wife Robin and I found ourselves in a deplorable physical and mental condition. We were in our mid-thirties, and eight years of hard work and partying had taken its toll. We were stressed out and drinking too much, and we had become mentally, emotionally, and spiritually unhealthy. We knew we had to change, so we redesigned our lives from top to bottom.

Cold turkey, we disciplined ourselves. We fasted. We read the scriptures of many lands, including the Bible, which we'd never read seriously before. We learned how to meditate, and through the fasting, meditation, and prayer, we grew closer to the Spirit—previously impenetrable passages in Scripture now leapt out with heightened meaning. It worked with every book we read, and our capacity to understand mushroomed. Surrounded by the Spirit day to day, we felt like children—as we used to say, "in the arms of Mom and Dad."

For two years, we drank no alcohol and took no drugs, not even aspirin. We declared a moratorium on all toxic consumables: we stopped watching TV and movies and shunned popular music, favoring the harmonizing effects of classical music instead. We also purified our diet, adopting, at first, the macrobiotic diet that excludes meat, eggs, white flour, and sugar (call this my monastic period). We later moved to a vegan diet, but the stringent macrobiotic experience was very healing and cleansing on many levels.

This was a dramatic shift for us, but extreme conditions called for extreme measures. We'd felt cut off from any form of spiritual life, as we had given up on the Church ages before (we were both raised Roman Catholic). We tried a variety of church services: Catholic, Baptist, Episcopal, UCC, and Unity—just to see if we could find the truth within the familiar forms that we had rejected. We learned a lot about forgiveness and about the individuality of priests and ministers.

But the only way I succeeded in not backsliding into my former self-indulgence was by adopting a rigorous spiritual practice. I adopted five daily sessions of meditation and prayer. It was a meditation practice in which I felt close to God and "informed" from within. (My meditation practice is described in chapter 10.) It wasn't a priest or minister who had brought this about, but my self-directed spiritual discipline and sincere desire to know the truth about myself and God.

When I first began to practice meditation, in the initial weeks it seemed like I was getting nowhere. By the third week, however, I found I was able to achieve a peaceful easy feeling. My concentration improved for everyday activities. I was less stressed. I became more discerning about people, habits, and entertainment. I believe that my basic intelligence improved. The shimmering light seemed to fill me like when I was thirteen. All I had to do was close my eyes and feel love, which I was able to feel so passionately that tears would run down my face. Eventually, I could feel love for one and all as easily as flipping on a light switch.

After a while, my meditations took on a life of their own. I discovered that I had a natural ability to engage in lucid, dreamlike meditations that were beyond mere imagination. Soon I was able to go into deep meditation almost instantly. I believed then as I do now that meditation put me in touch with the Spirit and opened my heart. Over the course of two years, I came to feel so close to the Spirit, I felt like I had an inner counselor guiding my every choice. I made better decisions in those years. I took the guidance for granted, but how I wish I had made it last.

The problem was that I allowed myself to run out of time. Choosing the Spirit of God was the most important decision of my life, but I allowed the demands of career to gradually wean me off my spiritual practice.

In the mid-1990s, I left behind the freewheeling life of a freelance writer and got a respectable job that required neckties and punctuality. I got swallowed up in the pressures and office politics, and left behind the joy-filled spiritual life that had been two years in the making. I got lazy, drawn back into the distractions of the world. Instead of the Spirit, I began to nurture my desire to experience the delicious buffet table we call life. Only after a number of my precious aspirations went south did I realize what I'd lost. Apparently, I had adopted attitudes that repelled the Spirit, such as "I can do this all by myself." I now know that life is much easier when breathing the atmosphere of the Spirit.

Now, my closeness to the Spirit occurs when I achieve some level of attunement. Researching and writing this book in 2005 brought me in close touch again. Tuned to the frequency of love, the Fire and Light poured freely into my mind. I was flooded with grand ideas of helping others experience God directly, and this book is the result. The Spirit awakened me once again, warmed me, inspired me, preserved me, shook free my conscience, and sharpened my common sense—with such a momentum that communing with the Spirit required little effort. Through the Spirit of God, I've had experiences in the brightest of light, shivering in awe, crying tears of joy. And in that light, this past year, I've known the fire of change.

I should point out that clean living and a spiritual practice didn't turn me into a saint or solve all my problems. The Spirit eased me away from addictions, emotional habits, and negative thinking, but it didn't take away the work required to keep myself in the light. It didn't entertain me when I got bored or uplift me when I got disgusted, depressed, or selfish. Nor did it sustain in me the faith in things unseen—you can forget the Spirit, I learned, even after having known it! Keeping aligned with the Spirit, I further learned, requires daily effort.

The Spirit did give me a lasting perspective, however. It provided a baseline for my thinking, feeling, and behavior by which I judge all my thoughts and actions. It gave me a handhold in that magnificent realm where eternal joy shimmers in the perpetual now. It gave me the knowledge that I came from there—that we all did—and will return there soon enough. The day you experience the Spirit for yourself, you will know what I mean.

The Spirit opened the door to guidance, and even gave me the gumption to follow it once it was revealed in my mind.

I was changed forever, and my later life as a writer has been an obsessive attempt to recapture that feeling, that experience, and convey it to others through my writing.

These days, many people are on their own search for direct experience with God, and the search is leading them beyond the walls of tradition and orthodoxy. If you break down all this searching to its essence, you find that the goal is always the same—knowing the Spirit of God, however you define it. But this begs a question: With over twenty-one thousand religions in the United States, is it any wonder that all this searching's going on?

A CHANGING LANDSCAPE

The experiences reported earlier in this chapter aren't typical by any means. Most of the Spirit experiences one finds in books tend to be conversion experiences, in which an individual has a "lightning strike" moment that deepens faith or converts that person to a new faith altogether. The fact is, more than a quarter of the U.S. population is not affiliated with any religious institution.[1] Perhaps this is a symptom of pandemic hunger for spiritual teachings and practices that nourish the soul, rather than just maintain the outward appearances. It may also be a reaction against the aggressive and political use of religious teachings for arrogant and bloody ends.

What else do the statistics reveal about spirituality in America? According to a 2005 CBS News poll, 36 percent of Americans said they combine the teachings or philosophies of different religions. In an interview with CBS reporter Byron Pitts, author and theologian Karen Armstrong said, "It's part of a giant universal human quest for meaning. That doesn't mean that they're abandoning their own religion, but they are quite naturally and spontaneously without any great fanfare turning to other faiths for wisdom."

In the United States today, there are nearly twice as many religions as twenty-five years ago.[2] Although 83 percent of Americans identify themselves as Christian, a third of them don't attend any particular church.[3]

U.S. evangelical pollsters traditionally fix American church attendance at around 45 percent; however, a study published in 1998 by the *American Sociological Review* showed that attendance is actually around 20 percent for Protestants and 28 percent for Roman Catholics.[4] In 2003, *Time* magazine reported that church membership is declining in Europe, and that in fact practicing Christians will soon be the minority there.

Some say this shows the disintegration of the churches or the diluting of faith, but it also shows that people are seeking genuine experience with the Divine with no strings attached, to slake their thirst however they can. Although church attendance is falling, belief and interest in God, as well as in personal spirituality, are on the rise. People are even willing to defy church authority to do what they think is right.

A case in point: On Christmas Eve 2005, in St. Louis, fifteen hundred people attended what the archbishop had declared to be an "illicit" mass. The mass was conducted by Father Marek Bozek, a priest who had been excommunicated for leaving his own parish to help the parishioners of St. Stanislaus Kostka Church. Eighteen months before, the archbishop had removed all the priests from St. Stan's to force the parish to conform to certain financial practices. He announced that anyone who attended Father Bozek's mass would be guilty of a mortal sin, which is quite serious in the Catholic Church. But that night, the crowds overflowed into adjoining buildings. People came from as far away as Oregon and Washington, D.C., to support Father Bozek and the little parish, including many lapsed Catholics who attended because they believed it was the right thing to do.

Father Bozek said he had agonized over his decision to help St. Stan's, but said the parish had been without a priest for nearly a year and a half. For him, going against the archbishop was a very serious decision of conscience.

"I will visit the sick and bury the dead," Father Bozek said. "I will laugh with those who are laughing and cry with those who are crying."[5] The story of St. Stan's shows that the Spirit draws people to itself, just as the Spirit within urges people toward unity and a genuine experience with the Divine.

THE DIVINE BREATH

To understand what the Spirit is, let's begin with the Judeo-Christian tradition, as it is familiar to most Westerners.

The word *spirit* comes from the Latin *spiritus*, meaning "breath" or "wind." This is a translation of the colorful Hebrew word *ruach*, whose derivatives include *riach*, "to cause to breathe or to blow," and a related verb *rawach*, "to breathe, have breathing room, or to be spacious." Although the Hebrew *ruach* is used often in the Old Testament, the phrase "Holy Spirit," *ruach ha kodesh*, is used only twice. It can, however, be found in the Talmud and Midrash. Most interestingly, in Hebrew as well as Aramaic, the language spoken by Jesus of Nazareth, *ruach* can also mean "the seat of the mind."[6]

The People of the Book—the Jews, Christians, and Muslims—make the most of the Spirit in the Torah, the first five books of the Bible that these religions hold in common. In the second line of Genesis, the Spirit makes its dramatic debut in the creation of the world:

> In the beginning God created the heavens and the earth. The earth was without form and void, and darkness was upon the face of the deep; and the Spirit of God [breath, wind] was moving over the face of the waters. And God said, "Let there be light"; and there was light. (Gn 1:1–3)

The Supreme Creative Mind, God, creates a visible universe by blowing the breath of its Spirit into the void. For example, it is my will to build a garage next to my house. I envision it, but in order to manifest it outside of my own mind, I use my hands to build it.

According to the Bible, the Spirit was the dynamic means for every aspect of creation. In Genesis 1:2 above, we read that the Divine Breath moved over the waters and, later, breathed the breath of life into the nostrils of humankind. The Spirit also gave physical and intellectual power to humankind.[7] In fact, the Old Testament says that all visible things were called into being after God sent forth the Spirit.[8] Even the wilderness becomes fruitful due to an outpouring of the Spirit.[9] Job 26:13 credits the Spirit for creating the beauty of the heavens and even forming the serpent. The Spirit gave amazing physical, intellectual, and prophetic powers to the prophets. All the elements of life— body, mind, and spirit—are attributed directly or indirectly to the action of the Spirit of God.

The Old Testament also refers to the Spirit as the binder of covenants;[10] the guider of judgments;[11] and hallower of people, places, and things.[12] And those are just some of the biggies. Clearly, according to the Bible, the Spirit is "God in action," creating the world and humans, too. In the Talmud, the Fathers first spoke about the Divine Breath that makes its presence known in a "rushing wind" or a "blazing fire." In the Midrash, the Spirit is referred to as the feminine presence of God and also the "fire and light."

In the New Testament, the word for Spirit changes from the Hebrew *ruach* to the Greek *pneuma*. (The Latin *spiritus* would come later.) The Holy Spirit becomes the Pneuma Hagion, which was personified as "he." In the Christian experience, Spirit seems to become more personal, referred to with a variety of names: "the Spirit of God," "the Spirit of the Lord," "the Spirit of the Father," "the Spirit of Jesus," "the Spirit of Christ," and "the Spirit of Truth." One source says that the Spirit became "Holy

Spirit" because the early Christians were actually Jews who were forbidden by law to write or utter the name of G-d.

TOWARD THE VOICE OF WATER

Some Christians believe that the Spirit belongs exclusively to them, but of course this can't be so. Judging by the scriptures of the world, it's safe to say that human beings deeply desire direct experience with some higher, responsible, creative power. As the Persian Sufi Rumi captured it, "We can't help being thirsty, moving toward the voice of water. Milk drinkers draw close to the mother. Muslims, Christians, Jews, Buddhists, Hindus, shamans, everyone hears the intelligent sound and moves with thirst to meet it."[13] People who believe the Spirit to be the personal property of their faith will be surprised to realize how well known the Spirit is in the world's wisdom traditions. Those who are educated in their faith know that the Spirit existed long before there were any institutions at all—in fact, before religions, and even before the world. Here are but a few references from other traditions:

> He whom the Spirit chooses for his own, only he can comprehend the Spirit. This Spirit is hidden in all beings. (Katha Upanishad, before 400 B.C.E.)
>
> ... [We cannot understand] what life is until we know what the Spirit is—the seat of the knowledge of God. (Al-Ghazali, *Alchemy of Happiness*, twelfth-century Persia)
>
> Because it calculates not, Spirit shines in lonely glory in what is beyond the world. ... Though Spirit lies beyond the world, it stays ever within them. —Seng-Chao (388–414), *Book of Chaos*

The Qur'an refers to the Holy Spirit as Ruh Al-Qudus (the Angel Gabriel): "Say, the Holy Spirit has brought the revelation from thy Lord in truth, in order to strengthen those who believe, and as a guide and glad tidings to Muslims." (An-Nahl 16:102)

Buddhists don't profess a creator-god, but they acknowledge a supreme reality that they call Amida Buddha. In Buddhism, Spirit is also known as the "breath of the Atman (soul), a function of the higher mental plane, the buddhic plane. . . ."[14] The religion of ancient Persia, Zoroastrianism, was one of the first based on one god. In the Zoroastrian tradition, the Holy Spirit (Spenta Mainyu) is an aspect of the Wise Lord (Ahura Mazda) and created all life and goodness. (There are 150,000 practicing Zoroastrians in the world today.) The sense of *ruach* meaning "seat of the mind" parallels the Sanskrit words *chitta* (consciousness), *ajna* (perception), and *atman* (the divine self, or soul).

The Spirit continued to breathe its inspiring breath through the time of the prophets. Throughout the four thousand years since Abraham, the Spirit is still the Spirit, and it is still operating in the world. How do we know? Through the amazing track record of the Fire and Light in human history, among people of all backgrounds.

The Divine Breath continues to touch people every day, and they're all around us, if we look for them. One day I realized that I know an uncanny number of them—enlightened people, holy people, from whom I have learned great lessons in my off-road search.

A FEW UNUSUAL FRIENDS

Whenever I read the world's scriptures, I sometimes experience that connection to God that I first encountered at age thirteen. In my travels, that feeling now wells up inside me in unexpected places. It bothered me, at first, that I was able to feel close to God whenever I saw a house of worship: church, stupa, synagogue, cathedral, zendo, mosque, or temple—it didn't matter. I didn't even have to go inside. Somehow, just the reminder kindled a warm feeling in my heart. Many times in my adult life, I've been overwhelmed with this feeling. It comes in the form of sudden inspirations and feelings of ecstasy in every cell.

I'm an incurable addict for these brief moments in which I feel close to God. I have felt this sensation while listening to a Baptist minister and while watching a Catholic priest hold the Eucharist aloft. I have felt it listening to the ancient, haunting Hebrew of a cantor's song as well as at a Friends' Meetinghouse among the "plain folk," Quakers who might stand when moved by the Spirit to speak, and who seek "the peace in the center." I have also felt it at a Hindu ashram, during a silent retreat, during a walking meditation through the cathedral of a forest, and while chanting in Sanskrit during *darshan* in praise of the Effulgent Light at the Core of All Being, or singing in a church choir. I have vibrated in the stunning energy and cacophony of a Pentecostal service and felt a shift in my thinking while bumping heads with a Tibetan Buddhist lama. I've been moved to tears while observing a Dominican friar praying softly on a bench in a quiet grove surrounded by azaleas in bloom. I've bowed my head in a Zen garden and cried at the tomb of Francis of Assisi.

If the Spirit exists, it surely isn't limited to hanging out in buildings. It would be everywhere. Research shows that the Spirit doesn't discriminate, the way people do, by gender, race, religion, church, or belief system. It seems to express itself through people who somehow make themselves even temporarily more like it. At least this is what I have learned from people who seem to know it. Despite my own checkered spiritual resume, I keep coming into contact with inspired people, and over the years I've assembled a stunning collection of friends and acquaintances in whom the Spirit of God radiantly shines.

How else can I explain my acquaintance with Rev. R. Scott Walker, Ed.D., a Southern Baptist minister and author in Waco, Texas, or Shigeru Kanai, a priest with the Buddhist Butsugenshyu sect in Japan? I've been friends with Swami Divyananda, a monk and devotee of the late Swami Satchidananda, the spiritual leader who brought Integral Yoga to the West from India and who gave the opening invocation at Woodstock '69. I once worked with Rev. Albert Wingate, former pastor of Unity of

Naples, Florida, and edited books for Rabbi Yonassan Gershom, a Hasidic rabbi and author from Sandstone, Minnesota.

In the 1980s, I began to visit churches of other faiths, finding to my surprise many astute ministers who seemed "turned on" by God. I first met Scott Walker when he was pastor of First Baptist Church in Charleston, South Carolina. What struck me about him was the fire in his eyes as he spoke—not from his sermon notes, or his expert delivery, but because I could sense in him a deep and profound connection with Spirit. His sense of humor regarding things Divine cinched it—this was one Catholic boy who had finally realized that the Protestants aren't destined to roast in hell, as I'd been taught in elementary school!

Scott is a trained psychologist and college instructor, and his sermons are alive with the truth. He speaks from the heart. Ask him a question, and he sometimes shrugs, "I don't know," something I'd never heard in a church before. From within this honest sense that he, too, was struggling through life right along with me, he passed on some advice that I needed—as though by intuition. Scott's sermons helped me to discover that those who truly know the Spirit are able to transcend doctrine while still honoring it. They are able to open the door to others so they, too, can make its acquaintance.

I met Rabbi Yonassan Gershom in 1995 when I was a book editor for a small Virginia press. At age forty-three, I had never met a rabbi before. As I edited one of his books, he coached me along in some of the basics of Judaism 101: my introduction to the Tree of Life, the true meaning of Kabbalah (the mystical teachings of Judaism, not the popularized fad), and the very direct unity with God that observant Jews celebrate on the Sabbath. He explained the importance of scholarship to Jews, and the Jewish foundations of Christianity. I have since come to believe that a study of Judaism is important for anyone who wishes to understand the Spirit of God. Jesus of Nazareth, of course, was a Jew who quoted the Torah quite a lot.

I met Sensei Kanai in 1996 while dining at Terra Bella, a now-defunct restaurant at the Virginia Beach oceanfront. After we'd finished eating, Kanai came out from the kitchen wearing an apron. He approached our table, bowed deeply, and implored us to tell him if we had enjoyed our meal. He wasn't asking as a merchandizing ploy. It was very important to him to know what we thought. The meal was great, but we didn't know that he was anyone more than a hired cook.

As I got to know Kanai, I learned that he was not only the chef and co-owner of the restaurant, but a Seventh Grandmaster in Goju-Ryu karate, a Reiki master, a meditation teacher, and a Butsugenshyu priest, a refined sect originating in Kamakura City, Japan, whose purpose is to teach the unity of all religions. The fire of spiritual energy burned brightly in Kanai, whether he was discussing a Buddhist teaching or the freshness of a garden salad. You could know him for years and not know his impressive background, as he never bragged about his accomplishments. His practice of quiet compassion and lack of perceptible ego further inspired me to understand that the Spirit's reach extends far beyond the borders of the Judeo-Christian tradition. Kanai had demonstrated humility—made it attractive and desirable. On Kanai, humility looked good, so I try it myself from time to time. When I succeed, it brings me closer to the Spirit.

If the Spirit is the means of God's communication, such communication must be available in all religious traditions. It was with this premise that I pursued an understanding of Vedanta, the sacred literature of the Hindus.

At a yoga workshop in 1996 I learned something about how we unnecessarily complicate our lives. The class was conducted by Sri Ram, a handsome Westerner who teaches Integral Yoga to corporate executives and managers. People who practice yoga know that the mental skill of focusing the mind is as important as the physical discipline of holding the yoga poses for the proper amount of time. You become intimate with the hot burn in your muscles and joints. You don't want to be the one in class who grimaces in pain, breaks a pose, or, God forbid, breaks wind.

Sri Ram's class was more advanced than I was used to, so I was "breathing into the pain" as best I could that morning. He kept repeating, "Only use the muscles you need to hold the pose. Release everything else."

After a while, I discovered that I was unnecessarily flexing muscles to compensate for the pain and fatigue. One by one I released them, and found the pose much easier to hold. But it was near the end of the class that the metaphoric value of his teaching hit me: we flex unnecessary mental and emotional muscles when we are involved in personal, social, and even business struggles.

"Only use the muscles you need to hold the pose . . ." or to solve the problem, complete the project, know the Spirit, or whatever ideals you hold in your belief system. Without Sri Ram's knowing participation, he had led me to another awakening by the Spirit to a basic truth about the spiritual struggle that is the lot of humankind. Despite my early training, I had missed the simple truth of the Spirit's proximity to us all.

My encounters with the holy people I've known have provided some important milestones in the off-road search: All people access the Spirit, communicate with the Spirit, and receive the benefits of such contact within their capability. Most important, I learned that the Spirit of God is apparently hidden in plain sight, and all we have to do is find it.

Chapter 2

ENCOUNTERS
with
THE SPIRIT

Human beings have always entertained some concept of a supreme, benevolent spiritual force. We hang onto the hope, faith, or even knowledge that some grand overseer created the universe and tries to communicate with us. Whenever we ask "Why am I here?" or "What is the purpose of life?" we assume that some überintelligence is holding it all together. Once in a while, if we're lucky, this intelligent "something" sidles up close and tells us, "It's going to be all right."

This is the Spirit of God, to me. It's the means by which divine intelligence is perceived, felt, and known in the mind and heart. On the basis of the stories of Santi, Nelson, and Frank, and what I've experienced myself, the Spirit seems to be a divine presence that intercedes in the thoughts, feelings, and understanding. In these cases, it cleared away confusion and brought clarity and peace. It occurs without warning, on no particular schedule, and without much regard to our beliefs or lifestyles.

To people who dismiss God and religion, such incidents are simply inspired ideas, synchronistic events, anomalies of the brain, coincidences, or strokes of luck. However, on this issue,

I side with biologist Edwin Conklin, who once said, "The probability of life originating from an accident is comparable to the probability of the unabridged dictionary resulting from an explosion in a printing shop."[1]

People who have already been turned on by experiences with the Spirit are convinced that they have communed with God. One thing is certain: the people I interviewed for this book say that interventions from the Spirit changed their lives in ways that they will never forget.

Those who contributed their personal stories couldn't be more different from each other. Though they use different words to describe it, they all encountered unexpected breakthroughs from the Spirit of God that provided fascinating trail markers for my off-road search.

STUNNING BREAKTHROUGHS

Joan Borysenko, Ph.D., is a Harvard-trained cancer cell biologist, a licensed psychologist, and the author of eleven books on healing and spirituality. The cofounder and former director of the Mind/Body Clinic at New England Deaconess Hospital, she has also taught at Harvard Medical School. She is a pioneer of mind-body health, and one of the leading authorities on women's spirituality.

In her book, *A Woman's Journey to God: Finding the Feminine Path*, she explores the Christian, Jewish, Buddhist, Hindu, and Muslim traditions, and cites many examples of how women have sought God in every age and culture.

THE WINDS OF GRACE

Dr. Borysenko was raised Jewish, but her philosophy of life has been influenced by a number of factors, including science, mysticism, Native American religion, mystical Judaism, shamanism, Buddhism, and Christianity. She was the first of several scientists who was eager to talk with me about science and the Spirit.

I asked her if she experiences a sense of the Spirit in her life. She answered,

> I can't separate it. I'm always encountering it because it's in everything. In every thought, every movement, every action, every deed, is for me, the movement of *ruach ha kodesh*, and, in Hebrew, that would really mean the blessed "Holy Wind." For me, there's an ineffable, unknowable aspect of the Divine because it hasn't manifested in form yet. But as soon as it takes manifestation, it has a movement and so that movement to me would be *ruach ha kodesh*. And the movement appears in the entire manifest world, in every thought, coming and going.
>
> So, any movement of that divine intelligence is a bit like a wind, it's always moving, it's always coming, it's always going. It's always there. And I guess Paul would have said in a certain way it's that in which "we live and move and have our being"[2] for me. And I have no concept from the Christian point of view what the Holy Spirit actually is, so this is entirely idiosyncratic to me.

She described a stunning healing experience she had as a child of ten. For a period of seven months she had endured a severe psychosis, an obsessive-compulsive disorder in which she lived in a state of complete horror, seeing snakes and scorpions and headhunters about to appear and kill her family. In the psychosis, she devised complex rituals that she had to perform in order to prevent certain disaster.

> So that went on for seven months when I was ten. There was no psychiatric help for this at that time. I recovered through an experience in prayer. I simply had an experience that I absolutely had no framework for at the time. Now I would say it was an experience of cosmic consciousness, an experience of divine union. And what I experienced was a total letting go. Complete safety. A sense of great harmony and things being the way they should be. Infinite mercy and compassion and an infusion of wisdom, when I knew clearly that I was going to recover from this, and I knew exactly how to do it. And over the next

maybe three or four days, I simply did what I had received in that state and the whole mental illness cleared up. Four days later I went back to school, everything was fine, no one said a thing. That was the end of it. It was amazing.

That experience led her to a lifelong fascination with psychology and the brain. I asked her what it feels like when she experiences the Spirit now, as an adult.

At times my consciousness feels very contracted, and at times very expanded. So I feel that sense of unity and that sense of being with things that are arising. I feel that as inspiration, and it's a wonderful sense and that's when I feel like "ahh" I'm having a moment. I'm having a glimpse, truly a glimpse of enlightenment. But for me it certainly isn't another entity, and for me it's not a "state" that's established. I spend time there. I come, I go, and my ego gets me and my patterns reassert themselves. And then the flow of creativity, I think Rama Krishna would have called these the "winds of grace" that are blowing all the time. And his point was that it's up to us to raise our sails.

Sometimes my sails are open and raised, and other times I'm just in my meanest, smallest, most reduced, less spacious sense of self. And it's become really kind of a curiosity for me over the years to just notice—what are the experiences, what are the frames of mind, what are the graces that seem not to be due to my effort—but maybe just simply letting go—that foster that state of what people would call different things—for me transparency is good. But I feel myself at least my god-self is always present. I just have a sense of when I am transparent to that.

Any attempt to put it in language gets confusing. It probably confuses all of us, and because different religious traditions have tried to "language" it in their own way, the language itself sometimes becomes an objectification that obscures the actual experience.

For me the most profound senses of the wind filling my sails are not the big spiritual experiences that I think anyone with "strange brain" can have. Paul probably had complex partial seizures on his road to Damascus, which opened him up to different varieties of reality. I don't have complex partial seizures, but I have "strange brain"—I've had migraines from my earliest memories and I tend to have experiences of divine light and mystical experiences. But that doesn't make you transparent. In fact, there's a good reason why the various mystical traditions have all had permutations of "If you see Buddha on the road, kill him." Because you just develop spiritual materialism. I think you get attached to those, to the powers, to the *siddhis* [miracles], to things that come but really aren't for me, a movement of what we're calling here, the Spirit, a sense of union with the Divine.

For me that happens when I forget my sense of self, during daily life when I'm not being self-referential, when I'm not worried about if people will like me. Am I being a good person? Is my motivation pure? When I worry about that, I'm stuck in my ego. So they are really usually just such simple moments of the heart opening and without thinking and without self-reflection, simply being in the flow of what is good? What is caring? What is loving? What is wise? What is nonreactive? And because it's such a simple state, I think generally I don't notice it. It's kind of like breathing air.

I asked her if that "transparent moment" brings ecstasy in addition to peace, and she smiled.

Very interesting. It feels like clarity. It's not always ecstasy. It could be terrible anxiety, in fact. And yet, there's a serenity there that comes in those moments because the battle has stopped. If I'm anxious or angry, I'm not fighting with myself, saying, "if I were just a spiritual person I would be in a blissful state." What I have is a sense of spaciousness that all states are divine states, all the divine intelligence, it's moving, it's changing, it's informing, and right now maybe I'm having an anxious state or a mean state, or something else, but as long as I don't get stuck in judging that state and I just give it space, like everything else, it comes, it goes, maybe it leaves a little wisdom in its wake. Maybe it doesn't.

But I would say there is a sense of serenity. Sogyal Rinpoche [a Tibetan Buddhist master] would say, "You can't stop the ocean from making waves," about the risings and the risings. And so whether I'm furious or contracted, I can see that and leave the risings and the risings, and then it mirrors a certain serenity that underlies that. A certain equanimity. A certain clarity. But that's it. The emotional state can be very variable and it's not always blissful. And there are wonderful blissful states. But I'm also aware that developing an attachment to bliss is just one more attachment.

Joan's experience at age ten and her description of transparency adds a dimension of continuing contact with the Spirit. In other words, these experiences are not limited to momentary events, but can linger, continue, or create a permanent change in consciousness.

INSTANTANEOUS ACTION

At forty-six, Kay Sturgis and her husband Larry found themselves trapped in a rocky run of bad luck. With nasty divorce experiences, children who had turned against them, and deaths in the family, they had reached their limit. Kay had just buried her mother after a long, horrendous illness, and on top of that, her twelve-year-old daughter, Kelly, was dying of liver disease.

After years of prayer and worrying about her mother and daughter, Kay was out of resources and out of tears. Feeling defeated, she signed up for a meditation workshop on the Holy Spirit. Already an experienced meditator, she went into a guided meditation during one of the exercises and asked the Holy Spirit for help. She explained,

I had achieved calmness in the meditation. My eyes were closed, but all of a sudden this bright hand rushed up to my face and seemed to pass through my head. At that instant, the anxiety was gone. I saw a beautiful image of my deceased mother, and knew she was all right. But then I saw Kelly. She was healthy and happy, and I thought it meant that she was going to die, too. She needed a liver transplant, and there was no donor in sight. Besides, we had no money or insurance, even if a donor appeared. After this experience, though, I felt that everything would be all right, even if it meant losing Kelly.

Tears flowed again that day, but tears of a different kind. It had been many years since Kay felt the exhilarating serenity of childhood—in the light of innocence, before the unpredictable burdens of adult life weighed down.

"The Holy Spirit visited me that day, there is no question in my mind," she said emphatically. "The action was instantaneous. The next day, an attorney called me who said an inheritance was coming my way. Within a week, a liver donor appeared, and my daughter received her transplant."

YOU'RE LEAVING! YOU'RE LEAVING!

Elaine Hruska is an author, massage therapist, and instructor for many types of therapeutic body work. She's also a professional editor who once worked for *TV Guide* in her native Texas. Elaine is a former Roman Catholic nun whom the Spirit inspired not only to join the convent—but also to leave the convent.

My first introduction to the Holy Spirit was in college. We studied that the Father was the creator, the Son was the word, and that the Holy Spirit proceeds from the Father and the Son. And, in the [Nicean] Creed, that the Spirit is the result of the Father and the Son, and it wasn't a separate individual entity, but came forth from them. Evidently that was controversial since the early days of the Church. Wars have been fought over it, trying to figure out where the Spirit fits into the Trinity. I've heard of other interpretations of the Holy Spirit being a subtle way for the Church (unconsciously) to define the feminine, trying to put the feminine in the equation.

I went through a period in my childhood when God the Father was more important to me. Then I learned about Jesus in grade school, and, in the convent, he became more real to me. And now the Spirit is more real. They were all important steps. The Spirit will be something that I maybe acknowledge more often or am more aware of. The insights, the intuitions, the flashes. That could easily be the Holy Spirit. That's how it happens for me sometimes. I think it's the Spirit that helps me that way when I meditate. I try to work with intuition, and when I hear other people saying "The Spirit worked through me," I think that sounds like the Holy Spirit.

I asked Elaine what made her decide to become a nun, and she recalled her early years in Catholic school.

> We were encouraged to think about God's calling for us. So in the seventh grade, when I read the autobiography of Saint Thérèse of Lisieux I was blown away.[3] When I was in fifth grade, I was really into saints and the stories of saints. But in Thérèse's autobiography, she seemed more real. I thought if she could do it, I could do it. I wanted to be a saint! In the eighth grade, a Maryknoll sister spoke to us and said, "The one thing you may be putting out of your mind could be the exact thing you should be." Being a nun was that very thing for me, so it caused me to ponder it.
>
> The idea to be a nun never came up when I was praying or when I was in church. It always came up at odd moments, when I was in school, or playing volleyball or something. It was not in spiritual experiences. I thought that was unusual. One day in school the thought kept nagging at me to "be a nun, be a nun." So I finally said, okay I'll be a nun. And it was an ecstatic moment. First of all, I felt this big burden lift, and I felt light, and I thought "What happened to me?" I was sitting in the middle of a classroom and feeling this overwhelming joy and love. I didn't cry or anything, it was almost beyond tears. It was an ecstatic moment, and I felt I knew this is exactly right for me.

For Elaine, this was an experience with the Spirit of God, though she attributes it more to an urge from the Spirit within. She had made up her mind to become a nun even though her family was against it.

Some relatives and friends and my sister were okay with it, but my mother thought I'd been talked into it. I wasn't. I had resisted it until the day I got that feeling of ecstasy. It was like when you push grace away. Grace is trying to come to you, and you say "no" and then finally the wall breaks down. When I stopped resisting it, there was like this ocean. So that feeling of ecstasy was a defining moment. It was overwhelming. I was a nun for six years.

With a spiritual send-off like that, I had to ask her why she left the convent, and she said that her leaving was also inspired by the Spirit. She said the turning point began during the Second Vatican Council—the sweeping changes to modernize the Church made under Pope John XXIII, in which the Latin mass was abandoned for vernacular, along with many other changes.

That was odd, too. Vatican II happened from 1962 through 1965, and in the convent we had a nun who was interested in all the changes. We had weekly meetings and people were leaving. We were rewriting our rules, trying to modernize, and be more relevant to the world. I was allowed to wear a modified habit. So we were experimenting.

We were also noticing people's reactions. Some older nuns had a problem with it because the founder of the order had had a vision that we'd be dressed in these habits. A lot of change, turmoil. People were leaving the convent.

I left because I had a shift, and I felt I no longer belonged there. It was almost the exact opposite of what I experienced when I was nudged to enter. I kept getting the feeling "You're leaving! You're leaving!" and I'd brush it aside. I always explained it away.

Finally it was getting more and more heavy to leave. I tried to resist. Then one day, I was at mass, and in the middle of the "Our Father" the thought to leave entered my head again. And I almost started crying. It was like a relief. All day, that's all I could think about was to try to figure out why this was different. Later, I asked another nun about it, and she said, "You know, you should talk to the other nuns who left and see if they have a room for you."

She was encouraging me to leave! I said, "But I haven't decided to leave." She said, "But isn't that what you're saying?" And then suddenly that same ecstasy came over me that this was right. I had decided to leave and hadn't realized it.

I left the convent because I had grown. There were other things I had to do. I still consider myself Catholic. I go to mass. Even though there are gripes against the church, it's not enough for me to leave it. I still feel a sense of community. I used to teach Sunday mornings. Maybe we think we can change the Church from within. I'm still a Catholic even though I don't believe in all their policies. Most Catholics I know feel this way.

In Elaine's case, the Spirit was the instrument by which she joined the religious life, but also the one by which she left it.

ALL IS VANITY

Retired since 1995, theology professor Franklin Takei, Ph.D., taught at Pennsylvania's Clarion University for thirty-three years. He taught in the areas of Greek philosophy, world religions, and Eastern thought, and I wanted to know if he'd had any experiences with the Spirit. He told me of one in particular that occurred while he was performing a mundane project. It was an experience that saved his marriage.

In the late seventies and early eighties, I was twenty years into my college teaching career. It was really ironic. I'm teaching authentic human existence, enlightenment, etc., but I discovered that I was basically clueless about the relationship between a man and a woman. I was fundamentally a left-brained person and approached all issues from that perspective. So, obviously, emotions were not in the picture, nor were feelings.

Dr. Takei had always been emotionally distant, but his apparent coldness had lately become a problem for his wife, Shelly. He explained how she had told him to seek counseling, but he refused because he, himself, still couldn't see the problem. It went on for years, until one day when he finally saw the light.

It was a Saturday morning. I was trying to install a new vanity in the first-floor bathroom. I was cussing some, and Shelley came in to find out what was going on. She asked me if she could help. I leaned back and told her that I did not know what was going on between us.

The frustration was too much for him to bear.

"At that moment, I started to cry," he said. "She tried to comfort me, but I would have none of it."

Then the unexpected happened.

"She walked out on me."

Franklin ran to catch up with her and relented. He asked her who she would recommend for counseling; it turned out to be a family friend. He had finally taken the first step toward dealing with his problem, and he believes the Spirit helped him understand something about himself that he had ignored all his life.

The counselor mentored and counseled me, until, fortunately, I got it. So, there was this opening up of myself to new visions of my own reality. And, this was possible only because I allowed the Spirit, which is the essence of all of us, to manifest itself. The whole process transformed my life from an intellectual/academic lifestyle to one of openness and fruitful relationships with my wife and children.

I had had an experience of enlightenment. I often reflect on this situation, and it certainly marked a significant turning point in my life. Ironically enough, it was this experience that allowed me to also understand what was going on in philosophy. I now understood what all the talk about enlightenment was.

Philosophy/religion/theology/psychology now had a different sense for me. Before, it always felt that much of the discussion was outside of me, that I could not get a handle on it. After this whole experience, I now understood all of this as inside my existence.

What is it about experiences with the Spirit of God that make them so different from each other, yet so intriguingly similar? People have been trying to understand religious and mystical experiences since ancient times, and some very good observations can be made ranging from the inspiring to the mystical, from the transcendent to the sublime.

ARE YOU EXPERIENCED?

After the initial interviews for this book, I realized that I was not alone in that "oneness" experience I'd had at age thirteen. Apparently the Spirit reaches through the veil to intervene in people's lives at seemingly random intervals, both in how they occur, how they manifest, and who receives them. But they all seem a little different. Just how many kinds of spiritual experiences are there?

Many such experiences have occurred over thousands of years among Christians, Muslims, Hindus, Buddhists, and others. The ones who wrote them down were called "mystics," and the ones who didn't faded into obscurity. The experiences of ordinary people can range from a grateful housewife who was alerted to her toddler wandering out the front door to intense revelations by people of all faiths. Direct experiences with the Divine seem to vary in depth, intensity, and duration. It's as though the individual capacity for spiritual experience plays a role in the degree of the Spirit's effect.

I wondered if the phenomena were peculiarly modern, or if there were records of such experiences from before our time. It turns out that people have been recording religious experiences since the time of Plato, and certainly before.

In the *Abingdon Dictionary of Living Religions*, H. N. Maloney offers a summary of religious experience:

> An encounter with what is seen as transcendent reality varies among major religious traditions. It can be theistic or nontheistic, individual

or group, passive or active, novel or recurring, intense or mild, transitory or enduring, tradition-centered or not, initiatory or developmental, expected or spontaneous. Types may include ascetic, mystical, or prophetic; either reviving, affirming or converting; either confirming, responsive, ecstatic, or revelational.[4]

That's a mouthful, but he seems to capture the broad range of the Spirit's action in people's lives. There don't seem to be any rules or ways to predict such an encounter. The experience is individual and serves to convince no one but the individual who has it. The phenomena are variously described as experiences with God, transcendent truth, nonlocal reality, "the All," or some other perception of numinous reality that's unlike any other human experience.

In his *Types of Religious Experience, Christian and Non-Christian*, published in 1951, Joachim Wach suggests three characteristics of religious experiences: (1) the experience is a total response of the total being (physical, emotional, spiritual); (2) it is the most intense experience possible for a human being; and (3) it usually gives the person some imperative to act.[5] Wach considered these universal elements of religious experience in all religious traditions.

In 1905, William James (the son of Henry James the social theorist and brother of Henry James the novelist) delivered a famous series of lectures that were later published as *The Varieties of Religious Experience*, a work that turned the psychological world on its ear. James observed religion and religious experiences as a psychologist (in fact, he founded modern psychology as a physical science, building the first laboratory for studying the mind). James advanced the philosophy of pragmatism and brought functionalism to psychology. His books and lectures are studied and debated to this day.

James wrote that religious experience often produces an undifferentiated sense of reality, a feeling of being in the presence of God or being "immersed in the infinite ocean of God."[6]

He identified certain religious experiences as "mystical," limiting the meaning of that sometimes-provocative word to four very specific experiences, all of which are included by Maloney. If Buddha's enlightenment beneath the Bodhi Tree were mystical, then most certainly the dove of the Holy Spirit descending on Jesus by the Jordan must also be mystical, along with Jesus' miracles, his return after death, and his Ascension.

James organized these occasions of intimacy with the Divine into four levels, which I paraphrase here:

1. Ineffability. The experience defies expression in words, and therefore must be experienced to be understood. These are more like states of feeling than intellect; for example, listening to music or being in love. Only the experiencer knows what it feels like.
2. Noetic quality. Along with the experience of feeling, these seem also to be states of knowledge or insights into deep truths untouched by intellect. They are illuminations, revelations, full of significance and importance. They also defy articulation.
3. Transience. The state doesn't seem to be sustained for long, except in rare instances. After a time, the clarity and intensity of the experience become difficult to reproduce in memory.
4. Passivity. The experiencer is usually passive and the experience unpredictable. The will is held in abeyance, sometimes grasped and held by a superior power. Afterward, there is sometimes no recollection of the experience. James said that it is difficult to make sharp divisions between them and their intensity varies.

These descriptions cover the experiences of Santi, Frank, Nelson, Drs. Joan and Franklin, Elaine, and, as we shall see, nearly everyone else I interviewed. They cover conversion experiences, healing experiences, and experiences of deep reassurance.

William James observed, "the founders of every church owed their power originally to the fact of their direct personal communion with the divine."[7] He also said, "It is as if there were in the human consciousness a sense of reality, a feeling of objective presence, a perception of what we may call 'something there,' more deep and more general than any of the special and particular 'senses' by which current psychology supposes existent realities to be originally revealed."[8]

With William James and Dr. Borysenko, the off-road search trespasses into the well-defended world of science. Although we will be looking at the Spirit in relation to science in chapter 8, the experiences of the following scientists show that knowing the Spirit is by no means limited to religious folk.

A SANCTUARY FOR THE SCIENTISTS

Nineteenth-century Canadian researcher and doctor R. M. Bucke, a contemporary of William James and friend of Walt Whitman, once described a whole range of spiritual events as "cosmic consciousness." He himself had a number of such events.

In 1872, he experienced an instance of what he called Illumination. He and some friends had been reading poetry that evening, and they turned in around midnight. He took a long drive in a hansom cab and felt a calm come over him. Then, all of a sudden, he found himself "wrapped around by a flame-colored cloud." For an instant, he thought fire had engulfed the City of London. He said that in the next moment, he knew that the light was within himself.

Another of his experiences was similar to the one I had at thirteen. He described it this way:

> There came upon me a sense of exultation, of immense joyousness accompanied or followed by an intellectual illumination impossible to describe. Among other things, I not merely came to believe but I saw that the universe is not composed of dead matter, but is, on the contrary,

a living Presence; I became conscious in myself of eternal life then; I saw that all men are immortal; that the cosmic order is such that without any doubt all things work together for the good of each and all. . . . The vision lasted a few seconds and was gone; but the memory of it and the sense of the reality of what it taught has remained during the quarter century, which has since elapsed. I knew that what the vision showed was true. . . . [9]

At first I assumed that spiritual experiences happen only to religiously inclined people or people in crisis, but it's not true. It happens to people in all walks of life, even to scientists who only believe in what they see. Psychologist Charles T. Tart, Ph.D., sponsors an online journal, The Archive of Scientists' Transcendental Experiences (TASTE) (http://www.issc-taste.org/index.shtml), where scientists can post their spiritual experiences—anonymously, if they wish. Interestingly, Dr. Tart says about half post anonymously—apparently desiring to avoid the censure of their peers or, even worse, the loss of funding for their projects. The site makes no claim whatever that these experiences come from God or are associated with the Spirit of God, yet the parallels to experiences with the Spirit speak for themselves.

At age thirty-two, a mechanical engineer who identified herself as "Lucky Laurel" on the TASTE website underwent a stunning experience with the Spirit that lasted for weeks. While sitting in a chair in her family room, she was pondering her abusive stepfather when, strangely, she felt compassion for him instead of loathing. Just as Santi Meunier forgave her first husband, Laurel inconceivably forgave her stepfather. She wrote:

Spontaneously, I entered an altered state of consciousness. I felt a total state of bliss (it is indescribable) and love that had no inkling of judgment. I felt as if I must be in the presence of God or "the light," as I began to understand it. This love without judgment was a surprise to me, as it was not in alignment with my childhood teachings of God. Being always the seeker, in my mind I began asking questions while in this state. Like how did the universe begin? I was shown that a loving thought manifested itself into a physical reality. I asked what happens when we die and felt myself being further pulled into the bliss. I stopped myself from total communion with the source because I felt to do so I would have to lose myself. I felt a bit saddened to realize that to become one with the "source of all things" meant that "I" would no longer exist. I immediately understood that there is no reason to fear death.

Without words, but by "experiencing knowledge," I was shown that we are all one. And that all religions are basically saying the same thing, but we fight over the details/language of our understanding.

She reported that she stayed in and out of that state for several weeks, experiencing sometimes overwhelming psychic experiences.

I continued to ask questions and be taught during my waking hours and even during my sleep. Things of the nature of "all of time is now," knowledge is endless, understanding paradox, and the experience of infinity. I say "experience," because there are no words to describe its meaning, only through the experience of it will one understand infinity.

The whole experience was overwhelming, especially because the understandings I had gained were not even remotely in my realm of thinking before the experience. I felt a bit crazy, but knew what I had experienced was real. . . . Now if I could just figure out how to get back to that experience, I have so many more questions to ask: Like what triggered the experience in the first place?

This experience has been life changing. And I am no longer fearful that I will be judged upon death if I don't hold certain religious beliefs. There is peace in knowing there is something so loving out there in the universe and that all of the events on the planet have meaning and purpose even though we might not readily understand why. It has become a mission of mine to understand why and how this experience happens and to find others to discuss their experience.

Dramatic spiritual experiences aren't limited to the Judeo-Christian tradition, either. Dr. Ranan B. Benerji, a retired physicist and mathematician, used his real name when he posted this event that took place in 1953. He experienced a kind of transcendence one day while on a ship in the Eastern Mediterranean. He wrote:

> I was on a boat plying between Australia and England. That morning, standing at the rail of the boat deck looking out at the ocean, I felt the utter smallness of our boat, indeed of ourselves. And yet, looking around the deck, seeing all my fellow passengers leading their everyday lives as if there was no great ocean out there, it seemed very significant to me as revealing the human condition, this shutting out of the entire universe beyond our little shells. It seemed to me that this was like Arjuna seeing "Viswarupa" (the nature of the world and of God; a oneness experience) in chapter twelve of the Hindu scripture, Bhavagad Gita. I felt a central purpose of the world leading all of us.
>
> A voice seemed to indicate to me that what I was doing and planning would be good for me in ways beyond my comprehension. At this time of my life, my agnostic feeling of self-sufficiency had received a jolt (I had recently been jilted in love). I was feeling very lonely. I had just met on board the lady who became my wife and a major influence in my spiritual and worldly life. I was confused as to how I should respond to my feeling towards her and was inclined towards making my feeling known.
>
> The "voice" was not an external feeling—it was more like a conviction seemingly coming from "outside of me"—but the conviction was still in my mind. I was in transition: leaving my native land for the first time to pursue a visiting research position in the United States, I was in the middle of a rather difficult decision—whether to propose marriage to a woman I had met only a week ago. All these tensions seemed to disappear.

The TASTE site contains many similar narratives, as well as other types of experiences posted there by respected professionals.

What these brief stories showed me was that the scope of this search for the Spirit included everybody—the Spirit excludes no one, and neither should we.

SAINTS—KNOWN AND UNKNOWN

So far, we've encountered a number of spiritual experiences by everyday people from a wide variety of religious backgrounds. But what about people who deliberately try to live the religious life? Are their Spirit events any more intense? Can examples from among the "saints" of various religions help us in our search?

Of course, if it's saints you want, the Roman Catholics have plenty. Over the centuries, the Church has canonized thousands of men and women for many reasons—because they were martyrs, ecstatics, or healers, people who had dedicated their lives to God in some unprecedented way, or because they had performed documented "miracles." Although some saint stories are based on legend, others are well documented. I thought a nondenominational look at the Spirit of God should include some mystics the Church acknowledges as well as some it doesn't.

Citing even a few of these extraordinary experiences of spiritual ecstasy reveals a pattern of how the Spirit worked with human beings long after the age of the prophets and the early Christian church—with people who were extraordinarily close to the Spirit by whatever means.

In nineteenth-century Italy, Don Bosco was guided by vivid dreams and demonstrated a gift of prophecy. Miraculous healings were attributed to him, and it was said that he could "read hearts." He dedicated his life to helping the poor boys of Italy. He was an expert juggler and acrobat, and happy, without apparent reason, all the time. He had so many varied kinds of experiences with the Spirit that Pope Pius XI said that in him, "The supernatural almost became natural, and the extraordinary ordinary."[10] It would appear that Don Bosco exhibited what today would be called psychic, extrasensory perception, or intuitive abilities.

Such abilities were known among a number of the Christian saints, including Catherine of Siena, a Christian mystic who defied the bishops and reformed the church—this in a day when women were reviled as unworthy in the church. Known as much for her mystical experiences as for her fearless confrontations with popes and cardinals, Catherine lived through the Black Death of the fourteenth century. The Spirit seemed to live in Catherine, as she underwent physical transformations and described astounding visions of God and Jesus.

There are many stories of saints that ring true, but for many more the evidence was the stuff of legend and hearsay. Besides, canonization seems to make these individuals into an elite priesthood—above and beyond mere mortals; out of reach, or contractually special to God in some way. So I wanted to venture beyond the official roster of the saints, and I found many others who were never canonized, yet whose lives were changed dramatically by the intervention of the Spirit.

In his *Ecstatic Confessions,* Jewish philosopher and theologian Martin Buber revealed nearly fifty personal testimonies by mystics of various traditions, whose stories were corroborated by historical documents. These chronicles of ecstatic experiences with God were written in their own hands, or in some cases by their "confessors," and came from all over the world.

To ensure authenticity, Buber restricted his collection, as much as possible, to diaristic records, even eliminating testimonies that seemed overwritten or too creatively expressed. The collection is a vital record of the workings of the Spirit in the lives of many kinds of individuals of various faiths. The term *Holy Spirit* is not mentioned in Buber's stories, but he does speak of ecstasy as a "fire," an experience of unity and oneness "outside of oneself."

He wrote of his collection, "I am including in this book the utterances of several individuals who are among those generally labeled mentally ill . . . but it does not interest me whether a doctor who examined Christin of Ebner would find her hysterical; what interests me is the way this female being speaks out of the urgency of her bliss. I do not know what madness is; but I know that I am here to listen to the voice of the human being."[11]

Amen.

SO GREAT A BRIGHTNESS

Even a few of the extraordinary experiences of spiritual ecstasy that Buber collected show a pattern of how the Spirit makes ordinary people extraordinary, whether they are called saints or not.

A simple farm girl in seventeenth-century France, Armelle Nicolas left a record of the day she experienced unity with the Spirit. The wretched girl had fled church because she could not bear to hear the horrific descriptions of the crucifixion of Jesus. Home alone, she tore around the house screaming for God to relieve her inner torment. She inexplicably found herself in the attic, where she threw herself to the floor.

"In the same moment God let a ray of his divine light shine into the depth of my heart," she later said. "Through this ray he revealed himself to me and let me know clearly that he whom I had so desired was entering into me and taking full possession of me. Then this grace occurred to me, I felt myself wholly clothed and surrounded as with a light."

Armelle was so changed, she hardly knew herself, and "felt such a contentment of all desires that I did not know whether I was on earth or in heaven." She wrote: "Since the Feast of [the] Holy Mother, I have seen my soul detached from all things, so pure, so solitary, so secluded, that it seems as if it no longer lives in my body, which, as it seems to me, seeks nothing except to follow the soul as if without feeling."[12]

The Hasidim tell many stories about the mystical experiences of the Eastern European rebbes. One such story reads, "It is told of one master that in times of entrancement he had to look at the clock in order to keep himself in this world; of another, that when he wanted to contemplate individual things, he had to put on spectacles in order to subdue his spiritual sight, for otherwise he saw all the individual things of the world as one."[13]

Buber also included the experiences of Angela Di Foligno, who lived in Italy in the late 1200s. Angela described in eloquent detail her experience with the Spirit:

> Once during Lent it seemed to me that I was very dry and without devotion. And I prayed God that, since I was empty of all good, he might give me of himself. And then the eyes of the soul were opened, and I saw love coming toward me.

Though never made a saint, Angela had stunning experiences of God in progressive degrees of abstraction: pure love, a sense of emptiness and allness. She described how these experiences felt:

> And immediately after God has shown himself to the soul, he reveals himself and opens himself to her [the soul] and expands the soul and gives her the gifts and the sweets that she never experienced before, and with far greater depth than I have said. And then the soul is drawn out of all darkness, and is given a greater recognition of God than I can understand the possibility of, and that with so great a brightness and with so great a sweetness and certainty and in so deep an abyss that there is no heart that could attain this.

The spiritual literature of Taoism, the *Tao Teh Ching* ("book of the way and its power"), is contained in a single thin volume of eighty-one sayings. It was written down around the fourth century B.C.E. by the ox-riding sage Lao Tzu, and it speaks of the power of God, which he called "the Way," saying "Those who know do not say; those who say do not know."

Lao Tzu's words seem to capture not only my own experience but also that of those whose stories appear in this chapter:

There is a being, wonderful, perfect;

It existed before heaven and earth.

How quiet it is!

How spiritual it is!

It stands alone and it does not change.

It moves around and around, but does not on this account suffer.

All life comes from it.

It wraps everything with its love as in a garment,

and yet it claims no honor, it does not demand

to be Lord.

I do not know its name, and so I call it Tao, the Way,

and I rejoice in its power.

—Tao Teh Ching, 25[14]

We'll be smart in our off-road search if we honor the wisdom of all traditions. We'll let the experiences of saints, sages, and contemporary people point the way.

THOSE WHO KNOW

According to those who know, the actions of the Spirit transcend every boundary. Such encounters occur, seemingly without prompting, prayer, or even particularly wholesome living, religious practice, or expectation. The Spirit floods into the mind, graces the life, and somehow elevates the individual's consciousness, often changing the course of his or her life forever.

In tracking down an understanding of the Spirit of God, we surely want to discover how the Spirit operates in people. But it will also help us to check out the Spirit's service record. Have experiences with the Spirit always been the same, or have they evolved as people have evolved? Was there ever a time when people freely experienced the Spirit? Did politics or historical events play a role in our interplay with the Spirit?

On the TASTE website, after her experience was over, "Lucky Laurel" complained, "Now, if I could just figure out how to get back to that experience, I have so many more questions to ask: Like what triggered the experience in the first place?"

Isn't that the question for all people, for all time? It is for me. How do we commune with the powerful, ineffable Fire and Light? I believe that anyone is capable of receiving contact from the Spirit to some degree.

Given my rebellious nature and spotty report card, it's a puzzle why the Spirit would bother with me at all. But somehow the circumstances of my life have placed me on a journey that keeps my spiritual eyes open and my heart loitering at large in the neighborhood of divine love. I believe that keeping an open mind is the key to both understanding and experiencing the Spirit—the universal force of creation that doesn't seem to be the property of any church, but that graces those who somehow approach its essence in some way. The Buddhist experiences the Spirit as a Buddhist. The Jew experiences the Spirit as a Jew. The Christian experiences the Spirit as a Christian. Even the atheist experiences the Spirit as an atheist.

To help us define and understand the Spirit of God, we've looked at people's direct experiences: everyday people, scientists, and even saints. But what about individuals who are allegedly selected by God to speak for God—the prophets? Maybe we can gain some insight about the Spirit's early track record through the prophets. Have you ever wondered what it is that makes a prophet a prophet?

Chapter 3

POWER
to
THE PROPHETS

By age twenty-five, folk singer Bob Dylan was a cultural and political icon who was selling out concert halls around the world. He has written over five hundred songs and recorded over forty albums.

In his early years, he was called a prophet and a savior.

"I never thought I was a prophet or a savior," he grimaced at broadcast journalist Ed Bradley in a November 2004 interview on *60 Minutes*. "I wrote songs, not sermons."

He said he wasn't the spokesman for anybody or anything.

Bradley asked him, "I understand you wrote 'Blowin' in the Wind' in ten minutes."

"Probably."

"But where did it come from?"

"It just came," Dylan answered. "I don't know how I got to write those songs."

He explained that his early songs were almost "magically written." That he couldn't write songs like that today.

At age nineteen he had felt destined for something great, and within a month of moving to New York he landed a contract with Columbia Records. His songs have been heard by millions, and, at age sixty-two he continues to play concerts nonstop.

Bradley asked him why he does it.

"That goes back to the destiny thing," he mumbled. "I made a bargain with it a long time ago, and I'm holding up my end."

He said he had made the bargain with the "chief commander of the earth and the world we can't see." In 1997, Dylan had said, "Those old songs are my lexicon and prayer book." Reverend Beth Maynard of Good Shepherd Church in Fairhaven, Massachusetts called Bob Dylan a modern-day "psalmist." According to an August 10, 2004, article by Jen Waters for *The Washington Times*, Maynard says the same of U2's Bono and the late Johnny Cash, too. Brian J. Walsh, campus minister and professor of theology at the University of Toronto, said that the Biblical psalmists were the rock 'n' roll artists of their day.

It would be amusing to imagine rock stars getting up every afternoon with plans to prophecy or increase the presence of the Spirit in the world, but in the age of satellites and Wi-Fi, perhaps songwriters have a prophetic effect. Can we really think of musicians as conduits for the Spirit of God? Maybe the question isn't as crazy as it sounds.

THE SPIRIT AND THE ONE GOD

I always thought a prophet was someone who predicted the future, but that isn't the only meaning. A prophet is also someone who speaks for or communicates with God and receives a message to give others. This doesn't mean any rank-and-file preacher or politician who makes the claim, but those with profound messages that elevate humankind and relieve suffering.

WHAT IS A PROPHET?

Most religions were started by prophets, and the Spirit manifested in these individuals in various ways: inspiring, informing, transforming, opening their minds to divine knowledge, or even bodaciously possessing them without warning. The Spirit opened their eyes to vivid visions and gave them the ability to foretell the future and distill abstract truth for practical use, and also to see into the future and know people's thoughts and motives. This was true for Abraham, Muhammad, and Jesus, as well as for Buddha, Confucius, Lao Tzu, and the founding saints of Vedanta. The Asian cultures, however, use different words for "spirit" and don't refer to their founders as prophets. We will be looking at these later in a different context, but in this chapter the off-road search pursues the Spirit among the Judeo-Christian prophets.

The Spirit intervention stories of the previous chapters helped me to imagine what it must have been like for the prophets of old when the Spirit intervened, guided, rescued, empowered, warned, impressed, and even chastised the Chosen People. The Spirit brought wisdom to Israel's leaders, seers, kings, and warriors, many of whom were living pretty ordinary lives. We find different words to describe the prophets of the Old Testament. For example, Samuel was a *ro'eh*, or "seer"; later prophets were *nabiy`*, meaning "spokesman" or "speaker." So unless the prophet had the clairvoyant powers of a Samuel, he or she was merely "one who speaks for Yahweh."

In his book *Everyman's Talmud*, Abraham Cohen explains that the Holy Spirit ". . . is employed to describe the endowment of a person with special gifts. Prophecy, in the sense of the ability to interpret the will of God, is the effect of which the Holy Spirit is the cause. Its possession also endows one with foreknowledge."[1] In some ways the Bible is the story of how the Spirit of God kept the Israelites away from the bad-boy cults that seemed to invent a new god for every change in the weather. The early Israelites found it easier to know Yahweh directly, to hear the admonitions, and feel the love of God. Yahweh had the ear of Adam, Cain, and Enoch, who conversed with God like neighbors chatting over coffee. Even until the time of Noah, if the Spirit wanted to get a message through, it didn't have to use the intermediary of a book or the unwieldy switchboard of some priestly bureaucracy. Pre-flood humankind was apparently within easy reach and a lot more willing to listen to Yahweh—that is, until things went wrong.

It's probably best not to try to imagine what the world had become before the flood wiped it out. You had "giants in the earth" and the "sons of God" taking to wife "such of the daughters of men as they chose"—perhaps not unlike the Hyatt after a Knicks game. Yahweh saw that things had gotten so out of hand, it was time to throw in the towel and start over.[2]

Following Noah's voyage, there was a long dry stretch without much contact from the Spirit. But Yahweh found a new foothold in Abram, whom he convinced that if he adopted the One God idea, he'd make his descendants as numerous as the stars. From Isaac on down, the descendants of Abram, now Abraham, would follow Yahweh's instructions, more or less, and the Spirit was instrumental in keeping the ball rolling. In agreements with Yahweh (called covenants), the Israelites worshiped One God with relative ease for several generations. The Spirit of God always seemed close at hand—that is, until Joseph died. That's when Pharaoh decided to enslave everyone.

"I AM THAT I AM"

Four hundred years passed before the Spirit made itself known again, and that came through the person of Moses. Filled with the Spirit, and after several dramatic transmutations of matter, he brought the Israelites to the relative safety of the desert, where on Mount Horeb, after a stunning conversation with the "burning bush," he asked Yahweh to tell him his name:

> And God said unto Moses, 'I Am That I Am': and he said, "Thus shall you say to the children of Israel, 'I Am' has sent me to you." (Ex 3:14, KJV)

And "I Am That I Am" helped Moses big-time when he came back down from the mountain, his face all aglow, and holding the famous tablets of much-needed laws. He needed the help, too, because he discovered the Israelites had resorted to dirty dancing and worshiping idols again. And that was only the beginning of more troubles ahead.

In the surrounding desert lands there lurked seductive tribes whose erotic cults turned debaucheries of every description into the very vehicles of worship—the porn of the day was "Live on the Sacred Altar" in the big tent just over the hill.

Maybe the pull of those cults helps explain why the Israelites were isolated for centuries in Egypt and later in the desert for forty years. If it hadn't been for this isolation, the One God idea might never have survived and the Torah never been written down. Despite the isolation, however, the Israelites continued to drift into this or that cult. Baal. Astarte. Moloch. The problem was that the kings themselves eventually joined in, and as we all know, wherever the king goes, so go the people.

Whether the Israelites were wandering in the desert, conquering Jericho, or suffering capture in Babylon, Yahweh used the *ruach* "blazing fire" (the Spirit of God) to preserve the Jews and their One God idea through the use of the prophets. Whether from birth or selected in midday without warning, these individuals suddenly became keenly "awake" in blinding closeness to Yahweh. It was human beings, like you and me, who awoke with the Spirit inside them, speaking new truth to a people in desperate need.

Many of the prophets started out mending tents, tending flocks, throwing nets into a lake, but once Ruach Elohim raised them in the Fire and Light of divine inspiration, their faces, voices, and eyes lit up. Personalities dissolved into dazzling inner light that got the attention of the tribes. These were the shepherds, warriors, wives, builders, and fishermen whom the "holy wind" lifted in understanding, cleansed with ecstasy, and transformed into zealous prophets, as warnings tumbled from their lips to stop the people Israel from straying into oblivion.

Yahweh was never going to be outdone, even as humans began making all the mistakes children tend to make. In the terrible twos there was disobedience (Adam and Eve); then tantrums (Cain and Abel); rebellious teenage pranks (selling Joseph to the Midianites); and you know how kids make idols of just about anything: coca leaves, hip-hop gods, rock stars, '69 Dodge Chargers, computer games, the Internet, and even death. The whole family was eventually ripped in two by divorce.

THE CHOSEN PEOPLE

After Solomon, and the division of Israel into two kingdoms, came hundreds of years of kings who misled the Jews into a labyrinth of golden calves, strange cults, and lugubrious practices best forgotten.[3] Through that long and troubled time, I can hear the voice of the Divine Parents scolding the Children of Israel through the prophets until they were blue in the face:

"Stop hanging around with those nasty Amorites this instant! And if I ever catch you eyeing that Baal-worshiping tramp again, you'll be in big trouble, mister!"

That's why I suggest that perhaps the captivities and wandering were the Divine Parents' way of giving the Children of Israel long "time-outs" to help the One God idea stick. Without them, the Chosen People might have seeped away like so much blood in the sand, lost forever, barely a footnote in history. There would have been no protected outpost of the One God culture into which a messiah would ever be born. So there would have been no Christianity, either, for Christianity is the godchild of Judaism—whether the Jews and Christians like it or not.

Through all the ups and downs of their history, the Jews believe now, as they always have, that they were specially selected by Creator God Yahweh to be the Chosen People on the earth. Observant Jews today believe in the vivid knowing of this special relationship whenever they read the Torah, the Talmud, and the other rabbinical commentaries. They associate themselves with God's universality, unquestioned unity, and direct contact with the world. They emphasize God's presence in the here and now and claim an intimacy with God, a Divine Father to whom each one can pray for his or her needs.

The Talmud introduces us to a sense of why the Spirit comes to an individual: "The Holy Spirit rests on him only who has a joyous heart."[4]

Recalling my own experience with the Spirit, I wondered whose heart could be anything else, once they know the Spirit of God firsthand. As I hunted for clues about the Spirit in the Old Testament and other sources, I was soon to observe the Ruach Elohim up close and personal through direct experience.

DANCING IN THE AISLES

I wanted to interview a local rabbi and ask him about the Spirit—*ruach*. My local paper, the *Norfolk Virginian-Pilot*, runs a religion column every Saturday morning: "Issues of Faith" by Betsy Wright Rhodes, which I read, well, religiously. In the column, I'd seen a number of letters by a rabbi who had been involved for many years in the regional ecumenical movement, Rabbi Israel Zoberman of the Congregation Beth Chaverim, the only Reform congregation in the area. (Reform is a liberal branch within Judaism that allows adaptation of Jewish practice to one's time and situation.)

I know enough about religion to know how carefully one must use language when discussing fine points of theology and enough about Judaism to know that there are few easy answers in such an ancient tradition with such a complex literature. So I composed a list of questions and refined them over several days. Not being Jewish, I felt a little nervous when I phoned Rabbi Zoberman, but his cheerful "Hi, Jon" set me at ease.

After introducing myself and explaining my book, I brought up the *ruach*.

"How do we categorize that?" he asked. "Judaism is a body of traditions that has various movements. Judaism is interpreted according to each tradition—the orthodox, the ultra-orthodox, the conservatives, the reformed, or the more liberal wings."

He said that the traditions interpret according to their understanding.

"There are key ways in how we interpret the *ruach*," he explained. "The prayers of the ages. You're talking about a very open-ended approach because we respond to *ruach* in such an open way. It's not as if one definition would suit our response to the *ruach*. It benefits through the entire body of Jewish heritage, which is very vast."

He thoughtfully suggested that I come and observe the Jewish experience by attending their worship service. It would be Friday night at eight o'clock.

When my wife Robin and I arrived at the synagogue, ladies and children were laying out snacks for later—lemon tarts, cookies, and other pastries. Feeling self-conscious, we entered the sanctuary. I'd attended Jewish weddings before, and I spotted a basket of black yarmulkes. I wanted to be respectful, so I put one on. We found seats in the back.

It was apparent from the program that we were attending a special service, one that was auspicious for me and the off-road search. That night was the annual consecration of the Torah—Simchat Torah—a celebration that follows the high holy days of autumn. (In addition to the first five books of the Old Testament, Torah also refers to the entire body of Jewish teaching.)

The service was an ending as well as a beginning, the rabbi explained from the podium. The weekly reading cycle of the Torah ended on that day with the death of Moses (Dt 34), but because the Shabbat cannot end with death, a reading of Genesis 1:1 begins the cycle again.

But there was more. It was the eve of the bat mitzvah of a twelve-year-old girl, the daughter of one of the congregation's families. The child was present at the altar throughout the service, dressed up and participating right along with the rabbi. It was moving to witness a worship service that so honored and welcomed a child into adulthood, but also into the worship itself.

Rabbi's effervescence and love energized the air as the service alternated between Hebrew and English, punctuated with lively songs of praise. The children of the religion class received certificates, and paper flags were handed out to everyone in attendance. The service burst into a joyous procession with two ornate Torah scrolls, one carried by the rabbi and the other carried by the young lady of honor, as the congregation danced behind them. My wife and I had never had that much fun in a worship service before.

After the reading from Genesis, Rabbi Zoberman and his music soloist, Jim, rewound the Torah scroll. During the rewinding, the rabbi explained that the Torah is never touched by human hands, and that this particular Torah had two stains, received during World War II when the Nazis confiscated it along with 1,500 others and stashed them in a warehouse in Prague.

The service ended with parents and children sharing bread and tastes of wine, and Rabbi Zoberman told the children that they were each a precious living Torah. My eyes filled with tears at the pure, vibrant truth of what I was seeing. In them, I saw all that history, all that suffering, proof of the covenants and the Spirit of God that broke through the veil to Abram some five thousand years before. I felt very close indeed to Ruach Elohim, for it had filled the sanctuary that night and poured from the people. It shone brightly in their leader and made us all One.

After the service, we sampled the goodies out in the lobby, and introduced ourselves to Rabbi Zoberman. I thanked him because the service had answered my questions about the Jewish experience of God. I had seen it that night alive in the families and children and worship service—a tradition over five thousand years in the making. Simchat Torah was a new beginning for me, too, amplifying my experience with the Spirit, and spurring me on with fresh excitement as I sought the Spirit among the ancient prophets, for it was in them that the Blazing Fire first manifested in ordinary people and made them extraordinary.

THE SPIRIT AND THE PROPHETS

As soon as the fire of the Spirit seized the prophets, they experienced a numinous ecstasy, a self-emptying, and other altered states that varied by degree. Some merely heard words; others saw visions. Some were completely "possessed" by the Spirit, even terrified at the power it had over them. Some prophets, such as Jeremiah, Ezekiel, and Jonah, didn't want the job and tried unsuccessfully to avoid it. Some, such as Saul, nearly lost their minds in the ecstasy of Spirit. Saul, in fact, lost the Spirit after he displeased the Lord by consulting the Witch of Endor.[5] For some, the Spirit manifest throughout the prophet's life; for others, only for a short time.

Prophethood wasn't limited to men, either. Look at Miriam and Deborah. The former accompanied Moses and Aaron in the desert, and the latter was a magnificent judge.[6] This should come as no surprise, because the Hebrew word *ruach* is both masculine and feminine, and the Spirit spoke sometimes like a man and sometimes like a woman (the Tree of Life has both masculine and feminine pillars). In these prophetic experiences, the prophet sometimes physically glowed. While filled with the Spirit, the prophet was able to know the truth in another's heart, receive superhuman powers, and see into the future. Perhaps the most dramatic event of all was when the Spirit blasted Elijah away in what was described as a "chariot of fire."[7]

OLD TESTAMENT RESUMÉ

The actions of the Spirit, in which the Spirit often imparted amazing physical and intellectual powers, are mentioned throughout the Old Testament. The phrase "Spirit of God" is mentioned in 378 verses (some count 389), in an interesting variety of ways:

- 131 physical manifestations, including air in motion or the wind
- 39 physiological representations, such as the breath
- 74 psychical connotations, emotional or mental aspects of experience, anger, grief, and the like
- 134 supernatural meanings, forces operating upon man from beyond nature[8]

Most often, the Spirit elevated the prophet to the status of "messenger of God." Given the stories of people in previous chapters, just imagine the experiences of the prophets as the same, but spiking way higher on the voltmeter. The degree of the Spirit's influence seemed to depend on the needs of the times and the effect upon entire tribes.

To help us get a picture of the Spirit's range, let's look at some of the ways the Spirit acted in ancient times:

- The Spirit entered Joshua upon Moses' touch and became the leader of the people.[9]
- Yahweh took some of the Spirit that was in Moses and gave it to seventy elders to help him deal with the people.[10]
- The Spirit of God inspired judges, such as Othniel, and warriors, such as Gideon.
- In the Hebrew, it literally reads that the Spirit "put on" or "clothed itself" with Gideon.[11]
- The Spirit came upon Jephthah, the son of a harlot, who was victorious over the Ammonites and gave Samson the power to tear apart a lion with his bare hands.[12]
- Like Joseph with Pharaoh,[13] the Spirit enabled Daniel to interpret dreams, after which he was exalted to a position of authority and power.[14] Daniel also predicted the future, as did Isaiah.
- Samuel was involved in creating an entire government.[15]

What can we expect from the Spirit for ourselves? The Spirit gives instruction (Neh 9:20), teaches (Ps 143:10), and provides a keen sense of judgment (Is 32:15ff) as well as devotion (Is 44:3–5). Ezekiel 36:26 says that the Spirit can clean away the filth of idols and give a person a new heart and a new spirit. Elijah and Elisha raised the dead[16] and multiplied food[17] through the Spirit. The Spirit also gave David the power to rule.[18]

After the Temple was destroyed, the people of Israel went into exile, and the Spirit returned to heaven as indicated in Ecclesiastes 12:77.[19] Jewish tradition holds that the Spirit withdrew from the world after the passing of Haggai, Zechariah, and Malachi. Why is this? It turns out that in Haggai 2:5, the Mosaic period is referred to as the age of the Spirit, "when ye came out of Egypt, and my Spirit abode among you." The apocryphal 1 Maccabees 9:27 laments the "departed age of prophecy." Perhaps Yahweh was just fulfilling the words of Genesis: "My spirit shall not abide in man for ever, for he is flesh. . . ."[20]

According to Jewish tradition, the era of the prophets came and went. There were to be no more prophets until the awaited Messiah came. The proximity of the Spirit was close in the time of Moses—face-to-face close—but that closeness deteriorated during the time of the kings.[21] It is believed that less direct means of communication with God have never ended, and, according to the Talmud, minor forms of prophecy still occur. Many Jews believe that the Spirit dwells only among worthy generations and only to the degree of their deserving. Such were the powers of the Spirit in the prophets. And such is the potential of the Spirit in you and me.

Some books by Christian authors tend to gloss over or patronize the theology of Judaism as merely a means to the end of Christ's birth. But I hope I can make clear my view that all the activities of the Spirit are a means to a universal end—of humans eventually uniting with God. In that light, I urge Christians not to overlook the exquisite spirituality of Judaism and the unique and stunningly vibrant experience of a people who were chosen by the Creator to establish a foothold for the One God on earth. They never stopped being chosen, and, like all people, they possess the potential to once again see God face to face.

THE FIRE AND LIGHT

On the basis of the way the symbols of fire and light are understood in various traditions, we can think of fire as "the fire of change and transformation" and the light as the "light of consciousness and understanding." From "let there be light" to the spiritual fire in the burning bush that did not consume, it's helpful to contemplate these properties of the Spirit. Spiritual fire purifies the mind and heart, and spiritual light imparts wisdom and understanding.

POWERFUL SYMBOLS OF THE SPIRIT

The symbols of "fire" and "light" appear universally in the literature of the world's religions.

In Buddhism, fire is understood as divine love, an aspect of the Buddhic, or Spirit, plane called Atma-buddhi.[28] Modern-day practitioners of Zoroastrianism, the religion of ancient Persia (Iran), uses fire (*asha*) as a symbol of the original light of God (Ahura Mazda); for them, fire is a symbol of purifying the soul from the desires of the lower self. In Zoroastrianism, founded by Zarathustra and one of the first religions based on the One God, priests continue to maintain sacred fires from centuries ago. (The "wise men" associated with the birth of Jesus were Zoroastrian priests.) Deuteronomy 4:24 says, "For the Lord thy God is a consuming fire." John the Baptist said Jesus would baptize with fire. Fire teams up with light as the action of understanding and change that transforms the mind and heart.

Light, too, is found throughout religious literature; here are just a few examples.

Christianity: "That was the true light, which lighteth every man that cometh into the world." (John 1:9 KJV)

Hinduism: "In the effulgent lotus of the heart dwells Brahman, the Light of lights." (Mundaka Upanishad)

Islam: "Allah is the Light of the heavens and the earth." (The Holy Qur'an, Sura 24:35)

Judaism: "The Lord is my Light; whom shall I fear?" (Psalm 27:1)

Buddhism: "The radiance of Buddha shines ceaselessly." (The Dhammapada)

Shinto: "The Light of Divine Amaterasu shines forever." (Kurozumi Munetada)

Sikhism: "God, being Truth, is the one Light of all." (Adi Granth)

Taoism: "Following the Light, the sage takes care of all." (Lao Tzu)

Zoroastrianism: "First I have made the Kingdom of Light, dear to all Life." (The Zend Avesta)

The divine breath blew softly as God whispered higher awareness into the ears of the prophets the world over. Spirit nourishes and inspires, educating the soul as the mind evolves and accepts progressively higher truth.

The world's religions don't talk about God in the same way, of course, but that doesn't matter much to the Spirit. For example, many Westerners believe Buddhism to be a godless religion, but this is not so. It's just that Buddhists don't dress God up in the form of some type of man. They refer to a concept not unlike the ancient Hebrew "One Who Is." Taoists, too, embrace a single reality called "the Way" of the universe. In China and Japan, the Spirit is known as the breath or wind of *chi*. To the Vedantist, the breath is *prana*. The Spirit of God is the life force that animates the world and fills the mind.

Westerners don't ordinarily associate the many gods of Hinduism with the concept of One God, but to Hindus Brahman is the Absolute. Not only that, but the Spirit lives in human beings as the Atman breath. The Supreme Spirit is called Adhyatma. With that said, Western religion doesn't hold the copyright on hypocrisy. India's cruel caste system, for example, bears little resemblance to the intent of the Vedas, just as those Catholics who believe that statues and relics can somehow answer prayers and grant favors have strayed from the intent of Jesus. Give Christianity three thousand more years to evolve and it, too, may develop a caste system—it has already used Scripture to justify the Inquisition, the Crusades, the enslaving of Africans, and the waging of war! But go back to the early Vedantist teachings, and you find the One God represented in Brahman (the Ultimate Reality), right along with its own trinity of Brahma, Vishnu, and Shiva.

The point here isn't about how these religions are practiced today, but about the original meaning of the teachings. The Buddhist farmer motoring his boatload of fresh veggies to the market in Phuket, Thailand, is not necessarily any more articulate about his religion than the Kansas farmer delivering his corn to a grain elevator outside Wichita. However, in every religion one can find members who intimately know the Spirit, individuals who find the universal light despite the often Spirit-numbing conventions.

THE SHEKINAH GLORY

As already mentioned, the Midrash identifies the Spirit as "fire and light," symbols that appear in every scripture in the world. The Midrash also associates the Spirit with something else: the Shekinah, the "Presence of God"; the visible glory that was seen around the Ark of the Covenant in the first temple in the Holy of Holies.[22] This is the visible glow of light that also appeared when the original name of God "descended."[23] It also refers to God dwelling in Jerusalem, on Mount Zion, and in the Temple itself,[24] which is called the "house of the Shekinah" in the Targums.[25] According to the rabbinical literature, the Shekinah protects, comes to the sick, and twice spoke with the prophet Jonah.[26] It's referred to in Isaiah 60:2 ("Arise, Shine: for your light has come, and the glory of the Lord has risen upon you."). The Shekinah manifested as light and sound and had wings, appearing in the form of a "dove," and those who acknowledged God took refuge beneath its wings.[27]

We will soon be looking at the Fire and Light in the New Testament, but it was the Shekinah glory that appeared at the baptism of Jesus and numerous other events in the New Testament. It is significant that Shekinah is a feminine word and that the Midrash indicates in places that the Spirit is feminine, wisdom—the feminine nature of God, a subject we will return to in the off-road search.

I believe I saw the Shekinah at two different funerals, long after I departed from Roman Catholicism. Perhaps significantly, they occurred at the funerals of my mother and mother-in-law. The first time was in 1975 at the funeral home during the viewing where my deceased mother lay in an open casket. I wouldn't allow myself to look at her because I wanted to remember her as she was, so I fixed my gaze above the casket. It was there that I saw a bright glow, like a polished gold bar shining in an arc light. It was vivid, standing out from the background of reality like a special effect in the movies. I wasn't inebriated in the slightest, nor had I ever seen such a thing before—I kept it to myself, too. I didn't realize what it was at the time, but that light took away some of my grief. I felt warm inside, and reassured, like I was somehow in good company. And my mother's face was suddenly smiling at me in the center of it. I knew she was happy and glad that I could see her there. She made an impression on me that will last all my life.

The second time I saw the Shekinah was in a Roman Catholic church in 1988 during the requiem mass for my mother-in-law, Betty, who had just passed away after a long illness. When the priest raised the chalice, an ovoid of bright golden light shone around and above the altar. I still wonder why it happened at all, as I wasn't living a particularly holy life at the time, and the young priest had irritated me, having mumbled impatiently through the service like it was a big chore. But again came the peace and reassurance. I didn't see Betty as I had seen my mother, but I felt her in the midst of the light. I don't know why I saw it that time either, but I remembered what happened at my mother's funeral. I remember thinking nothing of it—that it must happen all the time for those who can see it. I now believe that what I saw was the Shekinah.

A friend of mine, Avrum Levine, experienced a live demonstration of the fire and light. It was an experience that changed his life.

WATCHING THE DAWN OF CREATION

The Jewish theologian Moses ibn Maimon (Maimonides) maintained that the highest knowledge of God is achieved more through the imagination than through the intellect, but I believe both faculties worked together for my friend Herbert Avrum Levine, back in the 1970s.

Avrum grew up in a Jewish household in New York City in the 1920s. At age two, he found himself being entertained one day by a wonderful light during dinner.

"The family was around the table in the kitchen," he explained, "and there on the wall I suddenly saw these balls of colored light. I was fascinated. They made me feel happy and wonderful, and I felt like I was one with everything. I remember my twin brother, Daniel, trying to figure out what I was looking at. The moment lasted for quite a while and delighted me no end. I've never forgotten it to this day."

At eighty-five, Avrum chatted with me about the Spirit and his fascinating life. A gifted pianist while still quite young, he was directed by his traditional father to become an optometrist.

After a stint in the Army, he also got his bachelor's degree in social psychology, but these fields didn't hold him. What appealed was the sea, and one day he decided to join the merchant marine, where he spent the next fifteen years.

Then in 1972, a strange illness began to eat up his body. Believing himself to be at the end of his life, he had an experience with the Spirit that lasted nearly a month.

I was staying in a hotel in Puerto Vallarta, Mexico, and I was quite ill. Each morning I would go to the rooftop to watch the sunrise over the ocean. It appeared to me like I was witnessing the dawn of creation. Each time I went, it became more pronounced.

When you have a gut feeling, it is your inner brain and you had better listen to it. You don't have to know why you have the feeling. So I took the gut feeling to be my intuitive feeling.

So, I had this gut feeling, watching the dawn of creation scene down in Mexico. I'm seeing a nature display like the way an Indian would see it. It lasted longer than a month. I asked God, the inner God that is within each of us, "What am I going to do with this?" And the answer was, "If you look into it, you have a chance of living. If you don't look into it, you'll die a miserable death." To me, that was not much of a choice.

I was quite sick in Mexico. There was a deterioration of my glandular system. And as my body was invaded by organisms, I became more aware—I was in between life and death. I became more psychically inclined. While I was staring at this sunrise, morning after morning, I felt a deeper connection with the Indians from within myself. But it was more than that. Projected on the mountainside in Puerto Vallarta, I would see the face of an ancient Asian person, then that face faded out and I saw the face of a black boy, about sixteen. Then the face of a person high in the Catholic Church. These would be fading in and out up against the mountain.

Then I realized—I accepted that the soul continues. I realized from my feeling of the dawn and the story of the Bible and God said "Let there be Light"—that I was there at the creation of the world. This went on for a month. Later I learned that someone would give a king's ransom to have an experience like that, but I was never interested in being a king.

I later realized that I was not so out of tune with other people. I don't know that I ever got rid of the illness. It was a question of whether it could take hold of me. I knew this: that if I'm helping people, I'm helping myself. I love to help people and I have ever since.

Avrum's months-long communion with the glory of heaven in those Mexican sunrises eventually led him to study the clairvoyant readings of twentieth-century prophet Edgar Cayce (briefly described in the next section). For thirty years, Avrum kept himself healthy by practicing the holistic techniques described in that enormous body of work, and also taught others how to use them for themselves.

UNSUNG PROPHETS?

Where are the Samuels, the Isaiahs, and the Deborahs who will lead us out of our personal, social, and political hells? Let's hope they aren't twitching along the sanitarium walls doped up on Clozapine (which stops visions), Haldol (which dispels delusions), and Thorazine (which quiets "voices"). I don't mean to suggest that we should release the inmates, stop their meds, and see if a prophet emerges; however, if some gum-chewing patrolman had found Saul lying naked in the road prophesying, Saul would have been handcuffed pronto and led away with a lot of eye-rolling and head shaking.

Does it make sense to look for the Spirit in modern-day prophets? Judging by the experiences of ordinary people today, it seems clear that the Spirit of God has never ceased to knock at the heavily bolted door of the human will, though humankind may have grown more blind and deaf than even the Israelites under Ahab. But an Old Testament prophecy foretells the prophets of the future. Joel 2:28 predicts a time when just about anyone could be filled with the Spirit:

> And it shall come to pass afterward, that I will pour out my spirit on all flesh; your sons and your daughters shall prophesy, your old men shall dream dreams, and your young men shall see visions. Even upon the menservants and maidservants in those days, I will pour out my spirit.

And your sons and daughters shall prophecy? We don't have a Moses walking around today, at least that I can detect, but there have been individuals over the past thousand years whose activity could qualify them for prophet status. Whenever the mainstream populations of particular religions drifted into forgetfulness of God, or the teachings became so wooden as to have lost their meaning, mystics always emerged who, once again, "speak for God."

Here are a few of the many post-Biblical prophets who have brought the Spirit to others and changed the world.

MASTER OF THE GOOD NAME

Israel Ben Eliezer, known as the Ba'al Shem Tov (Hebrew for "master of the good name"), was the charismatic founder of Hasidism (c. 1750), the mystical Jewish movement that espoused Kabbalah ("tradition") and returned to what it believed to be knowledge of the unwritten Torah (the Tree of Life, and so on) given by God to Adam and Moses. Hasidism opposes rationalism and renounces mortification of the flesh, insisting on the holiness and joy of daily life, which included sex and other pleasures. Israel Ben Eliezer possessed deep spiritual insight and clairvoyance.

Other modern Jewish holy men considered by many to be prophets include Moses de León (1250–1305), de facto author of the *Sefer Ha-Zohar* (*The Book of Splendor*); Simeon ben Yohai (second century C.E.), reputed author of the same work; Isaac Ben Luria (1534–1572), the founder of Kabbalah; Moses ben

Maimon ("Maimonides," 1135–1204), and Rabbi Menachem Mendel Schneerson (1902–1994), the seventh Rebbe of Chabad Lubavitch.

JOSEPH SMITH

The founder of the Church of Jesus Christ of Latter-day Saints and other Mormon denominations claimed in 1827 to have been directed by an angel to buried golden plates whose engraved surfaces told a story of the Indians, describing them as descendents of the lost tribe of Israel. He was shown a key to translating the plates, which he said were written in a form of Egyptian. He believed his church restored the ancient, primitive Christian religion. Mormons believe their presidents to be prophets. In 2004, the Mormons numbered over twelve million members.

THE SLEEPING PROPHET

During the first half of the twentieth century, a fundamentalist Christian from Kentucky named Edgar Cayce conveyed millions of words of inspired knowledge on religious, health, and mystical matters while in a trancelike state. The "sleeping prophet," as he came to be known, gave over 14,300 readings that cover subjects ranging from the Old Testament times of the prophets to the New Testament times of the Christians, ancient and prehistory, and a consistent message of love, hopefulness, and healing for those who came to him for readings. The Cayce material is filled with teachings on the nature of God, Christ, worship, and spirituality. Richard H. Drummond, Ph.D., retired chair of the Department of Theology for the University of Iowa, Dubuque, called the Cayce information on spirituality "the finest devotional material of the twentieth century."

TRAVELING PROPHET MUSICIANS

So what of Bob Dylan? Is or was he a prophet? Have we seen the Spirit operating among the songwriters of our times, perhaps one or two who shake the tambourine on the popular stage?

The idea shouldn't sound so strange. Around the time of Samuel, people prophesied in "guilds," some of which traveled around in musical groups.[29] No kidding. For the Israelites at the time, this was the norm. It seemed that practically everyone was filled with the Spirit and prophesying. Sure, there were also a lot of charlatan necromancers, diviners, and fortune-tellers around, but almost no one had the amazing powers of one such as the "seer" Samuel. Samuel had crystal-clear, personal contact with God, who was speaking in his ear, basically every day. Samuel could see the future, read another's thoughts, and "remote view," a means of seeing what's going on in another place—a faculty being proved by scientists today.[30] But his was a time of strolling prophets, when the Spirit was abroad in the land, inspiring everyone, it would seem, to his or her capacity.

But did musical prophets actually travel in bands?

A scholar of comparative religion, Huston Smith, Ph.D., wrote, "Traveling in schools or bands, their prophecy was a 'field phenomenon,' which could occur only when the group was together."[31] Fueled by music and dance, the traveling prophets would prophecy in a collective ecstasy. As far as anyone knows, this "prophesying" may not have been more than an ecstatic frenzy.

Saul encountered such a group after Samuel identified him as ruler of Israel. Samuel told him he'd meet a traveling band, "with harp, tambourine, flute, and lyre" and be "turned into another man," and he surely was:

"When they came to Gibe-ah, behold, a band of prophets met him; and the spirit of God came mightily upon him, and he prophesied among them."[32]

But music and prophets had mixed earlier, after the Pharaoh's army drowned in the sea, when the prophetess Miriam, sister of Aaron, "took a tambourine in her hand; and all the women went out after her with timbrels and with dances."[33]

Could the influence of the Spirit of God explain how Bob Dylan wrote "Blowin' in the Wind" in ten minutes? Maybe it was in the same way that Georg Friedrich Handel scored the entire *Messiah* oratorio in three weeks and who, upon writing the notes for the "Hallelujah" chorus, "did see the heavens open and the great God before him." Maybe in the same way Julia Ward Howe jotted down all six verses of the "Battle Hymn of the Republic" minutes after she dreamt them in their entirety early one morning. (Could it be that Bob Dylan keeps on the move so the Commander doesn't ask again?)

In the Old Testament, artists, musicians, and craftsmen were often inspired by the Spirit: to build the tabernacle (Ex 31:2–4), make Aaron's garments (Ex 28:2–3), and build Solomon's temple (1 Ki 7:14; 2 Ch 2:14). So why can't a modern pop singer play the role of prophet in our time?

One can't rule it out, that is, if his or her songs somehow create conscience, enlighten, heal, calm, or motivate millions to love in a world chattering with a thousand contradictory messages— all it takes is one songwriter, one song, to make a people grab their tambourines and dance in the streets with Miriam.

In the 1960s, roving bands sang warnings against the militarism and materialism of the generation who had suffered the Great Depression and fought World War II. Songs promoted peace between nations and love among people. Some of Bob Dylan's early songs burned with a fire of truth that felt good in the heart and good in the belly. Despite his denial, Dylan's lyrics stirred the conscience regarding war, human nature, poverty, and even the human relations between lovers or friends. The message is present in the songs of others, too, such as Paul McCartney, who still campaigns for compassion for people and animals, and John Lennon—all he was saying was "give peace a chance."

Was Bob Dylan a prophet? Probably no more or less than Joan Baez, Joni Mitchell, Peter, Paul and Mary, Judy Collins, or Paul Simon, for whom "the words of the prophets are written on the subway walls." No more or less than any performer since, whose song lyrics urge integrity, love, compassion, and courage to stand up for the truth—yes, the Godly things. The troubadours, journalists, leaders, activists, and religious people today command the attention of millions through the power of the media, and it's up to each of us to decide for ourselves which ones "speak for God."

WHERE ARE THE PROPHETS?

Maybe by comparison, you could call today's prophets "Spirit lite," but there's a big difference between the time of the prophets and now. It's a difference in what was at stake. What was at stake then was losing Israel! Throwing away the Promised Land! The One God! The Chosen People—in whom was planted the fertile seed of Yahweh, "I Am That I Am"—would have vanished forever and given the world back to the wandering tribes that worship the bulls, phalluses, venery, and fecundity. At stake was the loss of the tribes in their entirety. But the tribes gathered around their prophet-leaders who shouted the message of the One God—one voice for thousands of ears.

What's at stake for us today? In terms of ideology, our world is fragmented, by country and city, by town and neighborhood, by temple and church. We are even fractured within our dysfunctional households and inside our divided, scattered, distracted minds. Now there are thousands of voices competing for the ears of each man and woman. Each individual of us is a tribe unto itself, wandering in a desert of disinformation with desires tugging this way and fears yanking that way; with reason enslaved by doctrine, prejudice, and illusion. What is the Spirit to do?

Where are the prophets, the voices that "speak for God"? While TV evangelists fleece their Sunday morning congregations, the political Sadducees demonize their opponents and manipulate elections in the name of God, and the harlot of the media profits from every change in the wind, the closest we have to prophets may well be the voices of those poets whose messages "speak for God" and all things of the Spirit, breaking through the gospel of grunge and metal, pimp and gangsta, and the eviserating jingles of advertising. Thank Yahweh that the Philistines didn't have cell phones and a TV network, or the kids in David's house wouldn't have stood a chance.

The Jewish tribes are now scattered throughout the world from inconceivable and horrific persecutions over thousands of years. The Christians have scattered themselves by their own divisions and infighting, just as the Muslims have.

In July 2005, Irish rocker and promoter Bob Geldof reenacted his 1985 Live Aid concerts for AIDS victims in Africa. The Live 8 Concert sponsored dozens of musical acts performing round-the-clock in ten cities all over the world (and was largely ignored by the American media). Their purpose? To awaken compassion among the conclave of kings, the G8, who were meeting in Scotland that weekend. Bono of the rock group U2 has been campaigning for years for the superpowers to forgive the debts of the poorest nations.

The Spirit seeks every open avenue for expression—in anyone with a voice and a will. As we shall see, that includes you and me.

So maybe we'll find today's prophets among those who give freely of themselves and their wealth to help the poor, the starving, the sick, the suffering, and the exploited. They won't have to do the heavy lifting of the prophets of old, but those who "speak for God" today, whose sails are filled with the Spirit, will match up satisfactorily with the teachings of Torah as well as the teachings of the Anointed One—Jesus of Nazareth, whose life and message was all about the Spirit of God.

the
SPIRIT
SET FREE

Our search for the Spirit next brings us to a fifteen-year-old Jewish girl named Miryam. She was startled one day by the sudden appearance in her room of a luminous being. The seraph informed her that she would have a son by the Holy Spirit—a child who would be given the throne of David.[1] The girl was "greatly troubled," as anyone would be, notwithstanding the appearance of a luminous being. But the Gospels ("God's talk"), which are four versions of the story of Miryam's son, explain more or less that this is how she became pregnant.

The paternity of Jesus will probably always be debated, reviled, and beloved. But if, through the Spirit, God created the world and the stars, breathed life into humankind, and gave Moses the power to part the Red Sea, then I don't see why the Spirit can't transmute matter and energy by bringing a soul into a womb without the physiological participation of a man.

The virgin birth, however, is not the toughest problem of this search for the Spirit. The hard part is cutting through the mythology and assumptions about Mary's son, Jesus of Nazareth, and understanding the specific role the Spirit played in everything he did. The New Testament is important in the off-road search because it is actually the continuing story of the Spirit of God, after it took to the streets.

A NEW KIND OF PROPHET

The Spirit underwent a name change between the Old and New Testaments. The Hebrew *ruach ha kodesh* of the Old became the Greek *pneuma hagion* in the New. In the Old Testament, the Spirit of God seemed to come upon individuals more for the sake of the tribe, the covenants, and national security—but not so much for the growth of individuals. The prophets were "carried up in spirit," a type of dissociative state that revealed exquisite wisdom, stunning insights, previously unknown knowledge, and amazing strength. At other times, the Spirit possessed the prophets entirely, filling their heads with sounds and visions, dominating their thoughts, or simply guiding them with a "still small voice."[2] In the New Testament, however, the Spirit got a lot more intimate with individual people.

THE SPIRIT'S LONG GOOD-BYE

After Malachi, the last of the Old Testament prophets (ca. 420 B.C.E.), came centuries of profiteering empires determined to utterly destroy Abraham's One God project. The Chosen People were conquered by the Ptolemies and then the Seleucids, whose Antiochus IV abolished Jewish law and contemptuously installed a statue of Zeus in the Temple. Next came the Romans, who thought the Jews were atheists because they only worshipped one god. In 40 B.C.E., the Romans installed their own "king of the Jews," Herod, son of Antipater, who some thought was the Messiah promised in Isaiah.[3] The Romans were simply horrible, and, after a few decades of occupation,[4] the Jewish temple became foul with corruption and hypocrisy (a condition that would befall the Christians a few hundred years later).

The Jews were desperate for a messiah, and at the time they had many to choose from. It was a scary age in which self-proclaimed messiahs could be found on every street corner. Judea was also overrun with bandits and terrorists,[5] mystical sects, and prophets, too.[6] Desperate for answers, people felt lost. As Latin would come to be in the Middle Ages, Hebrew became a language of the scholars and scribes. It was no longer understood by common Jewish people, whose most recent ancestors had adopted Aramaic during the Babylonian captivity.

The time was certainly ripe for a new kind of prophet, someone who could demonstrate that he had so perfectly fulfilled the Law, he was capable of teaching a way that could bring Ruach Elohim to the Chosen People and bring back that face-to-face light that had caused Moses to glow. It seems that the leadership had lost touch with "I Am That I Am" centuries before, and it was into this chaotic atmosphere that two new prophets were born, the likes of which the Jews had never seen.

OUT OF THE SHEKINAH GLORY

The first action of the Spirit in the New Testament wasn't actually with Mary. It was with an elderly Jewish priest and his wife. Like Abraham and Sarah, Zechariah and Elizabeth mysteriously conceived a child in their old age. They were told by the angel Gabriel that the child would be "filled with the Holy Spirit, even from his mother's womb."[7] While Elizabeth was carrying John, who would become the Baptist, Mary found herself pregnant with Jesus. (The story of Jesus' birth is well known.[8] Christians believe Jesus fulfilled the prophecy of Isaiah, whereas Jews do not.)

Christians make a big mistake in forgetting that the Nazorean was Jewish; if they hadn't, their faith would be far richer. By the time of his bar mitzvah, Jesus had learned the Torah so well that he was questioning the elders in the temple. There is no record of what Jesus did from age twelve to age thirty, although some, such as Nicholas Notovitch and Nicholas Roerich, claimed to have seen Tibetan records, now lost, of a St. Issa (Arabic for Jesus) from Palestine who studied and taught in India around that time. Whatever took place during those lost years, when both cousins reached the age of thirty they met up with each other at the Jordan River, where people apparently witnessed one of the showiest Spirit phenomena in history.

John had spent much of his adult life foraging in the desert, and until that day he had been just one of many prophets doing ritual water cleansings, "baptisms," for Jews who wanted to be closer to Yahweh. Among the crowd that day were religious politicians that John called "snakes," warning them that already "the axe is laid to the root" of unfruitful trees.[9] But when John saw Jesus emerge from the crowd, he told them that he, John, had only been sent to "bear witness to the light";[10] to prepare the way for one who would baptize "with the Holy Spirit and with fire."[11]

When John poured water over Jesus, the "heavens opened" and the Ruach Elohim descended over Jesus like a "dove." A loud voice was heard out of the Shekinah glory light: "You are my beloved Son; with you I am well pleased."[12] The Spirit had already been described as a dove long before in the Jewish commentaries,[13] but we can tell from the description that John, who must have already been intuitively open by the Spirit, perceived a fluttering light of spiritual energy as the *ruach* descended upon his cousin.

Judging by the description, the Spirit infused Jesus with the thoughts, desires, and actions of "I Am That I Am" like no other prophet before him. That day, Jesus, like Saul, became "another man." If Jesus' consciousness was transformed from human to that of the Christos, the awaited Anointed One, then Jesus was certainly the greatest prophet since Moses. (It shouldn't be a problem here to refer to Jesus as a prophet, as this is how he twice referred to himself.[14]) Imagine a flood of spiritual light transmuting the very cells of your body. It would be the most powerful infusion of the Spirit possible, consuming your personality and aligning your desires with the Divine.

THE LIGHT IN EVERY MAN

After the Spirit descended from the ethers, it led Jesus into the wilderness, where he spent forty days fasting and praying—an emptying of self that plays a big role among the founders of all the major religions (Buddha sat beneath the tree, Muhammad in a cave, and so on). In the desert, the Spirit enabled Jesus to overcome the lure of just how powerful he could be in the world with his new consciousness. As he was now "in the power of the Spirit,"[15] he began teaching almost immediately thereafter. In the temple, he read from Isaiah, "The Spirit of the Lord is upon me because he has anointed me to preach good news to the poor. . . ." and afterward said, "Today this Scripture has been fulfilled in your hearing."[16]

The Spirit spoke through Jesus everywhere he went, and it seems that the more he taught, the more of his humanness faded away. His human side was tempted in the desert, and he got angry with the moneychangers and sacrifices in the temple. In the garden, he had doubts about his fate, which was understandable, considering the cruel death he saw headed his way. At the eleventh hour, he even wondered, like Jeremiah, Jonah, and others before him, if there weren't some way out of this.

Ultimately, however, he acquiesced, giving up his life for Yahweh's mission, and this is what separates Jesus from the prophets that came before. He had lived the Laws of Yahweh (the Ten Commandments) perfectly, sacrificed his life for others, allowed his ego to be transmuted, and dedicated himself to love, showing humankind how they could find the "kingdom of heaven" within them. When Jesus fully became the Christos (fully infused, "anointed," with the Spirit by the time of his death), he revealed ". . . the true Light, which lights every man that comes into the world."[17] If we are to believe the story of the New Testament, Jesus showed the world how to become one with the Spirit, both symbolically and literally.

But just who was Jesus anyway? Was he the awaited Messiah? Was he a prophet? Some Christians say he was God. Because he conveyed the Spirit throughout his entire life and teachings, we'd better have a look at these questions.

IS JESUS GOD?

"I killed Jesus," she nodded emphatically, asserting her authority with a jut of her chin. Her unblinking eyes seemed to look right through the interviewer. "I killed Jesus, and I have to make people understand that Jesus is God and their Lord and Savior."

These weren't the irrational words of a tent preacher or even a Supreme Court judge. They weren't even the words of an adult, but those of a ten-year-old girl. She and her fundamentalist family were interviewed on network TV in 2004 during George W. Bush's bid for a second term as president of the United States. The view held by some Christians that they somehow participate in the killing of Jesus through sinfulness goes hand in hand with their view that Jesus himself was and is God. Can this be true?

I surmise the child didn't believe in reincarnation, as her statement implies that she was actually present at the crucifixion, so I can only assume that she was confused by well-meaning adults who were clueless about the Spirit's role in Jesus' work, and, in fact, about the name of God.

ANOTHER NAME FOR GOD

So far, my off-road search for the Spirit has reinforced my belief that we can't paint religious groups with one brush. That goes for the Jews, the Buddhists, the Vedantists, the Catholics—everyone—even the Baptists, among whom I found a trove of wisdom that is essential to understanding how we can know the Spirit ourselves. Most Christians believe the Spirit is a "person," one component of a divine trinity, even though no such trinity is defined in the Bible.

Reverend R. Scott Walker, Ed.D., pastor of First Baptist Church in Waco, Texas, said he doesn't side with the Christianity that's presented in the media.

> I am very much a monotheist in the tradition of Judaism, Christianity, and Islam. I think one of the major dangers that Christians have, really without knowing it, is almost becoming polytheist where you've got God the Father, God the Son, and God the Holy Spirit. And they've come to think of them as separate entities versus a holistic unity. Anytime I talk about the Holy Spirit, I have to emphasize the unity of God.
>
> So I think of "God as Holy Spirit," as a way of emphasizing that unity, and I think that's what the early Christian fathers leaned over backwards to do, acknowledging that God is experienced through the three entities Father, Son, and Holy Spirit. We're really not talking about the Holy Spirit—we're talking about God. And we're talking about how God is experienced as the Holy Spirit.

Scott's elegant explanation dispersed the fog of mystery, at least for me. Though he did not express it so, I can't resist the temptation to extend the concept out to every manifestation of God: God experienced through nature, through love, through all expressions that reflect the inclusive goodness and unity of the "One Who Is."

The search led me to a variety of detailed proofs by experts on both sides of the question of whether Jesus was or is God. Each expert presents his or her list of verses that supposedly proves it one way or another. Some emphasize the God-like attributes he demonstrated; others point out Jesus' human frailty. Still others assert what's called a "hypostatic union," which declares Jesus a being both fully human and fully divine.

But just as Jesus himself never claimed to be God, he also made it clear that through the power of the Spirit he ultimately became one with God. He spoke of the "father" as the one who sent him as well as the Holy Spirit, a "comforter" that the Father would send after Jesus' departure. Jesus said, "I do not speak on my own authority; but the Father who dwells in me does his works. Believe me that *I am in the Father and the Father in me. . . .*"[18] [my italics] In John 17:14 Jesus explained that he was not of the world, and in 17:5 refers to the glory (the Shekinah, presence of God) he had with the Father "before the world was." Although he said he and the Father dwell in each other, he later said that he and the Father dwell in *us.* Can this be true?

Clearly, Jesus wasn't alive before Adam, but the Spirit was.[19] Jesus told his followers that he'd pray for those who came into this understanding. Here he refers to oneness and the Shekinah glory, the presence of God within those who understand, "that they may all be one; even as you, Father, are in me, and I in you, that they also may be in us, so that the world may believe that you have sent me. The glory which you have given me, I have given to them, that they may be one *even as we are one, I in them and you in me*, that they may become perfectly one. . . ." Jn 17:21–23 [my italics]

So at some point Jesus, the man, became the enlightened, self-realized Christos, and even beyond that to oneness with "I Am That I Am." He became one with the Spirit, a process that began at age twelve. His human personality diminished until his voice and that of the Spirit were indistinguishable.

HE WAITED HIS TURN

Did you ever stop to wonder why John had been filled with the Spirit from the womb, but Jesus only received the Spirit at age thirty by the river? It bothered me a little. If Jesus were sent as he said, why was the supposed Messiah on a waiting list, standing in a queue at the Jordan River with the unwashed of Galilee? Even though the Bible says that as he grew up he waxed "strong in spirit,"[20] I wondered if the delayed official indwelling of the Spirit had been by design. For what purpose would the Spirit's grand entrance, after centuries of silence, be made such a specific public event?

The Bible shows Jesus' life as a process in which he was progressively infused with the Spirit. Moreover, he allowed his personality, human desires, and ego, and even his body to eventually dissolve into that Spirit. In the final months of his teaching, Jesus, the man, ceased to be, and his personality—perfected while practicing what he preached—remained eternally alive in the Fire and Light. His life was a demonstration of what every human being can do—transform the ego into "I Am That I Am" and adopt the qualities of the Spirit—the Christos—God. In other words, through the Spirit, all humans are capable of accomplishing for themselves what he demonstrated—we're chips off the old block.

According to the Bible, Jesus performed many amazing "miracles," but perhaps these events are overemphasized. Certain prophets of old had already performed miracles through the power of the Spirit: Moses had turned his staff into a serpent and parted the sea, Samuel could read minds, and Elijah and Elisha had raised the dead and multiplied food. Many examples of the Spirit's power exist in the ancient writings, but it was "God as Spirit," after all, that created the visible universe. Buddhists and Vedantists call miracles *siddhis*, the ability of an adept to transcend and transmute matter and energy. Their scriptures often describe examples of such mystical events.

Filled so completely with "God as Spirit," there wasn't anything that Jesus could not do. And he was determined to help others access that power, too.

CHRIST CONSCIOUSNESS

How do the experiences of those who shared their stories for this book, and even my own contacts with the Spirit, compare with those of Jesus of Nazareth? There seem to be parallels, just a smidge. If mine was a dewdrop of the Spirit, perhaps Santi, Joan, Kay, and Nelson had drawn a spoonful. Gideon drew a cup; Solomon a bucket; and Moses a lake. But Jesus became the ocean of the Spirit into which he ultimately united—body, life, suffering, everything. He was manifesting 24/7 what people today receive in tiny sips. Jesus was like all the prophets of yore combined, but on steroids. He was speaking for Yahweh and is equated with the Word of God—Divine Reason alive in a body of flesh. This is the Logos = Word = Divine Reason, the state in which he lived the entire last three years of his life.

Jesus frequently referred to himself as the "son of man," but in John, he allows himself to be referred to as the "Son of God." In *The Left Hand of God*, Austrian theologian and author Adolf Holl writes that later Christians came to believe Jesus was God because he referred to the Semitic Yahweh as "Father"—the very reason why others believe he wasn't God.

As we have seen, there are two ways to think of the words of Jesus: was the man speaking or the Spirit speaking? When Jesus said "I," were these the words (Word) of the Spirit? Jesus wasn't necessarily calling himself, his human self, "God," but describing the state of his oneness with the Spirit. The progression of his statements reveals that he identified more and more with the Spirit, finally uniting with it completely after his death.

I certainly mean no disrespect to Jesus Christ or to those for whom "Jesus is God," such as the little girl mentioned earlier who was interviewed on TV. It is in fact my love for the Spirit, and urgent desire to discover the barest, cleanest, most unshackled truth about the Spirit possible, that presses me to find new ways to express and understand it. It's time that people think outside the box about their religious ideas and seek a context for the Spirit that opens the door to direct experience of the Divine by all the sons and daughters of God. I think this is one of the main reasons why Jesus came. Why hold the claim "he died for our sins" above the thrilling realization that "he lived to show us that a part of us lives forever, one with the Spirit?"

The late Rev. Kieth VonderOhe was a pastor in the tradition of United Church of Christ. He was a fourth-generation minister whose faith was informed as much by Christian mystical teachings as by the Bible. He credited his decision to become a minister, as well as many other important choices he made in his life, to the Spirit.

> I don't use standard Trinitarian terms anymore. They're not that meaningful. I would go back and redefine God in terms of manifestations of oneness. To talk about feeling that oneness in a living, dynamic, and very present way, is the way I would talk about the Holy Spirit. A lot of what I think about is just the oneness of the Divine. Everything is really a manifestation of it, whether it's in us, in nature, in the being we call Jesus, or in the Christ Consciousness.

He explained Christ Consciousness as the pure state of Jesus' mind that we can all aspire to:

> . . . the ability to make that intimate connection with the Divine so that you realize you are a part of the One Force. Out of that flows a love that comes to you and a love that flows through other people. You can see it manifest in people's lives when that connection is made. Buddhists seek enlightenment. Vedantists seek self-realization. Muslims seek the clear mind of Allah. In the mystical aspirations of the Hasidim and other Kabbalists, some Jews even seek what is called "messianic consciousness."[21]
>
> The Holy Spirit, for me, is a particular manifestation of this oneness that seems to make the presence of the Divine more real, more immediately present and more meaningful on an emotional or feeling level. So that's what I would say the action of the Spirit is—to reach beyond us and at the same time into us. It's an immediate experience of the presence of God.

What Jesus did was something new for prophets: the practice and preaching of compassion, forgiveness, and unconditional love. In parables, he told people that the way to happiness was to forgive their enemies, love the One God, and try not to "miss the target" (the English word "sin" is used for *hamartia*, the Greek word of the Gospels, which meant "to be without a share in," and, for an archer, "missing the target"). He said that the "kingdom of heaven is within you" and, with simple clarity, that the Spirit would come to anyone who asks for it.

A PROMISE AND A WARNING

Jesus himself only uttered the phrase "Holy Spirit" five times, and perhaps the most important was his saying that Yahweh would give the Spirit to those who ask,[22] explaining that when a son asks his father for an egg, what father would hand him a scorpion?

To believe otherwise about the Creator separates human beings from God, leaving them to founder in a mere hope in some future deservingness of divine favor. It's worth rereading the Gospels from the point of view that Jesus was promising the kingdom of heaven through the Holy Spirit in the here and now, not in the sweet bye and bye.

TWO SIMPLE RULES

Someone once asked Jesus, "Teacher, what good deed must I do, to have eternal life?" And he said to him, "Why do you ask me about what is good? *One there is who is good.* If you would enter life, keep the commandments."[23] [my italics] This of course referred to the Laws of Moses, but Jesus added two new commandments to the mix.[24] He said, "If you keep my commandments, you will abide in my love."

Besides the Laws of Moses, which commandments was he talking about? He was referring to two new rules that he himself had given, "'You shall love the Lord your God with all your heart, and with all your soul, and with all your mind.' This is the great and first commandment. And a second is like it, 'You shall love your neighbor as yourself.' On these two commandments depend all the law and the prophets."[25] Observe these two, and the Ten Commandments of Moses are a piece of cake.

Perhaps we miss the greatest teaching of all by holding the man Jesus as an end in himself without understanding his most simple, practical message. Perhaps he was showing himself as a model, a pattern by which all individuals can achieve heaven, an elysian state of mind, by aspiring toward the ideals of the Spirit—the sublime Christ Consciousness that Jesus had achieved. He demonstrated the Christ pattern that all sons and daughters of God can emulate to find the kingdom of heaven within them.

A MYSTERIOUS WARNING

The Spirit was so vital to Jesus' mission, he uttered a strangely inflexible warning about it. The warning is quoted in all four Gospels, in which he said, "And whoever says a word against the son of man [Jesus] will be forgiven; but whoever speaks against the Holy Spirit [the Spirit of God] will not be forgiven, either in this age or in the age to come."[26] (Some scholars assert that this may be the only authentic reference Jesus made to the Holy Spirit.[27])

Why would the one who preached love and forgiveness everywhere he went, declare this one act to be unforgivable? What could he have meant but that speaking against the historical Jesus, the man who lived, would be of no real consequence, but that speaking against the Spirit of God would actually be self-condemning because it would speak against the divine, spiritual, eternal part of yourself—the Spirit within?

Jesus' stern warning no doubt had a lot to do with why two thousand years later Church authorities have never succeeded in defining the Spirit in an understandable way. I am not concerned that, by attempting it in this book, I myself have trespassed against this warning. Anyone, of any religious persuasion, who has been lifted up, altered, or reassured by the Spirit, would say the same. I am motivated to help people know this direct experience with God—to understand that their transcendent experiences, prophetic dreams, intuitive flashes, and comforting energy experiences are tastes of the Ruach Elohim, which seems to be operating more and more personally and intimately with individuals today, regardless of their belief systems.

THE PROMISE

People everywhere seem to be making an acquaintance with the Spirit, regardless of what they call it. Through Abraham, the Creator launched an initiative to bring humankind home to a loving sanity, one that led to a prophet who could reveal that the Ruach Elohim has been inside us from the beginning, even before we became "ashamed in the garden," when we, too, knew Yahweh face to face.

One can find passages in the Bible to justify anything one wants—slavery, domination over women, the supremacy of the white race, even war—but to call Jesus "God," and walk away from the deeper understanding of the Spirit of "I Am That I Am" forfeits the potential of "the kingdom of God is within you."[28] It ignores the role of the Spirit in Jesus' mission. To modify the well-known Buddhist metaphor, declaring Jesus "God" turns Jesus into a finger pointing at the sun, and all people can see is the finger.

MYSTERIOUS WAYS

This "blazing fire" or "mighty wind" that created the world also breathed life into humankind and gave Jesus the power to do what he did. And this same Spirit manifests in people today in various ways, as we find in the lives of three very different Christians. The evidence shows that their transcendent experiences vary widely by degree and apparent purpose, informed by their varied approaches to their beliefs.

First, let's look at Rev. VonderOhe's memory of an incident that took place during the 1990s in Italy.

I'd always wanted to go to Florence. But when I got there, I was incredibly unimpressed. The artwork was magnificent, but I saw all this scrub brush and all these brown buildings, and wondered what was so inspirational about this place where the Renaissance started. Then, I got on top of the cathedral, around the dome, and saw the whole Florentine countryside. That was the first experience I remember of my boundaries falling away and having a strong sense of unity and oneness. I can't explain that sense. But something happened to me that said there is a unity and harmony. That is one way in which Spirit works. Spirit is meant to bring unity.

Another time, I was sitting in my apartment one night, reading a book, and put the book down. For about thirty seconds all the boundaries dropped. I could feel a vibration in the room, the wall, the pictures, and in me. I know there was a part of me that had a separate consciousness. At the feeling level, I finally got to feel what it means to say we're all a manifestation of this one force, and we all express it in different ways. That was really a "feeling" experience of the sense of oneness.

HEAVENLY FRAGRANCE

Carole Lazur is a Pennsylvania writer and former Catholic high school English teacher who always felt close to the Holy Spirit. A startling contact occurred the night she thought she was going to lose her husband, Jim.

> We were packing for a trip to London to visit our daughter when my husband decided to go to his doctor to get checked for an annoying problem. He had been complaining about chronic heartburn that was keeping him up at night. When the doctor sent him for an MRI, we felt apprehensive because we were afraid to miss our flight. It turned out that he had an abdominal aortic aneurysm. It was immense—almost thirteen centimeters.

Carole said that the surgeon was astounded. He was afraid Jim might not make it through the night, much less the surgery.

They really didn't give us much hope of his survival. That night I slept fitfully. I was in as much shock as my husband. Early the next morning, prior to his surgery, I went to the hospital. The kids would arrive later, but those early morning hours were mine alone. I went into the ICU and prayed with him. When they finally sent me out to the waiting room, I sat there deep in prayer, which had turned into a silent meditation.

Suddenly, I felt comforted, warm, encased in the fragrance of roses. I opened my eyes thinking that someone had come into the room wearing this heavenly perfume. No one was there. I was completely alone. The fragrance of roses lingered, and I smiled to myself. Message received. I knew then that Jim would be all right. There was no need to worry.

Jim pulled through the surgery and made a complete recovery.

LIKE A SHOT OF HEROIN

Adam Ward is a forty-three-year-old Desert Storm vet and propulsion engineer with a major Virginia shipbuilding firm, who also works as an addictions counselor. Recently retired after twenty years in the Navy, he described how, in 1992, the Spirit saved his life and eventually led to his conversion to Christianity. He described how his wife, Linda, had left him, which plunged him into the most desperate crisis of his life.

"It was shortly after I got back from my last Med cruise during Desert Storm," he said. "The ship was finally in port, and Linda left. I spent a year and a half trying to gain love from people in various ways—everything from just being very nice to helping them out. I had reached a crisis of life and was in pretty dark despair at the time."

Adam grew up a child of alcoholic parents. Most of his six siblings were either alcoholics themselves or addicted to drugs. A couple of years before, while aboard ship, a chaplain had encouraged him to study the Bible. He attended study classes and was eventually baptized, but he had trouble connecting with it personally. By the time his wife left, Adam was at his lowest ebb. He found himself in the room of a friend holding a loaded gun in his hand and tearfully preparing to blow his brains out.

> I was just sitting in the room cracking up. I was sort of debating. There was a part of me that realized just how horrible this would be to do to my friend, so I was trying to figure out whether I should go out into the woods or what should I do. I was at my wit's end. And for whatever reason, I asked Christ to save me. And he said "Okay," basically, and my state of mind went from one of absolute despair to absolute joy in a split second.
>
> It was like I had taken a shot of heroin. I mean that kind of physiological change. And I don't think it happened because it was Christ. It happened because I was at the end of my ability to cope. I believe it was the Holy Spirit that moved me to ask Christ to save me. To me, Christ is the embodiment of the Holy Spirit. I believe that a lot of things were solidified in my understanding of spirituality and the universe that day. I went from pulling the trigger to the happiest I'd been in months. It was a real spiritual event. It was impossible for me not to believe any longer. There was no doubt.

Adam's conversion experience would sound like thousands of others you hear Christians tell, except that Adam had almost no religious training. Moreover, even though he considered himself a "saved" Christian, he still didn't attend a church. Neither did his present wife, who also had a conversion experience.

"It's not 'angry at the church' or anything like that," he explained. "But that experience was real. My relationship with whom I understand as Christ is real, but I realized that in order to believe the dogma, I would have to suspend my thinking. I totally believe that there's nothing exclusive about the Holy Spirit."

These experiences differ in manner and degree, ranging from a reassuring energy for Kieth, to the fragrance of roses for Carole, to an altered state for Adam in which his intent to commit suicide vanished on contact. Though different in many ways, these experiences with the Spirit have something in common—they are all reflections of the Spirit apparently manifesting according to an individual's capacity and needs.

THE SPIRIT SET FREE

The summit of Christian belief is that Jesus transcended death and continued to teach and help his followers in spirit form. He had achieved total unity with Ruach Elohim and explained exactly how anyone else can achieve the same, something that no prophet had done before. After reappearing in this spirit state, after what Christians call the Resurrection, he proceeded to deliberately fill others—initially his followers—with the Spirit.

If you accept the premise that Jesus was so filled with the Spirit that his body and personality were consumed by it, his appearing to people after his death doesn't seem any more bizarre than such claims about saints in other religions, the appearances of angels, or even the spiritual fire among the prophets of the Old Testament. Matter and energy are one, scientists have proved, so I say let the adepts make of matter and energy what they will in order to advance the freedom of humankind through direct experience with the Spirit, however it comes about.

RECEIVE THE HOLY SPIRIT

Three days after the cruel destruction of his body, Jesus, now free of the agony of his death, first appeared to a woman, Mary the Magdalene, telling her to inform his followers that he had returned.[29] Other accounts say various others saw him as well. However, he soon appeared in a room where a large number of his followers, both men and women, were hiding in fear. They were stunned to see him there, of course, but he had manifested a body solid enough for the doubters to touch him, finally convincing them of who he was.

Over the next forty days, he instructed them and, more significantly, infused them, too, with the Spirit. During one appearance, he breathed on them, saying, "Receive the Holy Spirit."[30] He charged them to go out and baptize, the Jewish ritual of cleansing with the Spirit and with water, but this time to do it with fire instead. He also told them, "I am with you always, to the close of the age."[31]

Jesus breathed the Spirit into as many as seventy people, some say, just as Yahweh had breathed over the waters, breathed life into Adam, and filled the seventy elders in the presence of Moses. In so doing, Jesus turned his followers from students (disciples) to messengers (apostles). He charged the messengers to go out and baptize with the Holy Spirit.

Now speaking as pure spirit, Jesus told the messengers that he would come to them. "In that day you will know that *I am in my Father, and you in me, and I in you.* He who has my commandments and keeps them, he it is who loves me; and he who loves me will be loved by my Father, and I will love him and manifest myself to him."[32] [my italics]

Jesus instructed his messengers to let the Spirit speak through them[33] and said, "Truly, truly, I say to you, he who believes in me will also do the works that I do; and greater works than these will he do. . . ."[34]

The messengers, too, were now filled with the Spirit, so when he says "I [am] in you" he's talking about the Christ Consciousness that the messengers now shared. Now they understood the meaning of "born anew"—the lower personality transformed into a "new man" by an infusion (baptism) of the Holy Spirit.[35] Jesus had truly baptized them with Fire and Light. They were so filled with the Spirit, they became as prophets.

CLOTHED WITH POWER

With the Spirit, they would also receive the power to heal sick people and perform other miracles (*siddhis*) as Jesus had done.[36] But he told them not to do so right away. At the end of Luke, Jesus tells the messengers to stay in the city "until you are clothed with power from on high."[37] This, too, was the Spirit—a mystery that would be solved on Pentecost, an ancient Jewish festival known today as Shavuot.

The disciples in the room were overwhelmed by the sound of a rushing wind coming out of the heavens. What was described as "tongues of fire" appeared over their heads, and they were overcome with emotion. They ran outside, where they found they were able to speak in all languages—the hearers, visitors to Jerusalem from all over the known world, heard them in their own languages. (Actual comprehension of the words distinguishes what the messengers experienced from the "speaking in tongues" that takes place in today's Pentecostal and charismatic church services.)

The denouement of Jesus' association with the Spirit is the Ascension, in which, after forty days of counseling his disciples, his body transformed into energy, and he vanished into the Shekinah glory of the divine realm—reminiscent of Enoch and Elijah, who were also taken up off the earth.

THE SPIRIT OF TRUTH

The New Testament has two books that focus mostly on God as the Spirit. One is Acts and the other is John.

The Book of Acts tells the stories of the Spirit operating in Jesus' messengers as they proselytized around the Middle East and Asia Minor and beyond. It also tells the story of Saul of Tarsus, who, as Paul, was perhaps the most influential of all teachers of Jesus' philosophy. Theologian and author Karen Armstrong wrote that Paul actually created the Christian religion.[38] So enamored of the Christos was Paul, so turned on by the Spirit, and so eloquent in explaining the new teaching, that he became for the future Christians what Padma Sambhava was for the Buddhists and the Talmudic Fathers for the Jews—a voice that explained the teachings of the prophet and how the struggling new Christian communities could apply them.

In the writings of Paul, the Spirit is referred to as the "Spirit of God," the "Spirit of Truth," and the "Spirit of Christ,"[39] because after the Ascension, the personality of Jesus was fully one with the Spirit. If the Spirit of the risen Christ was now synonymous with the Spirit of God, we gain a whole new perspective on many of his teachings, especially ones that Christians sometimes use to threaten non-Christians, "I am the way, and the truth, and the life; no one comes to the Father, but by me." (Jn 14:6) He wasn't speaking as Jesus the man but as the Spirit, the Spirit of Christ, addressing the potential or even the destiny of each individual to become the same, by whichever path he chooses.

One can see in the writings of Paul a Spirit that is no longer the proprietary catalyst for the occasional prophet—but apparently the Fire and Light are available to anyone who observes the two rules. He also states that Jesus had become the Spirit. Paul wrote, "The Lord is the Spirit, and where the Spirit of the Lord is, there is freedom. And we all, with unveiled face, beholding as in a mirror the glory of the Lord, are being changed into his likeness from one degree of glory to another; for this comes from the Lord who is the Spirit."[40]

MANIFESTATIONS OF THE HOLY SPIRIT

Paul and the seventy messengers performed many of the same miracles as Jesus, but the Bible lists many other benefits of the Spirit, called "gifts," that don't necessarily qualify as miracles. The gifts were known variously in the Old and New Testaments and are also experienced by people today. The difference, perhaps, is in the strength, power, or portion of the Spirit received or manifested. Paul often wrote about the "gifts," and I've found it helpful to be familiar with them in my off-road search.

THE GIFTS OF THE SPIRIT
The Jewish Book of Wisdom equates wisdom with the Spirit; in Psalms and Ezekiel the Spirit gives a "new heart."[41] Isaiah 11:1–5 gives a list of six "gifts" or manifestations of the Spirit:

Wisdom	Strength
Understanding	Knowledge
Counsel	The fear of the Lord[42]

In subsequent verses, the Spirit confers a force or effectiveness with words and of justice with the oppressed. The Roman Catholic Church added piety to the preceding list, completing its list of only seven that it identifies today.

However, quite a number of other talents, abilities, and strengths are described in the letters of Paul and in other New Testament literature. In the First Letter to the Corinthians he mentions celibacy (without being ruled by lust) as a gift from the Holy Spirit[43] and in 12:8–11 describes these:

Words of wisdom	Prophecy
Words of knowledge	Distinguishing of spirits
Faith	Tongues
Healing	Interpretation of tongues
Miracle-working	

In chapter 12 of Paul's Letter to the Romans, these gifts are given:

A positive attitude about such gifts	Exhortation
	Giving
Gifts of service	Leadership
Teaching	The showing of mercy

Other manifestations of the Spirit include peace, prophecy, grace, wisdom, and ecstasy. Perhaps one of the most important is that the Spirit helps one to understand holy writings—it has certainly helped me understand the holy books of many lands and cultures.

GOD'S SPIRIT DWELLS IN YOU

Rev. Walker identifies five major manifestations of the Holy Spirit referred to in the Book of John: "the most common is the Paraclete/helper (Jn 14:16–18), another is taken out of a court scene, showing God as judge (Jn 16:7–11). God can also be a witness (Jn 15:26) and teacher (Jn 14:25). The fifth is God as a guide (Jn 16:12–15). John uses all five of these words, and it's illustrative of how God as Holy Spirit works."

Perhaps the most important message of Jesus' new teaching came in his promise to send the Spirit in another form, saying, "And I will pray the Father, and he will give you another Counselor, to be with you for ever. . . ." The quotation goes on to say, "You know him, *for he dwells with you, and will be in you.*"[44] [my italics] This statement confirms an interesting component, mentioned above, of many other world religions—the Spirit is in us. Paul wrote "Do you not know that you are God's temple and that God's Spirit dwells in you?"[45]

Rev. Henry Van Dusen was a leader in the twentieth-century ecumenical movement who founded the World Council of Churches. In his book *Spirit, Son and Father: Christian Faith in the Light of the Holy Spirit*, he wrote, "Indeed, the Spirit is, above all, the agency of moral transformation ('sanctification'), and that transformation is into the likeness of Christ, because the Holy Spirit, which is the Spirit of God, is the Spirit of Christ."[46] To me, this is the capstone of all the writing, teaching, history, and scripture: the Spirit is God, Christ, the Messiah, the seat of the mind "I Am That I Am." It has been all along, and all we have to do wake up and realize it.

By giving powers of the Spirit to the messengers, Jesus seems to have fulfilled the prophecy of Joel quoted in chapter 3, that "your sons and your daughters shall prophesy." It was a time when the Spirit filled ordinary people and gave them the abilities known by the prophets of old.[47] Contacts with the Spirit are on the rise in our world today, and, as we saw with Santi, Joan,

Kieth, and others, many of them transcend the boundaries of dogma.

To the Spirit is attributed acts of regenerating, quickening, enlightening, convicting, comforting, drawing, strengthening faith, indwelling, teaching, cleansing, leading, witnessing, sealing, and preserving, and the list goes on. The more one experiences the Spirit, the more one is open to the thrilling possibility of more contact with the Spirit in one's own life. I find that the more I seek to know the Spirit, the more I, too, experience the ineffable oneness known by anyone who has risen in consciousness in a way that brings one closer to a direct experience with the "One Who Is," the Ultimate Reality, God.

Rev. Van Dusen wrote that the Holy Spirit is the Comforter that finds "expression in speaking with tongues, experiences of ecstasy, prophecy, miraculous healings, and various paranormal events. It has inspired extraordinary courage, insights, skills in lucid argument, and even business acumen. The Holy Spirit has been associated with personal guidance, and the sharpening of all our conventional powers of intellect, physical strength, and spiritual awareness. It is the inexhaustible discloser of 'new truth.'"[48]

Jesus of Nazareth gave the Spirit freely. He never demanded belief in a theology or membership in a church. By his own life, he demonstrated the Spirit's full power in order to provide a perfect pattern that any human being with a heart full of love can aspire to, whatever religion you practice, or whether you have a religion at all. We can all imbibe of the Spirit and set it free for others by finding the Divine in them as well as ourselves and relinquishing the black-arts judgments that only one's own religion contains the truth. Follow two simple rules, he said, and you have the Spirit in your pocket.

Chapter 5

THE SPIRIT
in
CAPTIVITY

In the previous chapter, engineer Adam Ward described how the Spirit had intervened to save his life. He was certain that his experience with the Spirit and with Christ were real, but was afraid that by hooking up with a church, he would somehow have to suspend his critical thinking. He didn't want to expose his "new truth" to the scrutiny of an institution. In essence, he was saying he needed to protect his direct experience with God from the Church!

To me, this is a startling testimonial for the Spirit of God. Stranger still is the observation of Nelson Linaburg, introduced in chapter 1, who has played the organ and directed choral music for a variety of Christian churches as well as a synagogue. He says the Spirit is sometimes hard to find in Christian services.

I find that the acts of some ministers do little toward inviting the Spirit in," he said. "In churches today there's much that tends to be political, keeping your standing with congregants, and picking carefully what you say. It's politics, not religion. In the cases of many ministers, the name of Jesus is called on, but not often is he there. To say nothing of calling on the Spirit and asking for that presence.

How did the simple, original, unrestricted access to the Ruach Elohim become so muddled? How did people lose their awareness of the Spirit since the time when it was so freely available? How did over twenty thousand religions come to claim God as their own, lock, stock, and barrel, with so little understanding of the engine—the Spirit— that makes it all work? Eighteen hundred years of infighting, splintering, debate, theological sleight of hand, politics, and wars might have something to do with it. And a race. A race that began two centuries after Jesus lived, to see who could be first to lash the Spirit to the yardarm of doctrine. If the Spirit of God had been truly set free for all by the Nazorean, how did access to the Spirit disappear, apparently within only a few centuries after his death? To find the answer, let's follow the trail of the Spirit just before it was captured, in turn, by doctrine, book, and creed.

FREE AS A BIRD

The early Christians didn't have an easy time of it, what with thousands of them being roasted, flayed, crucified, and devoured by wild animals in the arenas.

But in terms of contact with the Spirit, those early years after Pentecost were a lot more fun than the churches would have you believe. During the first century or two after the Shekinah flames flickered over the heads of the messengers, they began passing the Spirit freely to others as they spread Jesus' two simple rules. It's not often emphasized, but average people were experiencing "God as Spirit" as intensely as the messengers themselves.

THE SPIRIT PEOPLE

History shows that people were awakening to a strange new awareness. They were the *pneumatikoi*—people filled with the Divine Breath. They were experiencing the ecstasy of the Spirit as intensely, say some accounts, as did the prophets of old. The Word was spreading by word of mouth, and pockets of people were waking up with a new light in their eyes, discovering the "kingdom of heaven"—the reality of the Spirit alive within them.

In those early days, the church was more like a mystical union of scattered souls than a meeting place with a bell tower and pews. There were a few early bishops (overseers) and priests, though guys like Anthony were striking out into the desert to live alone. These weren't mere believers—they were experiencers of the bliss of the Spirit. They wanted to isolate themselves to protect that wonderful "feeling" against the corruptions of places such as the lascivious Corinth, which would have made Las Vegas seem like a quilting bee.

True Spirit communities were forming here and there in Asia Minor, the Middle East, and Egypt. They were truly turned on by this new baptism of Fire and Light. The Spirit hadn't been that conspicuous in human society since the time of Samuel, when the wandering guilds played music in their ten-city tours. After the Ascension of Jesus, boy and girl bands were dancing down Main Street to the sounds of flutes and the jingle-jangle of tambourines. They were prophesying and spreading the message in the atria of rich men's homes and in the cafes and the public parks.

By the end of the second century, Jesus' followers were still free of broad doctrine on the subjects of creation, the nature of the soul, the Holy Spirit, Christ, and the nature of God. The church was developing on its own, but there were so many people prophesying, and so many communities forming their own churches, some of the leaders became alarmed. They decided they'd better regulate spiritual phenomena before it got out of hand. Even Paul of Tarsus (he was originally a Pharisee whose Jewish friends called him Saul) had to tell the Corinthians to quit using the Spirit's gifts for their own ego gratification.[1]

SANCTIONS AGAINST THE SPIRIT OF GOD

The Church soon began to regulate the unauthorized download-ing of the Holy Spirit, beginning with prophecy itself, which was actually administrated into a specialized "office."[2] (I'm not making this up.) Prophets were tested, categorized, and ranked, and, of course, sorting them out from the false ones got to be a FEMA-sized problem.[3]

In the mid-second century, a Phrygian prophet named Mon-tanus had attracted thousands. He and two prophetesses, Maxi-milla and Priscilla (women were very much a part of the Spirit movements of the early centuries), who were so filled with the Spirit, they became "possessed by God"—God spoke through them in the first person, like this: "I am the Lord God omnipo-tent, who have descended into man. . . ." and "neither an angel, nor an ambassador, but I, the Lord, the Father, am come. . . ."[4]

Among their prophecies was the second advent of Christ and something like the appearance of the New Jerusalem at Pepuza (in what is now western Turkey). Pilgrims gathered from miles around on the appointed day, but the moment came and went. A lot of people were glancing at their sandals, embarrassed, and the Church decided to put a stop to prophecy once and for all.

"In principle," writes Adolf Holl in *The Left Hand of God*, "after the Montanist prophecy, virtually every instance whatso-ever of possession by the Spirit was stigmatized and rejected for the next thousand years. The couriers and messengers of God, both men and women, disappeared into the underground, the Holy Spirit became a theological abstraction, and the liturgy in the basilicas proceeded without further interruption."[5]

Popular, self-serving cults came and went, though some, such as Mani, attracted many followers. The Manichaeans believed that Mani was the "Apostle of Light," and had followers through-out Asia Minor and as far as China (Mani's influence is still felt in western religion today). Another smaller group, the mid-fourth century Enthusiasts, were women who used a type of breathing technique to infuse themselves with the Divine Breath. They cut their hair short and dressed like men, proclaiming Jesus' teachings and setting the Spirit free to the many who listened. They taught that communion with the Holy Spirit was for them more pleasurable than the act of physical love.[6]

The Enthusiasts were eventually condemned for their views on baptism and some other points, but their activities contributed to a universal ban on Holy Spirit experiences. Belief in an indwelling of the Spirit was finally listed as one of the "thousand falsehoods" sewn by the devil into sound Christian teachings. Walkin'-around prophets, at least any that the Church could endorse, disappeared from Christianity along with those ecstatic Spirit raves the people of the first centuries had enjoyed. People ecstatically filled with the Spirit were deemed insane or evil, or simply shunned to the fringes of society. This is what happened to individuals such as the medieval Armelle Nicholas and Angela Di Foligno mentioned in chapter 2, and countless others.

THE SPIRIT AND THE BOOK

Unlike the religions of Asia, the teachings of Jesus did not come with a "how-to" manual. There were no instructions, for example, for how to discipline one's mind, no techniques for taming the emotions, transforming the desires, conserving and rechanneling sexual energy, or even for practicing Christ Consciousness. It fell on Paul alone to explain Jesus' teachings to those who were trying to emulate their Lord. Paul was constantly dashing off inspired, encouraging, and even scolding missives to fledgling Christian communities by original snail-mail to Thessalonia, Galatia, Colossus, Philippi, Ephesus, Rome—seven in all—just to try to keep everyone on the same parchment. His writings reveal a man who was effervescent with the Spirit. Some say Paul, himself, created the Christian church single-handedly.

HOMEMADE GOSPELS

"Jesus had insisted that the 'powers' of God were not for him alone," writes theologian and author Karen Armstrong in *A History of God*. "Paul developed this insight by arguing that Jesus had been the first example of a new type of humanity. Not only had he done everything that the old Israel had failed to achieve, but he had become the new adām, the new humanity in which all human beings, goyim included, must somehow participate."[7]

The Jews have the Talmud, which explains every aspect of daily life relative to living the Torah; the Vedantists have the *Baghavad Gita*, yoga sutras, and many other guidebooks; and Muslims have the hadith and other texts. But aside from Jesus' own words, which had begun to circulate in various drafts and versions, Paul's letters were the only "how-to's" that the struggling Christians had. So practically by themselves, Paul's letters kept the fledgling communities from flaming out. A century or two after Paul, however, it became apparent to Church leaders that the scattered Christians desperately needed their own Bible in order to keep the movement alive.

During the first centuries after Pentecost, there was no standard primer for Jesus' new path to the Spirit. In the far-flung cities and villages, people were writing down the stories they heard from traveling disciples, and these diaries became the Bibles for those towns. Other than the Torah, which had been translated into Greek in 282 B.C.E., they relied on the locally produced books.

Some of these homemade "gospels" were accurate, some incomplete, and others incompetent, but one thing they could all agree on was that there were no original manuscripts of the Gospels, only Greek translations, some of which diverged widely in detail. Planning began as early as 185 C.E., when Bishop Irenaeus suggested candidate manuscripts for the four Gospels that would be included in an eventual New Testament that they hoped everyone would agree on. But the early Church Fathers would debate for almost three centuries, not only on the content of the Bible, but how the international population of the time could be corralled into a singular belief system.

THEY NEEDED A BOOK

At this point, the Spirit was still free as a bird, at least in individuals everywhere to whom Jesus' Comforter had opened the doors to understanding. But with those early communities developing theologies of their own, the teachings could very well have disintegrated into superstitious hearsay if some authority hadn't taken the reins.

Over the next few centuries, a lot of ideology was debated. In 367, four manuscripts were finally chosen to be the official gospels. The names of Matthew, Mark, Luke, and John were affixed to them (after scholars decided that they were derived from original manuscripts authored by them).[8] Decisions both good and ill occurred along the way. However, many Christians to this day believe that the Spirit guided the overall process, even as imperfect men, working centuries after the death of Mary's son, edited, shaped, and pieced it all together. Others allow that the inserts, deletions, and errors, even the choices of which books to include (the Book of Enoch, for example, was at one time included) yielded a Bible which, although it is indispensable to the study of Jesus' teachings, may be remembered as having passed through many human hands and some grueling politics.

In 408, a comprehensive Latin Bible was finally produced by St. Jerome and two women (whom later writers referred to as the "venerable brothers" because they didn't want it known that women had played a major role in it). A complete Bible, with all the separate books bound within a cover, only became available around 550. Among other miscellaneous books, it usually contained Jerome's Old Testament translation from the Hebrew and his revision of the Gospels. The Latin Vulgate (version) has been subject to revision and correction ever since, even as late as the 1960s.

This off-road search for the Spirit of God certainly respects the authority of the Bible on the life of Jesus, while encouraging people to read it for themselves. However, as a caution to literalists, I mention this quote from the *Encyclopedia Britannica*, pertaining to the letters of Paul: "Of these, Romans, I and II Corinthians, and Galatians are indisputably genuine. Most scholars also accept Philippians, I Thessalonians, and Philemon. Opinion is divided about Ephesians, Colossians, and II Thessalonians. The Pastoral Letters (I and II Timothy and Titus) are held by many scholars to have been written considerably later than the time of Paul."

In his book *Lost Christianities*, Bart D. Ehrman, chairman of the Department of Religious Studies at the University of North Carolina, Chapel Hill, discusses a wide variety of credible early church documents and sources that would have changed the course of Christianity had they been chosen instead of the twenty-seven books that the New Testament now comprises. Ehrman writes, "Scripture passages dealing with Christ, his Father, and the Spirit were carefully examined, combined, amalgamated—all in order to make sense of the Trinitarian mystery."[9]

As the Bible was being developed, however, another bit of creative theology was unfolding that would not only change Christianity forever, but imprison the Spirit, right along with the Father and the Son, for a thousand years.

THREE CREEDS TO THE WIND

By the mid-third century, the Spirit was still flowing unfettered, but thinkers began to argue the fine points: Was Jesus equal to the Father? Less than the Father? And what was the Holy Spirit, anyway?

Enter a pagan general, Constantine, a native of what is now Serbia, who wouldn't have known a prophet from a sibyl. Before the Battle of Milvian Bridge (312), he saw what he believed to be a vision of Christ, so he painted crosses on the shields of his soldiers. Against bad odds, he won the battle, and as a result he adopted Christianity. Soon becoming emperor of the entire Roman Empire, he declared Christianity the official religion of the Eastern and Western Empires, dismissing all other religions as heresies.[10]

Constantine is still revered as a saint in the Orthodox Catholic Church, but in at least one sense, Christianity was a spoil of war. Commendably, Constantine put a stop to the recreational torture of Christians and even went easy on his enemy captives, which was unheard of in those days.

When he took control, there was already a lot of confusion about Jesus, Christ, the Father, and the Spirit. Some believed them to be of the same divine substance, others a hierarchy; still others thought they were just different names for the same being.

ARIUS AND ATHANASIUS

The Bible manuscripts made no mention of a trinity of three divine persons. However, the concept had already been discussed in the second century by Theophilus of Antioch, Origen of Alexandria, and Tertullian. This is because the idea of a divine trinity was familiar from ancient times: the Egyptians worshiped Osiris, Isis, and Horus; the Vedantists, Brahma, Shiva, and Vishnu; in Babylon it was Nimrod, Semiramas, and Tammuz; and in Platonism, the Unknown Father, the Logos, and the World Soul. How would the overseers juggle the divinity of Jesus, the Christ, the Father, and the Spirit? Trouble was brewing.

Around 320, an Alexandrian presbyter named Arius was gaining support promoting the idea that Jesus was human, citing the Nazorean's statement that the Father was greater than he. However, Arius's longtime assistant, Athanasius, turned on him, insisting that Jesus had to be God. Athanasius was all over the newly Christianized Constantine, urging him to stop Arius in his tracks. The emperor, tired of the aggravation, sent a courier to order Arius and his thousands of followers to cease and desist, but they refused.

"Arius believed that Christians had been saved and made divine sharers in the nature of God," writes Karen Armstrong. "This was only possible because Jesus had blazed a trail for us. . . . If Jesus had not been a human being, there would be no hope for us. There would have been nothing meritorious in his life if he had been God by nature, nothing for us to imitate. It was by contemplating Christ's life of perfectly obedient sonship that Christians would become divine themselves."[11]

But Athanasius flipped that coin, saying that Jesus had to be divine, otherwise there would be no divine mediator between God and man—Jesus would be in the same boat with men, so to speak, and would be unable to save humankind from self-annihilation. Missing the point that the Spirit was the intended new mediator (Comforter) between God and humankind, Athanasius concluded that Jesus had to be made of the "same stuff" as God. This view virtually eliminated the potential for humans to do what Jesus had done, and this was the view that took hold.

The deed was done in 325 at the Council of Nicaea, which created an oath by which all Christians would swear that God and Jesus were the same and that the Church had the power to say so. Few Christians at that time would actually have agreed with Athanasius's view of Christ, writes Armstrong, but the Nicean Creed became the official statement of faith for Christians, as it is today, and forevermore.

The Nicean Creed, at that time, concluded with these words:

> . . . We believe in one Lord, Jesus Christ, the only Son of God, eternally begotten of the Father, God from God, Light from Light, true God from true God, begotten, not made, of one Being with the Father. And we believe in the Holy Spirit.

Right out the window went Jesus' various statements that he had been "sent" by the "Father." Out went an earlier Apostles' Creed, based on the Scripture itself, that did not presume to define what God was. Out went Jesus' humanity and the down-to-earth value of what he accomplished and what he taught. Gone was the idea that Jesus had provided the pattern for how individual humans could themselves unite with the Ruach Elohim that created the world and could live forever in the bliss of Spirit.

Historians agree that though Constantine was educated, he had no understanding of theology. Out of 318 churchmen attending the Council, only three had been invited from Rome, and these spoke no Greek, so they were confused from the beginning about the Trinity. (This was a confusion that would last until Augustine put his stamp on it in the fifth century.) The emperor threatened banishment for anyone who did not sign the document, and the only abstainers were Arius and a couple of companions. After the papers were signed, Arius (deemed a heretic forevermore) was not even invited to the wrap party.

SQUEEZING IN THE SPIRIT

The Creed didn't catch on right away, and debate continued for another sixty years. "Unfortunately a dogmatic intolerance was creeping into Christianity," writes Armstrong, "which would ultimately make the adoption of the 'correct' or orthodox symbols crucial and obligatory. This doctrinal obsession, unique to Christianity, could easily lead to a confusion between the human symbol and the divine reality."[12]

Some people thought it odd that after all that, the Spirit was barely mentioned in the new Creed. In fact, it was only added last as an afterthought:

And we believe in the Holy Spirit.

In the late fourth century, three scholars from Cappadocia wanted to do something about that. Basil and the two Gregorys reasoned that because Paul spoke of the Spirit as renewing, creating, and sanctifying, these were activities of God. Therefore, they thought, the Spirit, too, must be divine.[13] God was an incomprehensible reality that expressed itself in three ways that humans can understand, so the Cappadocian Fathers solved the conundrum by devising a concept that the Father, Son, and Holy Spirit were three persons in one. A trinity of "three divine persons" was cast in stone, even though it was based on deduction and not Scripture.[14]

Jesus was no longer the man of humble origin who had resurrected himself into immortal oneness with the Spirit of God. The Spirit that hovered over the waters wasn't Elohim anymore, but a "person" in "his" own right. The Creed, and its subsequent revisions over the centuries, effectively put God in a three-piece suit, elevated the Christos out of the reach of ordinary people, and shrouded the Spirit into an inaccessible abstraction. Any further claims of being filled by the Holy Spirit could land you in hot water. Christians had officially traded their direct experience with God for a world-class dogma.

In *The Christian Agnostic*, the late Leslie D. Weatherhead, pastoral psychologist and longtime pastor of The City Temple, London, had this to say about creeds:

> May I suggest to you, my reader, that in some quiet hour you write out your own creed? Do not copy anybody else's. Do not try and make yourself believe what to you seems absurd. Do not have anything foisted on you at all. Write out what for you is true.[15]

A church confident enough to legislate God and declare itself the sole conduit for communication from the Divine would have to find ways to ensure its absolute power. Such a church would have to determine and design and administer every spiritual need. To do that, it would require a solid, iron-fisted Homeland

Security organization, a doctrine dictated by a lengthy canon of laws and rituals that could weather any storm, and, additionally, a priesthood empowered to dispense salvation and forgive sins. Any further challenges to theology would be a challenge to the autonomy of the Church itself, and easily silenced.

As the Catholic religious philosopher Søren Kierkegaard wrote, "Christendom has done away with Christianity without being quite aware of it."[16]

A SIX-LETTER WORD FOR GOD

The problem with any chat about the Spirit lies in trying to use modern human language. Interpreting ancient writings about the Spirit in modern language, especially English, expresses the subtleties and ecstasies of the Spirit with all the eloquence of a sportscaster calling a football play.

In my interview with him, Baptist pastor Rev. R. Scott Walker commented on the importance of language:

> Words are always inadequate to convey spiritual truth. Because of the limitation of our intelligence perception and also because of the limitations of our words, we are always having to talk about analogy. A "picture form" to point to a truth that is beyond our understanding. The Trinity is an analogy. It makes no attempt to be taken absolutely literally, and that's why we get into the problem of turning God almost into three gods. Because we're dealing with an analogy that we call the Trinity. And in that analogy we are saying God is experienced in diverse ways by humans.

Ten people will describe their experiences with the Spirit in ten different ways—they might even go at each other's throats over perceived insults in the telling. What else can one expect from a mental and emotional phenomenon that originates in the mind of the Ultimate Reality?

PESKY PRONOUNS

Because the New Testament refers to the Spirit as "he," it's unavoidable for literalists to plaster the Spirit with humanlike traits. In simple logic, they apply human qualities due to certain passages in the Bible: the Spirit teaches, has a mind, can be grieved, must be obeyed, can be lied to, insulted, and so on. How else could the Spirit be explained to a primitive humankind? This is the reason why Jesus explained his theology using symbols, such as sowers, Samaritans, fruit trees, and virgins. It's like the old Yiddish proverb that says "If triangles had a God, he'd have three sides."

As we have seen, some people believe that development of the modern Bible was under the direct control of God, the frailties of men included in the plan. Others offer proof that the book has errors in translation and, as we saw above, was even tampered with for political, liturgical, or convenience sake. It's hard to ignore the charges, but another problem lies in the language itself.

The Gospels show that Jesus referred to the Spirit as "he/him," and a literalist has no other thought but that the Spirit must therefore be male. On one hand, calling the Spirit "he" and "him" anthropomorphizes the Deity. On the other hand, what were the early church fathers to do? They couldn't change Jesus' preposition to "It," so "He" would remain "He." Because of the difficulties of language, they painted themselves into a linguistic corner.

God is referred to as "He" throughout the Bible, and so, of course, is Mary's son, who was an in-the-flesh human male. The syllogism that created this dilemma is amusing, because it made the leap from "He" to "Person" an easy one. If you're happy with "He," then use "He," but the Spirit that brooded over the waters could in nowise have been some type of man. Some people don't think the pronouns matter one way or the other, and I side with them.

OYATE

This is just one more example of the problem of language, especially the English language, which is woefully inadequate for expressing abstract spiritual truth. I once attended a talk by a Lakota elder who referred to English as an "evil and dangerous language."

Why would he say a thing like that? Maybe because the meanings of most of our words stem from other languages. To understand the meaning of the English word "philosophy," for example, you have to look up its Greek roots: *philos-* (love of) *-sophia* (wisdom). Most of our other words derive from Greek, Latin, French, German, Scandinavian, and even some Arabic words. A Lakota word for community is *oyate*. Its meaning is clear. A Lakota child doesn't have to look up its Latin origin in a dictionary to know what *oyate* means. If the child's name is Moon Wolf, he doesn't have to consult a name dictionary to see what it originally meant back in Europe.

You can find perhaps the most exquisite use of English in the verses of Shakespeare, but you won't find a practical lexicon for conveying the ways of the Spirit. I've already mentioned the fact that by the time of Jesus, the Jews were speaking Aramaic. But as we know, contemporary records of Jesus' teachings don't exist—he never wrote anything down. People only started writing down what he said decades after his death. They wrote in Greek, which was eventually translated into Latin. Then the Latin was translated into English, which, at its best, is great, unless you want to do more than order lunch. If someone were one day to discover the missing Aramaic diaries of Jesus, perhaps only then would we understand how our language has failed us.

LAYERS OF MEANING

Translations of the Bible into English were forbidden until King James turned that around in 1611. John Wycliffe had tried it in 1380—and was executed. A Reformation later, in 1534, William Tyndale tried it—and was hanged. However, Tyndale's version contributed greatly to the form and substance of the King James—a far cry from the Greek and Hebrew manuscripts of over a thousand years earlier, and even more remote from the Aramaic that Jesus actually spoke.

"Like its sister languages Hebrew and Arabic, Aramaic can express many layers of meaning," wrote Neil Douglas-Klotz in *Prayers of the Cosmos: Meditations on the Aramaic Words of Jesus.* "Words are organized and defined based on a poetic root-and-pattern system, so that each word may have several meanings, at first seemingly unrelated, but upon contemplation revealing an inner connection. The same word may be translated, for instance, as 'name,' 'light,' 'sound,' or 'experience.'"[17]

He writes that each word or phrase needs to be examined from various angles, explaining, "Jesus showed a mastery of this use of transformative language, which survives even through inadequate translations."

Douglas-Klotz cites the example of our word *heaven*. Modern Christians, Jews, and Moslems think of a promised paradise, a realm where the deserving go after they die. Clouds. Golden harps. For some Muslims, seventy-two virgins. The Aramaic word for "heaven," however, evokes something quite lovely: "The light and sound shining through all creation." Jesus' promise of the "kingdom of heaven" within you suddenly takes on a fresh, vibrant meaning: "The light and sound shining through all creation" within you.

Heaven, therefore, may be more an eternal condition of the heart and mind than an appointment with St. Peter. It's too bad there isn't some special language that could perfectly express spiritual ideas, abstract by their very nature, which would distinguish between degrees of human perception, give names to the numinous qualities of God and the nature of the soul, and eliminate vagueness.

BLISSFUL REALM

Well, there *are* such languages. Hebrew and Arabic are two of them, Aramaic another. Another is Sanskrit, a language that was deliberately refined for the purpose of describing spiritual phenomena and conveying theological ideas. (A 1976 article by Prof. Madan Mohan Shukla of the Oriental Institute at Baroda, India, provided evidence that Hebrew and Sanskrit share considerable vocabulary.)

I checked a Sanskrit-English dictionary, and found dozens of entries for "heaven"—such as *sukhavati*, for "blissful realm." But I also found the following:

> Brahman: the Absolute Reality; existence-knowledge-bliss; God
>
> sva: heaven or paradise
>
> nada: the primal sound from which all creation emanated; the first manifestation of the unmanifested Absolute
>
> brahmajyoti: the light of God
>
> mahat tattwa: cosmic intelligence; Christ Consciousness; the firstborn
>
> chidakasha: pure consciousness in the all-pervading continuum
>
> nirvana: liberation from the necessity to live on earth; a type of ascension
>
> turiya-turiya: the Absolute Consciousness of God behind our individualized consciousness (recalls the name of Yahweh: "I Am That I Am")

There seems to be no subtlety of divine reality that cannot be clearly expressed in Sanskrit. Think of the "sound" shining through all creation as the "Word," which would be the Sultan-ul-Azkar to the Muslim mystics; the *nada* or *udgeet*, meaning the "song from above" to the Vedantists. The "Word" referred to by John as a synonym for the Christos is the sound and light active through all creation: the Logos = Word = Divine Reason. The active principle of Elohim that first moved in the beginning.

Surround yourself with Spirit for sixty centuries like the Vedantists have, and you'll find yourself craving a more grown-up language to understand the Spirit, in its essence, at its core.

I'm not saying "Let's translate the Bible into Sanskrit." I'm saying only that as we read the Bible, or any English-language rendition of a sacred teaching, we should read between the lines and ask Spirit to convey the deeper understanding, because the King's English may only provide a scant outline of the "spirit" of the original teaching. Mistranslations such as "ghost" for "spirit" just don't help.[18] "Holy Ghost"? Sure, now everyone can relate.

Anyone who has worked in a business or church group knows that once a committee turns a teaching into a policy, they anaesthetize it, pith it, dissect it, and then reassemble it into something they can manage. The committee codifies the teaching, conforms it to some structure, and eventually pins it to a display board for others to scrutinize. Then they turn their attention to what the other guys are doing wrong, and war is usually just around the corner.

THE CHURCHES AT WAR

Rev. Henry Van Dusen wrote, "Thus, we see what Christians believe about the Holy Spirit is involved in virtually every major problem of Christian faith."[19]

In the centuries after Constantine, an action adventure unfolded in which groups took turns imprisoning the Spirit, only to be eventually rescued by outraged reformers, who would then imprison it again in new ways. It's ironic that the unifying force of the One God would become a wedge not only that divided one religion from another, but cleaved them into bitter factions within themselves.

After the passing of their founding prophets, well-meaning organizers passionately drove onward. Paul knew this would happen, writing, "The written code kills, but the Spirit gives life."[20] It appears that this pattern occurs in every religion.

RELIGION DIVIDES

Inspired by the Spirit, Buddha created an enlightened new religion in reaction against the cruelties of Hinduism. Within a century of his death, however, early Buddhists began to argue over whether Buddha was God or human—sound familiar? The religion split into many divisions, three of which are prominent today. Theravada is an orthodox view that values wisdom over compassion, believing that Buddha was a man who became a saint through such effort—a goal all individuals can attain. The goal is to achieve nirvana for yourself. Mahayana Buddhists value compassion over wisdom and believe one should strive for enlightenment in order to help others.[21] Vajrayana Buddhism, found mostly in Tibet, is the "thunderbolt" path to Nirvana that teaches the direct experience and inner knowledge (gnosis) of the Divine.

Islam divided, too, into Sunni and Shiite, the former believing Muhammad's successor should be an elected leader, the latter believing his successor should be a blood descendant. Shiites believe further that such imams are divinely appointed by God. Judaism divided into three main divisions: Reform, which allows adaptation of Jewish practice to one's time and situation; Orthodox, which insists that the Law is fixed and cannot be altered; and Conservative, which allows for modernizing some aspects of practice. Islam, Judaism, and Christianity also have their mystical branches, and we will grapple with those in chapter 9.

EAST FROM WEST

Perhaps no religion besides Hinduism has divided into more splinters than the Christian church. The six centuries after

Constantine saw a tug of war among five competing capitals of Christian authority: Rome, Constantinople, Antioch, Alexandria, and Jerusalem. They continued to argue about the relative humanness or divinity of Jesus and their relationship to the forever abstract God the Father. For a few centuries they ignored the tough one, the Spirit, but eventually they were forced to deal with it.

The East and West had been feuding about which pope or patriarch was the rightful descendant from Peter, and the Spirit became the pickle in the middle: the Roman Church cast in stone that the Spirit "proceeds from the Father and the Son," whereas the Orthodox Christian Church insisted that it "proceeds from the Father" only. The Roman Church decreed that the Spirit was active only in their church members through the dispensation of the priests. The Eastern Church believed the Spirit was freely available to any church member.

These disagreements and others led to the first true theological split in the Church in 1050, when the Eastern and Western factions excommunicated each other. The Eastern Church wasn't about to be told what to do by Rome without even being invited to the table. The Roman Church's excommunication of the Orthodox Catholic Church was only revoked by John Paul II, who tried to heal the rift—JPII was the first pope ever to enter a synagogue and an Orthodox church.

But Rome's problem with total control had only just begun. Over the next five centuries, discontent grew among the faithful as the Church attempted to legislate every aspect of life: to reinforce guilt and sinfulness, broker forgiveness, and dispense indulgences that could lessen the penalties—for example, one could pay the local friar in cash to reduce by a few years one's inevitable sojourn in hell.

The Spirit of God was the principle authority in Christian faith from the beginning, but once it was held captive by Rome, the debate that led to the Reformation had begun. Van Dusen wrote that the split dividing Catholicism and Protestantism came down to whether the Holy Spirit's primary authority lay in the Bible, the Church, or one's individual conscience.[22]

REPAIR MY HOUSE

In 1205, one of the first reformers of the Roman church emerged. A wealthy young man from Assisi was praying one day when he heard these words: "Go, Francesco, and repair my house which, as you see, is well-nigh in ruins."

Francesco abandoned his wealth and family and spent the rest of his life trying to restore the original teachings. He and his followers rejected money and even honored God in nature. The Church fought him until people started following him, and then, against his wishes, absorbed the Franciscan movement as one of its own.

Three centuries later, Martin Luther and John Calvin rebelled against Rome. One of their tenets was that the Holy Spirit didn't belong to the Church and its priesthood but strictly to Scripture, in which the faithful could read its message for themselves. The Reformation was the second major split of the Church, and the reforms attempted to free the Spirit the way it used to be. They also established for their followers that forgiveness of sins came through grace from God directly, rather through confession to a priest.

The Church launched its Counter-Reformation with the Council of Trent, culminating in 1563, in which the Church declared itself on equal authority with the Bible. This, along with centuries of the Inquisition, might have scared off a skittish reformer, but Luther and his friends, it seems, would imprison God again—this time trapping the Deity in the literal typography of the Bible. Enter Radical Protestantism, in which a whole new wave of Spirit-filled interpreters attempted to bring the Spirit back to the people the way it was in the old days.

Later reformers and dissidents believed that the operation of the Holy Spirit was not an arm of the institutional Church, but came directly to "expectant and contrite" souls in our time as it has through all the ages. They believed that the Spirit was not confined to Scripture, but could give "new truth" that God desired to reveal to everyday people.

What was the Roman Church to do? It had already declared itself equal in authority to the Bible. By 1870, there remained only one option to ward off all further debate. Pope Leo XIII declared himself infallible, and this went for all future popes, too. The Church cited biblical, historical, and theological grounds, which Protestant theologians have disputed ever since as self-serving and without foundation.

The explosion of Spirit-inspired theologies of the nineteenth century found ways to once again free the Spirit to inspire individuals in their daily lives; we will look at some of these in chapter 7. Some, such as the modern-day charismatics and Pentecostals, believe they have returned to the Spirit-party atmosphere of the first centuries. (It's well known among evangelicals that since World War II Pentecostalism has been the fastest-growing religion in the world, particularly in Latin and South America.)

WORDS TO THE WISE

Dissatisfaction with the churches is at an all-time high. My off-road search actually brought me into contact with people who are frustrated and angry, who don't know where to turn for direct contact with God, even if they believed it were possible.

Psychologist David Gordon, Ph.D., of Norfolk, Virginia, told me, "Without generalizing too much, the Christian church tends to be fear-based and shame-based, so my clients are getting that from their families. But they're also immersed in a church that says God agrees. So it's a deep negative condition. It's a sense of 'I'm not really adequate or worthy of love.'" The psychologists I interviewed agreed across the board that many of their Christian clients have deep-seated problems with guilt and shame, the child-molestation scandal of the Roman Church notwithstanding.

In *The Christian Agnostic*, Leslie D. Weatherhead wrote, "Not for much longer will the world put up with the lies, the superstitions and the distortions with which the joyous and essentially simple message of Christ has been overlaid."[23]

He likened the modern church to the legendary pipe the young Moses played to gather Jethro's sheep. The pipe was later adorned with gold and revered as a holy relic. However, once the pipe was gilded, it no longer played.

Weatherhead continued, "So the message of Galilee is overlaid with creeds and ceremonies and doctrines, and what with denominational squabbles, mutual disapprovals, and intolerances, one can hardly catch the message of the Son of Man or be lifted up and strengthened by its beauty and power."

Rev. VonderOhe summed up a sobering warning to the churches.

The whole interpretation of Jesus' life, death, and resurrection has been focused on human unworthiness, human guilt, and basic human shame, and that somehow God has intervened in a special way, and it's the only way.

I think this theology has to change, and I think it will change. If the Church doesn't change it, it will become obsolete within the next fifty years. People are beginning to realize that if you say you are a spiritual being that has an ultimate connection with the Divine and that you're here on a life journey to fulfill that, you basically shouldn't have that sense of unworthiness, that sense that God is separate or angry at you.

I think that theology has to change because it undermines the heart of the true church in many ways. I don't think you can do that without changing your interpretation of the life, ministry, death, and resurrection of Jesus. But I think that's what the church has to hear if they are going to continue to be relevant beyond the middle of this century. It doesn't mean that suddenly those churches won't exist, it just means that for the spiritual life and vitality of people, they are going to be obsolete and irrelevant.

Another Norfolk, Virginia, psychotherapist John Mein, Ph.D., commented on what the churches should be:

> The ideal role of the church would be to be loving and accepting, to be less judgmental and guilt-provoking. I realized a long time ago that I don't go to church for spiritual reasons. So let the churches become more spiritual. And I think mainstream churches should be doing healing work. That's what people are seeking. They get up on a Sunday morning and other than this fellowship of being with friends, there's a part that's yearning to be fed and is not being fed. So they should be more spiritual.

David, Kieth, and John got me thinking about the prophets of old and how they might comment on our age. Where are the prophets with the vision of a Moses, the insight of a Samuel, the heart of a Jesus, or the sheer strength of a Samson or Mary? If they were with us today, such prophets might point accusing fingers at those who wage war in the name of the Lord and condemn the sons and daughters of God to bleak lives of separation from the Divine.

Over the millennia, the Spirit has drawn humankind closer to itself just as humankind has inched toward the Ultimate Reality, the "I Am That I Am"—God. Maybe it won't be some external prophet who wakes up a dozing humanity, but the internal prophet within each of us during this time when awareness of the Spirit is on the rise. Perhaps the real congregation of the Spirit of God is only just beginning to awake on its own—an awakening congregation that has no name, no church, and no temple.

the
SPIRIT
WITHIN

My off-road search has already yielded some intriguing observations. Clearly, "I Am That I Am" has informed human thought since the beginning, all the while trying to get a Word in edgewise. The flame of Spirit, within us from creation, fuels our very consciousness, and its influence seems at first glance to unpredictably appear and disappear, shrink and balloon again. Despite the political chicanery of the Dark Ages, the Spirit has never ceased to comfort, inspire, thrill, and guide, while it empowers those who would set it free and pass it on to others.

Direct contact with the Spirit has never ceased, and such contacts may actually be on the rise because of a growing urgency in people to know the Divine. Though they describe their experiences variously as God, Jesus, Christ, the Spirit, an angel, a bodhisattva, an avatar, a benevolent being, a god, a helper, the "higher self," the soul, or simply a wrinkle in the space-time continuum, the labels don't matter much. The Spirit doesn't even require a church, temple, sect, or religion—just a willing mind and a deliberate open heart.

And hearts are opening everywhere—all kinds of hearts. Some of the most dramatic Spirit events reported in this book came from people who had little or no religious background, like engineer Adam Ward, introduced in chapter 4, and psychotherapist Dani Vedros, whose story follows shortly. People of every stripe are awakening to their divine nature. They don't know each other, yet they collectively form a type of unified congregation—an awakening congregation of the Ruach Yahweh that may well have been the ultimate payoff of the One God initiative that began with Abraham.

THE AWAKENING CONGREGATION

Two months before I interviewed him, Rev. Kieth VonderOhe was diagnosed with cancer of the liver. By August 2001, the disease was progressing rapidly. The introspective thinker had always been highly intellectual, but during the ravages of chemotherapy, his direct experience with the Spirit brought clarity. He explained,

> For the past two or three years, I'd been feeling disconnected from Spirit and from people. My meditation life had seemed to stall, and I had difficulty getting focused. I started feeling very disconnected from the universe. I was becoming more and more introverted and frustrated. But when I was diagnosed with cancer, I found people reaching out to me. I started opening up again through meditation, receiving laying-on-of-hands experiences, and within a matter of a week or so, I felt surrounded with such an intense presence and love like I never felt before in my life.
>
> Now it takes just about a minute or two to feel that intense light or whatever it is you call the presence of the Divine. You can call it the Spirit, you can call it the presence of the Divine, but it's a sense of being surrounded and loved, and knowing that I really am loved unconditionally by a force that knows everything I've done. I've had the intellectual

knowledge of that, but now I feel it to the depth of my soul. This is what's important for me, for anyone, to get in touch with.

Although he was trained in an orthodox Christian tradition, he came to think of the Spirit as a "manifestation of oneness in a living, dynamic way in people's lives." He thought the experience needed new language because, increasingly, experiences with the Spirit are occurring outside of religious institutions.

If you look back at church history, the Holy Spirit is not something that church establishments wanted to deal with when the Spirit really started to be active two to three centuries after Jesus. People would say they were inspired, but this would upset the establishment considerably.

All branches of Christianity are finding themselves threatened with new thinkers and controversial books containing things that the established churches don't want to hear. So when you look at the movement of the Spirit, it's almost regardless of which sect or whether it's the conservative or liberal fringe; getting people back into a direct experience of the Divine is upsetting to the establishment.

I think this Spirit we're talking about is the "Comforter" Jesus spoke about. I can't imagine what else he was talking about if he wasn't talking about the living presence that comes through what people call the Holy Spirit. People have a sense that sometimes they have an actual picture or sense of the presence of Jesus, you could also call that the Comforter. Some people don't have that. They feel this living presence in different forms.

If I've learned anything during the off-road search, it's that people feel the living presence of God in different ways. They range from flashes of being one with the universe, to an exhilarating comfort during traumatic times, to visions, to extended feelings of love and blissful transports to experiences of profound conversion that transform their lives.

Like Lewis Carroll's Alice reaching her hand through the looking glass, we are surprised when smacked with tangible proof of the Spirit. We know its intelligence and love, but our relationship with God resembles a rocky romance. Like Alice, we don't know what to think about the unseen until we experience it for ourselves. Like the bridge in the musical *Brigadoon* that appears and disappears, our direct experience of the Divine comes and goes. As Jesus said, "The wind blows where it will, and you hear the sound of it, but you do not know whence it comes or whither it goes; so it is with everyone who is born of the Spirit."[1]

We continuously look for a sign, and more and more people every day are feeling the effects, however they personally acknowledge it. People who have experienced the Spirit in their lives are united by a common knowing that the Spirit has reached through the veil, opened their awareness, and touched them. Perhaps the experience resides in that person's consciousness. Perhaps in the collective sense, people of every tradition who have been awakened by the Spirit in some way form a hidden congregation, united in the experience of the Fire and Light that they share.

The Spirit manifests to this one but not that one. To one member of a family but not another. It manifests to believers and nonbelievers, all of whom were doing something right with their hearts on a given day. The Spirit's scattered congregation is united in consciousness through their experiences. The hidden congregation spans the boundaries of organized religion, whose only members are those who have been expanded to some degree—a little or a lot—by the Fire and Light. Maybe this is the congregation that will ultimately prevail. The original congregation of humankind that will eventually include everyone.

It is a congregation that will never meet on the church lawn, at a fish fry, at a Sabbath seder, or at bingo. But they have one thing in common, whatever their background and whatever their beliefs: they've all been "taken up" to some degree. Whether in meditation or dreams. While walking down the street, or gazing off into the ocean on a cruise, or working in a scientific laboratory.

Whether its members ascribe to a religion or not, live in the jungle and wear no clothes, babble in tongues on Saturday night in a church, counsel patients, take the host at communion, bring fruit to the altars of Shakti or Buddha, bow toward Mecca, reject neckties and fancy cars, eat mushrooms in the Yucatan, espouse atheism, praise Jesus, dance with rattlesnakes, curl their sideburns, or whirl in ecstatic circles, the only true congregation may be the scattered one of people who have seen and know the Spirit in their own hearts and minds. They are those whose eyes shine with a new light because they've been lifted up and have glimpsed the All and their part in it. They've tasted the Oneness of the name of God, YHWH, the unity of "I Am That I Am" inside and outside. They are the congregation who has cried real tears because its members know what they know, firsthand. It's no longer about what they "believe." They've moved beyond faith, because now they *know*.

Peter described the members of the church as the "elect," a "royal priesthood, a holy nation, a people for God's own possession."[2] The "elect" is variously used to describe the Chosen People or angels, but also a human community of believers, the people of God, or people in some way aware of the Spirit. Perhaps the elect are those who have been awakened or touched by the Spirit, and this is what Jesus meant by being "born-anew." This then is the meaning of baptism by the Spirit (understanding) and by fire (transformation).

Is the Second Coming of Christ—Christ Consciousness— taking place right now in the awakening congregation? Is it unfolding directly in the minds of people who don't know each other by name, but who have in common their inner knowledge of divine thought? Perhaps they know each other in the transcendent oneness; the blessed, exhilarating, and reborn experience that opened their eyes to higher truth and raised them closer to oneness in "I Am That I Am."

I wanted to explore this idea of an "awakening congregation," and the inner experience of the Spirit. How does the Spirit operate in individuals? If the Spirit is within us, how does it behave? For an answer to that question, we need an independent source. The experiences and views of someone who grew up unencumbered by religious training of any kind.

THE WONDER OF ONENESS

Dani Vedros didn't grow up in a religious household. In fact, her parents were self-avowed atheists. She has never attended a church service or received any religious instruction. But she has had many profound experiences that are consistent with the Spirit of God, although she doesn't use the words "Spirit" or "Holy Spirit" to describe them.

> When I was eleven years old, we were living in a neighborhood of Southern Baptists. All my friends' parents were churchgoing, and it was quite a scandal that we were the radical atheist family. The church moms would always try to talk me into going to church, and I remember one telling me, "I don't understand if you don't believe in God why you don't just go out and kill people." And I remember thinking, my God, lady, I hope you never lose your faith.

Apparently, Dani had escaped the childhood training that teaches people what *not* to expect from the Divine. I thought it would be a help in the off-road search to relate some of her experiences and what she believed them to be. She told me of an event that occurred in 2004.

> I had this vision in which I felt like what someone may describe as a near-death experience (NDE). I was kind of traveling through the cosmos toward this blue pulsating mandala [a geometrical painting used in some Asian religions to symbolize abstract spiritual concepts]. It seemed like a mandala of souls. Just this beautiful jewel-like blue,

and my emotional experience was absolute awe and curiosity. And I had this kind of feeling, you know when people describe NDEs and they're "moving toward the light."

In that moment, I fully understood that the pull towards that exquisite pulsating entity was so strong and so beautiful, and I felt so much curiosity, and so connected, if I had just moved into it, I would have become a part of it and expanded into it. And I wanted that so, so badly. It was just amazing, like I understood that that's what moving toward the other side is like. So it was like an NDE without actually having to die or have a traumatic injury.

After the experience, my fear and anxiety and sense of death has completely changed. It's like I really understand it to be a transition. It was an experience that actually changed the way I view moving on to the other side.

Dani is a therapist in private practice who works with sex offenders. She and her husband, David Gordon, Ph.D., founded the Studio for the Healing Arts and the Women's Healing Collective in Norfolk, Virginia. I asked her if she felt the experience was a function of something within herself or caused by some outside intelligence.

"An outside intelligence," she said emphatically. "It was grace. There was no effort on my part, and I didn't ask for it. Something outside acting. I've had [visionary and psychic] experiences in meditation, but not like this. I was physically exhausted that day. It was absolutely nothing that I had worked for. It was just a gift."

I WISH I COULD

Dani next described an experience she had in Berkeley while attending a workshop on dreams with David. She was relaxed and in what she describes as an "open" condition.

We were sitting in a restaurant near the Embarcadero. I suddenly felt such a sense of nonduality or unity with everything in the entire restaurant. Then later, out on the sidewalk, everything took on a shimmery glow, and it felt like a complete experience of openness, so much so, that after a while it became necessary for me to consciously shut it back down. It felt like I was too open.

Dani and David walked into a wooded area, where the experience continued.

> Then I just had this sense that we all have our own obstacles. Some of us need to experience struggle, and others are supposed to help, so maybe my role is to help others, and that's why [being compassionate] is so easy. The ease of it scared me, and at exactly that moment I looked up and saw a man in a wheelchair, and, of all places, he was trying to move through this path in the woods. His wheel was stuck, and he asked me to help get him unstuck and guide him along the path!

As I listened to Dani describe this, I couldn't shake knowing that she didn't grow up in a religious household. One of the first things that strikes you about her is her naturally compassionate, loving, and nonjudgmental attitude. Because I am suspicious by nature, I wondered if she weren't just carrying some practiced clinical style into her social life. But talk with her for five minutes, and you realize that's the way she is. She says,

> I never thought that a religious dogma was required for a person to have compassion. And I think my family had an ethic of service and morality. They were deeply involved in the civil rights movement. I was raised among religious people who were hypocritical racists, so when I was a child, I began to see religion itself as being evil. I really thought it important to integrate our own morality and our own sense of compassion, not based on fear of retribution or the desire to gain favor, but because that's what human beings do to coexist in society.

I asked her if she consciously looks for ways to help people. She exclaimed "Definitely, definitely," and then said something that stunned me a bit—it was something I'd heard religious people say. "And if I feel like I'm not doing that enough, then I feel selfish and that I'm not on the right path."

Dani seems to feel more than just a sense of compassion, but also a palpable, almost mystical connection to everything and everyone. To me, any inner drive toward compassion is the Spirit at work.

Dani related a profound, extended oneness, or non-dual experience; a loving state that persisted after she returned from a weeklong meditation retreat.

> It became difficult for me to manage this experience of non-duality. I became aware of my thoughts as being illusions and part of something larger. It was disorienting and frightening. Because if you really embrace that, then your ego does dissolve, and that's a frightening thing. So I've had transcendent experiences, and, on an intellectual level and on a heart level, I feel I understand them.

(We'll look more closely at the idea of duality in chapters 7 and 8.)

Recognizing that Dani had perhaps more frequent and intense experiences than many of the religion-oriented people I interviewed, I asked her what may be one of the most persistent questions of all time: "Can you create this transcendent experience on demand?"

"No," she smiled. "I wish I could."

Stunning experiences like Dani's don't happen every day, but she got me thinking about how the Spirit reveals the oneness among people—the "kingdom of heaven within." Rev. R. Scott Walker had some important comments on this idea of oneness.

UNITY: THE QUEST OF LIFE
Scott Walker told me

> The quest of all human life is unity. The experience of birth itself is separation; the major dialectic dynamic in life is thus "separation seeking unity." That's what a Buddhist is basically about. That's what a Jew is basically about. That's what a Moslem is about. What we are seeking is unity. It comes through friendship, marriage, and sexuality. It's the unity that comes in solitude, but ultimately all of that is leading to a unity with that which we call God. Now the desire to lead a spiritual life, if you want to use that cliché, is the desire to be in harmony, unity, and conversation with God as Holy Spirit. What that really is seeking is unity. And that's what I would say is the common core of almost all religions. I think that's what God as Holy Spirit is all about.

If Dr. Walker is right, and the Spirit is "God experienced as Spirit," then perhaps Dani Vedros is one freelance *pneumatikos* from whom anyone can take a lesson. Perhaps Jesus' "back to basics" talks on the One God were really meant to lead individuals directly into contact with the Spirit. Genuine inner experiences can neither be legislated, canonized, analyzed, purloined, restricted, judged, nor qualified—but they can be suppressed through limiting doctrines. Spiritual experiences are real to those who experience them, and those experiences can't really persuade anyone else until those individuals awaken in their own good time. The mystics understood this more fully, though they usually come across as a little nuts in the debriefing. The adepts of the East understood spiritual enlightenment long ago. Enlightenment was the original state. It just is. Always has been. Always will be in the ever-present "now." It is up to individuals to find the Spirit of Truth and to understand and experience enlightenment. Someone once asked the Buddha, "When is the time for enlightenment?" He answered, "Now."

Because the Spirit was the agent of action by which God created the world, and because the Spirit had been influencing humankind long before Abraham, why should we disbelieve that it was the Spirit that flooded Buddha with Fire and Light beneath the Bodhi Tree, or Muhammad in the cave, or Lao Tzu perched on the back of his water buffalo?

Over the millennia, the Spirit has become more and more personal to humankind, first awakening the prophets, then guiding groups, and finally inspiring individuals themselves. The "awakening congregation" unfolds with or without our help, but the more aware we are, the faster the Spirit reveals it.

We already know that the Spirit is within us, so how can we find it, know it, and recognize it? These questions pushed me on in search of practical answers, and they weren't easy to find. I didn't just want answers for anyone. I wanted answers for *everyone*, and I found them in what I like to call the Library of the Spirit.

THE LIBRARY OF THE SPIRIT

The People of the Book don't have dibs on the Spirit of God. No way. I checked. The Spirit has been breeching the stubborn human will since the beginning, through a stream of prophets and teachings and millions of anonymous people as well. Because the Spirit existed long before there were people, let alone churches, it makes sense for an off-road search to see the Spirit's mark in the wisdom literature of other cultures.

The world's wisest leaders recommended it. Mahatma Gandhi wrote, "It is the duty of every cultured man and woman to read sympathetically the scriptures of the world. If we are to respect others' religions as we would have them respect our own, a friendly study of the world's religions is a sacred duty." Christian theologian and author Arnold B. Come concurred. In his book, *Human Spirit and Holy Spirit*, he wrote, "The Christian must listen to and so really know the non-Christian if the will of their common Lord and God is to be accomplished for all."[3]

As a student of philosophy, I've been studying the sacred literature of other lands for many years. In those holy books, I find abundant evidence of the Creator's benevolent contact with humankind. I call this collection of books the "Library of the Spirit." It's a vast and noble body of work that breathes in perfect harmony, like the Divine Breath itself.

This Library of the Spirit provides the world with guidance, comfort, teachings, methods of disciplining the mind and body, and rituals to help the generations remember their spiritual heritage and identity. The library contains the words of prophets, simple monks, mystics, ascetic hermits, kings, traveling teachers, lightning-struck loners, saints, sages, and martyrs, as well as ordinary people like you and me. It is the storehouse on earth of the Logos = Word = Divine Reason, the myths and parables, histories, travels of prophets, poetry, rules for healthy living, and practical laws. This library is the magnificent record of God's interaction with the human race. It is the transcript of divine thought, written down in human languages for people to study.

Almost universally, the Library of the Spirit says that we are replicas of God, made in God's "image," looking upward for a sign while looking inward to the soul. In the scriptures of many lands, Spirit permeates everything from the human mind to the stones and the living things, to brain cells, the soul, the stars and planets, electrons and neutrons, and the supposedly empty spaces in between. This Spirit of Truth is a radiant corona that invisibly surrounds and permeates humankind, whenever we are willing and able to absorb it.

THE TRUTH IS ONE

In spring 2001 I interviewed Yug Purush Swami Paramanandji of Haridwar, India, believed by his followers to be an enlightened master. Hindus do not subscribe to the idea of a Spirit of God, but the Swami teaches the concept of Universal Oneness.

Dressed in a floor-length orange robe, he also wore an orange babushka tied in a knot under his chin. His thoughtful eyes peered compassionately through square-framed glasses. Through a translator, I asked the swami if he thought there would eventually be a single, one-world religion.

"People have different levels of understanding," he said, "so people cannot be expected to be under one religion. But the day is not far away that people will realize that the truth is one."

In India, Paramanandji dedicates his life to service. He builds communities to house India's living saints. He established a unique series of homes for orphaned children—babies picked up from the gutters and streets who are cared for by volunteer "mothers" in proper homes. He also oversees twenty schools for poor children and started a college for girls, for which the Indian government gave him a grant of forty-two acres and funds for a road and electricity.

Swami Paramanandji said that experiences of awakening to higher truth are realized through God through special grace and also by association with saintly persons. These experiences, in which God's mind seeps into our mortal consciousness, occur in people who achieve grace through merit, their good work in the world, their curiosity to know, and reading the words of scripture. He is not fussy about which scripture one reads.

The swami explained that our enlightening experiences actually release inner knowledge that we already possess. Awareness occurs in different levels of consciousness, limited or enhanced by our individual capacity to know or apply higher knowledge of God. He said that through God's grace and by achieving merit through living the dharma (our duty to do what is right), we can achieve "higher consciousness"—a deeper understanding of the truth, which is one of the gifts of the Holy Spirit found in the writings of Paul. Act right and live a good life, in anyone's language, and the Spirit of God snuggles up to you.

Dollars to donuts, some readers out there will balk at the suggestion that there is nothing in the Vedantic teachings that contradicts the simple rules of Jesus. The attitude of forgiveness and service to others is unmistakable. The Breath of the Spirit of God has worked through the sages of every religion, through whatever lens that population, in its time, was able to see.

What makes Swami Paramanandji so insightful into the universal ocean of the Spirit? An event occurred in his life that caused him to dedicate himself to the concept of oneness. The event was that he became "self-realized," a state of spiritual lucidity he achieved after doing seven years of penance. The self-realized mind unites with the Spirit of God, revealing the potential for Christ-Consciousness. This message is not unlike that of my friend the late Sensei Shigeru Kanai, the Butsugen-shyu priest introduced in chapter 1 whose refined Buddhist sect was founded for the very purpose of teaching the unity of all religions. Universal oneness of all religion is also the fundamental teaching of the Sufis.

When the Spirit takes hold, the individual is inspired to a way of thinking and living dedicated to others, not to the stingy desires of the lower self. If we can believe that the Spirit, the "I Am That I Am," inspired the Rishis (the sages of India) and their predecessors, then we can respect a perspective on unity with God that predates Abraham by a thousand years or more.

SELF-REALIZATION

Self-realization could be a useful way to describe what happened to Jesus after the Spirit descended on him. When you think about how his human self united with the Spirit to give birth to his Christ self, the consciousness by which he transcended physical death becomes more understandable. For insight into the ideas of a spiritual Self and a lower self, I draw on another Vedantist, the late Sri Swami Satchidananda, founder of Integral Yoga in the West during the 1960s. His community at Yogaville, Virginia, features the beautiful Light of Truth Universal Shrine, by the James River, built in the shape of a pink and blue lotus blossom. On the upper floor is a prayer room, surrounded by ten altars for the known main religions, one for all other religions, and one for the religion yet to come. Swami Satchidananda often referred to the importance of the impersonal "divine Self," as opposed to the "little self" of the ego. He once said,

> You can't see your own Self directly. You are the Self, but you have never seen it. But God created you in His image, and wanted you to see your image. So, He gave you a built-in mirror. Do you know what that is? Your own mind. Your own mind is the mirror. That's why you say, "As the mind, so the man." If the mind is clean, you will see your Self as clean. The Self is always clean; it never gets into any problem. So clean the mind, and see your Self: "Ah, I am the ever pure, ever clean Self." That is Self-Realization.[4]

Perhaps Jesus came to demonstrate his Christhood as a remodeling of the ancient idea of self-realization—the potential for all people to unite in Spirit.

A RELIGION OF KINDNESS

In the Library of the Spirit, Elohim beats a single drum: Oneness. This is unity, compassion, effort toward perfection, also known as divine love, without all the fine print. All actions of the Spirit in the world of this great, ineffable One God, unify and heal and enlighten anyone who draws near its principles. It's love. Love that blazes from a single point, consuming all other points in unification and wholeness forever. Complicating it further is only useful to those who profit by dividing the Spirit from people, separating them from God, separating them from their best Self, or who profit from war, slavery, and ignorance.

It seems that if we can look for the Spirit in people, rather than where they go to church or what oaths they've sworn, we can begin to see the Spirit in action. The Dalai Lama Tenzin Gyatso, exiled leader of Tibetan Buddhism, said, "My religion is simple. My religion is kindness." The Sufi poet Nazir wrote, "From separation I passed into Unity; all the illusions of life disappeared like a phantom show. Now whenever I cast my glance,

I see Him alone, and none other. The Muslim, the Hindu, and the Jew have all become the same to me—they have all merged in the glory of my once Beloved." The Lakota elder Black Elk said, "For the Great Spirit is everywhere; he hears whatever is in our minds and hearts, and it is not necessary to speak to him in a loud voice."

If the message is compassion, cohesion, unifying, nurturing, healing, forgiveness, acceptance, and love, it's a safe bet that it's congruent with the Spirit of God. Slash the religions into ribbons of "isms," plaster them with labels, condemn them, exalt them, or even give them more credit than they deserve, but this search for the Spirit of God is discovering the unity of a single message: the message of "I Am That I Am."

Spirit is the universal engine that generates understanding and transformation through its Fire and Light. It is the invisible divine force celebrated in the Library of the Spirit, and presented to humankind through a variety of lenses. Let people everywhere take the blinders off and know that they can begin to experience the Spirit through the light that comes from reading the Library of the Spirit. The supreme gift of all knowledge is always at our fingertips. It is the power that disciplined a tribe to survive forty years in the desert, guided them to build a temple, made of simple men mighty prophets, empowered the Nazorean, and opened the eyes of sages the world over. The Spirit allows ordinary individuals to think extraordinary thoughts, to make the right choices in choosing a spouse or career, or to lighten a stranger's loneliness with a smile at a busy shopping center.

In our pursuit of the Spirit, we seek concrete evidence of our human birthright—not a legacy of sin, but knowing that the Spirit that brought all this into existence is the very Spirit that resides within us. As we have looked at the Spirit in history and in various religions, let's see if we can deepen our understanding by looking at the Spirit within. If we possess the Spirit, its nature will be evident in the Divine Image—the image of God in which Genesis says we are made.

CREATED IN THE IMAGE OF GOD

The Book of Genesis states without further explanation that human beings were created in the image and likeness of God (Gn 1:26), and this has had theologians in a tizzy ever since the Old Testament first came out in paperback. When you think about it, the entire foundation of western religion, from Abraham through Jesus and Muhammad, rests on how one defines this Divine Image. It sets forth the very purpose, essence, and potential of life.

In a handful of dusty volumes, one can study the history of the arguments about the Divine Image, ranging from God having a physical body like ours, to the image being merely our ability to have relationships, to exercising our dominion over the animals, and to the most popular: because human qualities are attributed to God in the Bible (that is, God is pleased, is moral, vindictive, angry, and so on), God must be like us. I wanted to see if the Divine Image isn't far more intimate in our consciousness than that—and how the "Spirit within" plays a role.

The importance of the Divine Image in our search for the Spirit is enormous, because understanding it could free us from millennia of misunderstanding about the purpose of life, the meaning of "sin," and the way we understand God and ourselves. It could even dissolve that nasty, separating duality mentioned by Dani Vedros earlier. Think of it: by dissolving the illusion of duality, we can be one within ourselves, with the Creator, and with each other. What if we discovered that duality is a mirage, and that the Spirit has been very close at hand all along?

My off-road search led me to seven elements of the Divine Image that I think reveal God within us:

- Immortality
- "I Am That I Am"
- The Spirit Within
- Free Will
- Love
- Masculine and Feminine
- Creativity

IMMORTALITY, THE SPIRIT, AND "I AM THAT I AM"

If God can't die or be killed, then the Divine Image in us certainly can't die or be killed either. The human body has been described as a temple, but it lasts only eighty or ninety years, if you're lucky. The image, therefore, can't be the physical body. It must be something immortal, eternal—the soul, the "I Am That I Am" (Ex 3:14) consciousness that we share with the Creator. Documented near-death experiences prove that the soul, our pure self, survives death. Our immortality, then, is one part of the Divine Image in which we are made.

Another important element of the Divine Image is that the Spirit is within us. It inspires us, heals us, tries to make us like it. Consider the many ways in which we experience God. The Trinity concept can help us in this. The Son (Christos) and Father are in us, too—like the Spirit, Jesus said he was with the Father in the beginning, before the world was (Jn 17:5), and loved us from the beginning. ("In that day you will know that I am in my Father, and you in me, and I in you." Jn 14:20) Thus the Spirit within is also part of the Divine Image.

Yahweh told Moses that his name was "I Am That I Am." Yahweh could have given Moses any name, and the Israelites wouldn't have raised an eyebrow no matter what it was. God could have told him something awesome, such as "The Creator," "The Lord of All," "the Ultimate Reality," "the Ineffable," or "the Unknowable Effulgence of Universal Being." But no. Yahweh gave a much more personalized answer that is very intimate in human and all sentient life. The divine name is a statement of "being" and the simultaneous "awareness of being." "I Am That I Am" is God being aware of God.

"I Am That I Am" is clearly a part of our own awareness of being. Prove it to yourself: Say aloud, "I Am That I Am." You have awareness. You are the witness. In that alone, you find your unity with the Divine Mind. If all these elements of divinity lie within, then it should be possible to understand the Divine Image within ourselves and, maybe more revealingly, within each other. It's the perpetual observer in the human mind that's always watching, whether we are awake, asleep, comatose, thinking, analyzing, or feeling.

"I Am That I Am" is really quite beautiful when you think about it. Strip away interpretation, and you realize that the Ultimate Reality within us is our awareness itself; not awareness of something in particular, but just awareness—the perpetual motion machine of consciousness. Yahweh didn't merely tell Moses a name, but identified the presence of mind we hold in common in the furnace of all thought. It's a phrase that, when we utter it, speaks the name of God within us—the image of God in which we were made. Psalms 82:6 reads, "I say, 'You are gods, sons of the Most High, all of you. . . .'" I prefer to think there is no contradiction to say "sons and daughters" of the Most High, which I believe we are. Chips off the old block, or, as the Jewish fathers said, "divine sparks." Paul wrote:

> The Lord is the Spirit, and where the Spirit of the Lord is, there is freedom. And we all, with unveiled face, beholding as in a mirror the glory of the Lord, are being changed into his likeness from one degree of glory to another; for this comes from the Lord who is the Spirit. (2 Cor 3:17–18)

This doesn't mean that the rumpus room of your head on Saturday night, while hollering at your spouse, or in a fog at work Monday morning is God-in-you at its best—you have a proud, cold-forged, new and improved, fortified-with-iron personality that's always trying to keep itself validated. The Divine Image is the "I Am" awareness underneath it that fulfills in you every promise of every prophet who ever walked the Earth.

For me, realizing this was tough because I was analyzing it with all my human baggage. But once I sat still, stopped "looking" for it, and simply enjoyed the knowledge that "I am aware," it hit me how alike we all are. Perhaps simple awareness itself defines the awakening congregation—everyone is included.

Jesuit priest, paleontologist, and theologian Pierre Teilhard de Chardin expressed it neatly: "We are not human beings having a spiritual experience, we are spiritual beings having a human experience."

LOVE AND WILL

Some things seem clear: "I Am That I Am" never dies, is never wasted, and never withdraws—humans withdraw through the illusions and distractions of the world and the gullibility of the five senses. We use "I Am" to do everything: everything from making love to making war—that is the license of our "free will," another important component of the Divine Image. Through I Am, we can choose: to create or destroy; to join or separate; to make good or make evil in the world. God is unlimited, and so is God within. Such is the power of the will to burn the inexhaustible fuel of the Spirit.

In addition, we demonstrate a third element of the Divine Image: our capacity to love. Love must also be a component of the Divine Image, because nearly every tradition in the world describes God as love.

"God is love," wrote John, "and he who abides in love abides in God, and God abides in him."[5] The *Tao Teh Ching* offers this: "World sovereignty can be committed to that man who loves all people as he loves himself." The Upanishads make many references to love: "True religion is to love, as God has loved them, all things, whether great or small." The Sutta-Pitaka of Buddhism asserts: "The ninth perfection is: Loving-kindness." Love, therefore, is perhaps the fifth component of the Divine Image.

We have the capacity to love. Perhaps we approach the Image whenever we demonstrate our love for love and our love for the Spirit in ourselves and others. Perhaps this best explains the Divine Image and best defines the Spirit of God. (These are, essentially, the two "new rules" of Jesus.) In terms of love, God is self-realized in every human creation, and humans are self-realized whenever we demonstrate love—we become more like the Spirit whenever we do so, in our efforts to uplift, heal, assist, and care for others. The more we identify with the "little self," mentioned earlier by Swami Satchidananda, the more we withdraw from the Fire and Light of universal love. Love for God is the nature of the soul, which is the mirror of the mind. For when we give in to love, what is the soul but God loving God?

THE DIVINE HIS AND HERS

Genesis reveals something else about the Divine Image that's rather startling. There's more to the image than the elegant statement of being "I Am That I Am," immortality, the will, the spirit within, or even of love. It has to do with an obvious part of this image of God that's been swept under the rug far too long—our genders of male and female.

Everyone is familiar with the Adam and Eve story, but what may be the best-kept secret of the book of Genesis is that we were created not once, but three times. Not three creations, but humankind was created in two specific steps plus the final step in which we were given physical bodies to live in.

> And God said, Let us make man in our image, after our likeness . . . So God created man in his own image, *in the image of God created he him; male and female* created he them.[6] [my italics]

Here's another problem of pronouns: "we" and "our." The plurality comes from the word *Elohim*, a Hebrew plural, though it's interesting that "we" are speaking when "we" created them. ("We" also finds voice in the Qur'an.)

Nevertheless, in the first two creation scenarios, we are created male and female from the get-go. It says "in our image, after our likeness." How can this be anything other than asserting that the masculine and feminine are complementary components of the Divine Image? This statement comes before the creation of Adam and Eve, before humans were placed in physical bodies on the Earth when we took on our "coats of skins." (Gn 3:21)

The embarrassing part for the reigning patriarchy is that the Genesis statement makes it clear that God is both masculine and feminine. Gnostic Christian sources maintained that not only does God comprise the essences of both genders, so does each human being: each of us possesses the essences of both masculine and feminine.[7] Childhood training with cowboy hats and dolls seem to be required in order to separate the behavior of boys and girls. So much for the illusion of the patriarchy.

It is only in the Genesis "rib" story (Gn 2:18–23) that physical creatures are placed on the physical ground, so one can contemplate the idea that "Adam" was created as a spiritual being first, before descending to the earth and inhabiting a physical body. God is no more two gods than three—this merely indicates that the whole of humankind, male and female, is One like the One that created them. The apparent distaff appearance in the physical may well have been the beginning of the illusions of duality and separation. After all, everyone didn't get cast out of heaven, only the rebellious angels who thought they were smarter than "I Am That I Am." Pretty dopey.

In Genesis 5:2, the fact of our maleness and femaleness is restated: "Male and female created he them; and blessed them, and called their name Adam, in the day when they were created." For those who disbelieve that God is also a mother, Jesus himself made a point of it: "But from the beginning of creation, God made them male and female." (Mk 10:7) Please notice the detail: he doesn't say we were male and female when "man" was created, but from the beginning of creation itself.[8]

In the familiar Garden of Eden metaphor, Adam falls asleep and a woman is fashioned from his "rib" (in one reading of the Hebrew, the word for rib, *tsela`*, means "side"—Adam's female side, which can mean "nature," as in his "female nature").

Our combined maleness and femaleness therefore must be considered another component of the image of God in which we were made—and whatever nuance you wish to attach through interpretation, it tells us that men and women are equal in the sight of God. The Jewish mystical source, Kabbalah, sees the masculine and feminine as equally important pillars in the Tree of Life. Taoists understand it as the yin and yang, opposites making up a singular whole. This also explains how masculine souls can end up in female bodies and vice versa. It also means that everyone is beloved by God—everyone is loved because God loves all of the divine sparks unconditionally.[9]

When will the People of the Book awaken to the spiritual reality of their feminine population?

It was shown in chapter 3 that the Hebrew word *ruach* is feminine and that the apocryphal Book of Wisdom equates the Spirit with Sophia—Wisdom. In the apocryphal Wisdom of Solomon, the Spirit is also equated with the feminine quality of wisdom. Clearly, God is neither a human man nor a human woman, yet out of God came a male and female humankind.

The principle is magnified and exemplified in the prophets. The lives and teachings of the Buddha and the Christ show a perfect blending of masculine and feminine traits. The manner in which they taught in gentle parables exudes with the nurturing, compassionate, healing, and soothing caress of a mother, yet with the exacting, uncompromising assertiveness of a father. Jesus' actions and teachings were a perfect blend of masculine and feminine—he was father and mother to everyone he met.

CREATIVITY

Just as God created the world, so do we, godlike, create in the world whatever we conceive. We can create a garden, people it with children, and call it good. The Spirit within us is all powerful, the only limitations being our brains, our hands, and our imaginations. We have built the pyramids, and the aqueducts, the Great Wall, and the Louvre; an interstate highway system and the colorful wonder box of the desktop computer. We have developed language and writing, and laws, and books, and government, and religions, and fashion, and art, and music, and the Spirit thrives in the good things we have done. But through the will, we can also use that I Am power, the knowledge of the Spirit, to create war, and slavery, and usury, and deceit to acquire power and riches. We can use our creativity for anything we like.

In 1991, Father Matthew Fox published his book *Creation Spirituality*, which asserts that we are cocreators with God and that God is within us. This Episcopal priest—who had been dismissed from the Dominican order by Cardinal Joseph Ratzinger (now Pope Benedict XVI) for his radical views—wrote

> Creativity is not a noun or even a verb—it is a place, a space, a gathering, a union—a where—wherein the Divine powers of creativity and the human power of imagination join forces. Where the two come together is where beauty and grace happens and indeed, explodes. Creativity constitutes the ultimate in intimacy for it is the place where the Divine and the human are most destined to interact.[10]

The Spirit has been within us since the beginning. It is the active part of us that we make most visible when we're at our best—when we demonstrate love with free will through our I Am awareness. The Spirit is the very substrate of all thought and feeling. It is the essence of the Ultimate Reality.

The Spirit opens hearts and seeps around the seams to enlighten us wherever we are, whatever our beliefs, and within our self-imposed limitations. The truth will set you free, as they say, and you can find the truth in the strangest places. Whenever the accepted doctrine loses its meaning, the Spirit flows through every open portal to manifest itself once again in the glorious display of human thought. The problem in this for humankind is that one man's gospel may be another man's heresy.

Chapter 7

NEW *and* IMPROVED HERESIES

Where the Spirit is concerned, it seems that the churches, temples, synagogues, mosques, stupas, sanghas, dojos, and the occasional rural compound really can't help but eventually make a mess of things. Division and debate are inevitable and usually begin before the prophet's body grows cold. As soon the living Spirit is forgotten by a people, the Spirit emerges again through some new visionary or prophet, labeled a heretic, to fill the vacuum. If his or her message catches on and people find nourishment in the new heresy, the Spirit once again comes alive in the heart, and the heresy becomes the new accepted teaching.

Once the teaching is calcified into doctrine, however, the light of the Spirit gradually dims and a new heretic must step forth to strike the flint of truth. It's a pattern of four stages that occurs in most religions:

1. The prophet provides fresh direct experience with the Divine.
2. The prophet dies; teachings are interpreted; doctrines and dogmas formed.

3. Direct experience with the Spirit is forgotten.
4. Reformers emerge to restore the prophet's original intent.

Nowhere has the Spirit of God changed hands so frequently, or with such devastating consequences, as in the West. Today's vague and human-like concept of the Spirit is the direct result of the third stage, which reached its peak of dissatisfaction in the 1960s, when millions began searching for the Spirit anywhere they could find it—a trend that continues today.

Tracing the root causes of this dissatisfaction helped me understand, in two important ways, how so many people feel disenfranchised and cut off from the Spirit. First, it helped me understand how the Spirit persists in the world—a world of greed, religious hate, and war in which millions are desperately seeking the Spirit outside formalized institutions. Second, it led me to the rap sheets of some of the most influential modern heretics, whose stories demonstrate the wide variety of ways in which the Spirit persists, in the prophets, the "heretics," and, most important, ourselves. The truth is that as historical Christianity lost its everyday knowledge of the Spirit, it chose instead the most stultifying teachings of all—the persistent belief in guilt, shame, and sinfulness, along with the demonization of women and sex. In this chapter, we'll look at some of the "heretics" who fought against these shackles, but first let's look at two very influential mystics whose work exemplifies the contradiction that has become today's concept of the "Spirit of God."

TWO MYSTICS FROM NORTH AFRICA

In 1945, thirteen ancient leather-bound manuscripts were found in Egypt. They revealed an early Christianity that had been previously unknown. These Nag Hammadi manuscripts, hidden for some sixteen hundred years, revealed the principles of Gnosticism—a mystical understanding of the teachings of Jesus, the nature of God, and the nature of the soul, shared among communities all over the Middle East and elsewhere.

Until the Nag Hammadi material came to light, the only information we had about the Gnostics were the diatribes written by their accusers.[1] Around the time of Athanasius, the authorities were burning every Gnostic book they could find, when some alert desert librarian, perhaps nudged by the Spirit, took the hint and stashed some of these books in earthen jars.

Gnostic traditions were many and varied. The wide range of beliefs were sometimes quite fanciful, but one common thread valued the direct experience of God—that you could find God within yourself by knowing your true self (the Divine Image), and that God was both Mother and Father.

Gnosticism focused on gnosis, "inner knowing" of the Divine, which was achieved through disciplined living, contemplation, and study.[2] They also generally believed that human misery results not from sin but from ignorance, and that the virgin birth and resurrection of Christ should be understood symbolically as well as literally. The transition from the Gnostic view to one of utter suppression can be seen by contrasting two of the most influential Christian theologians—Origen and Augustine.

ORIGEN: A SPIRITUALITY OF LIGHT

Christianity's first systematic theologian was an Egyptian named Origen (185–251), whose writings influenced the early Church for hundreds of years after his death. He was biblically rooted,[3] but his theology harmonized Neoplatonist philosophy and certain elements of Gnosticism, as well as principles of the East, particularly Zoroastrian and Buddhist.[4]

"Origen developed a theology that stressed the continuity of God with the world," writes Karen Armstrong. "His was a spirituality of light, optimism and joy. Step by step, a Christian could ascend the chain of being until he reached God, his natural element and home." Origen believed there was a "kinship between God and the soul: that knowledge of the divine was natural to humanity." It could be "recollected" and "awakened by special disciplines." Souls were created before the world, Origen taught, and entered physical bodies during the "creation of Adam."[5]

Origen believed that all souls could eventually ascend, step by step, into the "pure light world above." He believed that eventually all humankind, even evil people, would be redeemed into the One and be restored to their pure, original state of spiritual perfection. The dualistic separation between God and humans, maintained by the Gnostics, would vanish. He believed that the Spirit became powerful through the Nazorean and that the Spirit is "the spirit of the Godself,"[6] who permeates all creation and gives power, comfort, and joy to those who follow the Golden Rule. Origen wrote in his *De Principiis*, "The highest good, they say, is to become as like to God as possible."

For over two centuries after his death, Origen's views were accepted by early Christians, who believed they were true to the teachings of Christ. Had this view lasted, the crisis of the late twentieth century—and many others—may never have happened. Origen provided unlimited potential for uniting with the Spirit of God through free will, a potential that Augustine, Bishop of Hippo (354–430), would soon take away.

AUGUSTINE: TURNING SEX INTO SIN

The ideas of Origen and Augustine affected how Christians experience the Spirit of God to the present day. The contrast is important because it shows how a vast segment of Christianity became strangers to the Spirit.

Like Origen, Augustine was a North African mystic. He was born a century after Origen's death and, as Origen's teachings had not yet fallen out of favor with the Church, Augustine was influenced by him. Augustine shaped Western theology more than any other, but although he gained much for Christianity by creating the entire "Latin, Catholic paradigm" as it is known today, in the process, he also threw out the proverbial baby with the bathwater.[7]

Augustine's first great conversion occurred at age thirty-two in a flash of inspiration in which he spontaneously perceived the connection between human reason and divine reason (the Greek concept of Logos and the Logos of John 1:1 (Logos = Word = Divine Reason). The experience inspired Augustine to be baptized, and that was a big step, because in his early life he had accepted Manichaean and Neoplatonist teachings. After hearing St. Ambrose preach in Milan in 391, Augustine drew some of these concepts together with the Gospels and began to see Christianity as the ideal path.

Already a successful teacher and writer, at age thirty-seven he was essentially forced to become a priest by admiring friends and an ailing local bishop. He eventually became bishop himself, but a celibate bishop, due to his weakness for the fair sex. (In his *Confessions*, he wrote about how lust had controlled him most of his life.) Celibacy was rare in an age when most bishops married and had children. Augustine felt he had no choice but to live in a strictly ascetic circle of close celibate male priests and associates, which eventually became the norm for priests.

In all fairness, the most far-reaching limitations that Augustine's philosophy imposed on Christians didn't occur because of some stingy or vengeful nature on his part. He would, after all, one day write of the Holy Spirit, "In no other subject is the danger of erring so great, or the progress so difficult, or the fruit of a careful study so appreciable."[8]

The problems came because of political pressure to solve certain crises in the early Church. For example, as Bishop of Hippo, it fell to Augustine to help broker a deal between two groups in Carthage, the Catholics and Donatists, who split hairs on certain points in theology. He employed the police to enforce the reunification of the church there. Augustine later wrote that he advocated the use of force within the church against divisive groups based on a statement of Jesus in the great banquet parable (Lk 14:23) about compelling people to come into the banquet. Augustine chose to translate "compel" to mean "force."

"Augustine . . . was to be produced down the ages as the key witness," wrote theologian and author Hans Küng, "the key witness for the theological justification for forcible conversions, the inquisition and the holy war against deviants of all kinds. . . ."[9] Condoning force against the Donatists would eventually extend, of course, to using force against non-Catholics in the Inquisition, still some seven centuries away.

But Augustine didn't stop with force. On the basis of the sin of Adam and Eve and Paul's letter to the Romans, he concluded that human beings are all guilty of original sin. Not only that, but we really don't have free will; in fact, that our fates are sealed: we are predestined, a few to be blessed but most to be damned! This would later be used to justify so many offenses against humanity (remember Manifest Destiny? Remember slavery?). Augustine was also the one who instigated a policy of demonizing women and sex. He projected his own weakness for the flesh to be the center of all human sin, and he laid that guilt upon Christians forevermore. These policies—claiming as they did that humans' very nature is hateful to the Creator—serve, perhaps more than anything else, to disconnect people from the Spirit.

Princeton theologian Elaine Pagels writes that Augustine derived his attitude from the Adam and Eve story, "that sexual desire is sinful; that infants are infected from the moment of conception with the disease of original sin; and that Adam's sin corrupted the whole of nature itself."[10] Augustine actually cast in stone a misogynistic attitude toward women begun by Paul:

> As in all the churches of the saints, the women should keep silence in the churches. For they are not permitted to speak, but should be subordinate, as even the law says. If there is anything they desire to know, let them ask their husbands at home. For it is shameful for a woman to speak in church. (1 Cor 14:34–36)

In *A History of God*, Karen Armstrong writes that Augustine further entrenched this denigrating attitude toward women—in fact, toward humankind in general.

> Augustine left us with a difficult heritage. A religion which teaches men and women to regard their humanity as chronically flawed can alienate them from themselves. Nowhere is this alienation more evident than in the denigration of sexuality in general and women in particular. Even though Christianity had originally been quite positive for women, it had already developed a misogynistic tendency in the West by the time of Augustine. The letters of Jerome teem with loathing for the female, which occasionally sounds deranged.[11]

"What is the difference," wrote Augustine to a friend, "whether it is in a wife or a mother, it is still Eve the temptress that we must beware of in any woman."

The Muslims came up with the best solution of all for the problem of men's sexual weakness: cover the women from head to toe and forbid them to do much of anything at all. This was the thinking, further reinforced by Thomas Aquinas, that shaped modern attitudes toward women in Christianity and further distanced the Spirit from access by ordinary people. It's important for modern men and women to know this, because of the separation it placed between women and the Spirit of God in terms of their spiritual identity. Armstrong wrote, "Western Christianity never fully recovered from this neurotic misogyny."[12]

In all fairness, I should acknowledge that Augustine himself wrote of many direct contacts he had with the Spirit. He was motivated to do the right thing by his beloved church and his concept of the Lord's will, and he accomplished much in unifying and solidifying the Christian church in a time of schisms and power plays. He renounced sexuality as evil around the same time he himself withdrew to the chambers of the rectory. One could conclude that when he lost himself in the study of Scripture, he also lost touch with human beings. And so we can credit him with the suppression of sexuality, the continued subordination of women, and the turning of grace into something earned through the sacraments and priestly benevolence. Augustine very effectively placed severe limits on people's access to the Spirit simply because he didn't know any better.

Direct access to the Spirit of God was now abstracted behind a wall of guilt and self-loathing that Christian schoolchildren would be taught for centuries to come. These principles became the driving force of Christianity, requiring the luckless faithful to now rely on the institution of the Church to dispense grace and salvation. Direct experience with the Spirit would be gained through the bread and wine and by repeating the Rosary.

Like Origen, Augustine had found a place in his theology for the Neoplatonic concept of the all, the One, and a few other points, but he rejected Origen's easy access to the Spirit within, which in his day had been freely accessible to anyone.

In the Second Council of Constantinople (553), Justinian declared Origen's theology heretical and tossed it out completely. Gone was Origen's cosmology and gone the idea that souls were created before the world. Gone was any further mention of women in the clergy or the concept of God as Mother. Gone were married priests and the returning soul—you had only one shot at salvation and were predestined to blow it. If you blew it, hell was holding a place for you. Out the window went the "spirituality of light, optimism, and joy."

In the early church, it took a total of about five hundred years to make the transition from direct experience with the Spirit of God to one of suppression and oppression. For the next several centuries after Justinian, access to the Spirit would be a vague theory that even the theologians didn't want to bother with. Spiritual dispensation became pay-as-you-go. But like the patterns of old, the Spirit would find new heretics in whom to light the lamp of truth.

BE YE PERFECT

The way history tells it, the Spirit of Truth has never ceased to find ways to reveal the Fire and Light in its original simplicity and purity. In the early Middle Ages, centuries before Martin Luther, hundreds of Spirit sects came and went. Most were wiped out in the name of political expediency, but some groups so desired to keep the Spirit alive among them that they couldn't let it go. The lesson here is that what these groups did back then, we can do now—as groups and as individuals.

THE PERFECTS

In the twelfth century, the Cathars emerged with a mystical Christianity that would eventually draw nearly half a million followers. The movement, informed by the Gnostic traditions of early Christian Egypt, centered upon the Spirit as the path to Christ, rather than the person of Jesus. To them, this constituted the original teaching of the Nazorean, especially where the Spirit was concerned.

The Cathars formed sturdy communities in southeast France and northwest Italy. The "official" histories, however, malign them for many perceived heresies. For example, the Cathars rejected the sacraments wholesale—the group actually condemned the Catholic Church of its day as a work of the devil (a belief that would be shared by some Protestant faiths after the Reformation). The Cathars regarded the world and physical body as evil, but allowed that the soul, divine in nature, could free itself from bodily life by attaining perfection through the practice of love. The Cathars believed that every soul would eventually unite with God.

The Cathar church was made up of "Believers" and "Perfects" ("Parfaits"). Those believers who demonstrated a level of purity in their belief and practice could qualify for a baptism of the Holy Spirit called the Consolamentum. Such believers could attain the title of Perfect through this ritual, during which it was believed that the Spirit filled the Perfect's mind and physical body with its essence. These rituals were always performed by another Perfect through laying on of hands. Not just anyone came to the altar rail for this ritual, but only those who proved to the Perfects that they had sufficiently achieved Christ Consciousness. The Perfects wore black and lived the rest of their lives in the Spirit, abstaining thereafter from wealth, the consumption of meat, and sex. The Perfects adopted poverty and preached to others, and ordinary believers venerated them.[13]

The Cathars aspired to perfection not out of arrogance, but because Jesus had insisted upon it. The Bible refers to perfection in many places beginning with Genesis, but in Matthew 5:48 Jesus said, "Be ye therefore perfect, even as your Father which is in heaven is perfect." (References to being perfect appear in dozens of verses in the Old and New Testaments.)

Paul's letter to the Corinthians explained how the Spirit reveals the higher knowledge of the Divine to those who achieve the "elite" status. Paul wrote:

> Howbeit we speak wisdom among them that are perfect: yet not the wisdom of this world, nor of the princes of this world, that come to nought:
>
> But we speak the wisdom of God in a mystery, even the hidden wisdom, which God ordained before the world unto our glory:
>
> Which none of the princes of this world knew: for had they known it, they would not have crucified the Lord of glory.
>
> But as it is written, "Eye hath not seen, nor ear heard, neither have entered into the heart of man, the things which God hath prepared for them that love him."
>
> But God hath revealed them to us by his Spirit: for the Spirit searches all things, yea, the deep things of God. (1 Cor. 2:6–10, KJV)

The "perfects" weren't elected or appointed, nor did they buy their way into the inner circle. They genuinely achieved the deeper wisdom through the Spirit as a natural step of living a disciplined life dedicated to God.

At their peak, the Cathars had eleven large communities. They built their own churches, had their own bishops, and were supported by the nobility. They also believed that until one was a Perfect, one could live again until perfection was achieved. (The concept of the returning soul had also been a part of Origen's theology.)[14] Aside from those philosophical principles, Cathar services resembled normal Catholic services. At least that's what St. Bernard wrote after witnessing one.

In Cathar services, they placed emphasis on the Gospel of John—which tells the story of the Holy Spirit—over all the others. (The Gospel of John was quite nearly excluded from the Bible centuries earlier because of its mystical content.)

Rev. Kieth VonderOhe had a keen interest in the Cathars.

> The whole Albigensian crusade was against the radical Cathar movement in Southeastern France. It wasn't against the Muslims or the Turks in Palestine. It was wiping out the Cathars in Southeastern France because they were a very independent free-thinking group who talked a lot about this personal connectedness with the Divine. They didn't have a formal priesthood, and you didn't need to have someone intervene between you and God. It was a very radical interpretation of the Gospel of John that at that time undermined the power of the Catholic Church completely. They had healings, and people were trained to do that. We would call it psychic phenomena now, but people were recognized as having the ability to heal, and trained. So it really was a major threat to the Catholic Church.

The Cathars rejected the authority of the pope and paid no dues—that, of course, spelled trouble. They were eventually slaughtered because of it. Pope Innocent III and others killed as many as five hundred thousand in the cruel crusade of 1244. Thousands of men, women, and children were burned, tortured, and otherwise killed. Ironically, many thousands of Catholics were also intentionally slain along with them, as one could not distinguish a Catholic from a Cathar by looking at them. In a report to the pope during the massacres came the famous war cry, repeated to this day, "Then kill them all. God will recognize his own."[15] The killing of the Cathars was an early experiment in genocide that, along with Augustine's approval of using force, paved the way to further internal cleansing crusades and helped fuel the genocide programs of the Inquisition.

BURNING THE SPIRIT AT THE STAKE

The next two centuries saw a veritable explosion of Christian mystics, especially in northern Europe.[15] With the rise of individuals and groups claiming intimacy with the Spirit, there came a resultant pogrom against Spirit experiences. The age saw the rise of Meister Eckhart, the Beguines, and passionate communities that refused to give up their intimacy with the Spirit of God. Imagine, for example, living among the Free-Spiriters, who knew the Spirit as we know the air.

THE FREE-SPIRITERS

One of those communities was the Brothers and Sisters of the Free Spirit, closely aligned in principle with the Cathars and also focused on the Spirit. The movement, scattered here and there around Europe, sought religious perfection through imitating the apostolic life and achieving union with God while still on Earth. Hundreds of these communities dotted Europe, consisting of men and women, boys and girls, who clustered in loosely networked villages or neighborhoods in cities and small towns.

The Brothers and Sisters of the Free Spirit also rejected the church and sacraments, believing that God was in everything and that only faith in Christ was necessary in order to achieve eternal life, not dispensed by some institution. They taught that it was possible for each human soul to realize its divine nature and that those souls who possessed the awareness that they were one with God would automatically be free from sin.

They, and others like them, adopted a peculiar view of a threefold spiritual history put forth by Joachim of Fiore (1145–1202) and others before him, in which (1) the Old Testament was the "Father" period, (2) the time of Christ was the "Son" period, and (3) the time after that was the period of the "Holy Spirit." In this final period, Joachim promised that the institutional church, hardened in the letter of the Scripture, would be replaced by a community filled with the Spirit. Of course, the Free Spiriters, too, were condemned and killed, many by burning at the stake. Records show that they willingly gave themselves up to the flames, smiling and singing like the martyrs of old who were put to death in the Roman arenas.

Joachim's time of the Holy Spirit spawned an amazing number of revolutionary Spirit movements, including the Hussites, followers of the sixteenth-century reformer Thomas Muntzer, and others who celebrated freedom and liberty at one with the Spirit, freeing people once again to the gifts of prophecy that the messengers enjoyed after the Ascension of Jesus.

BEGIN THE BEGUINES

During the Middle Ages, a lot of people fell through the spiritual cracks. In that era of filth, ignorance, and crushing poverty, people everywhere were trying to find the direct experience with the Spirit that many believed had been lost after Constantine.

Protest movements were everywhere: in addition to the Brothers and Sisters of the Free Spirit, you had the Waldensians (whose vows of poverty made the wealthy and acquisitive Church look bad), the Lollards (who committed the no-no of translating the Bible into English), the Spiritual Franciscans (of whom I'll soon have more to say), and various groups of flagellants who thought that whipping themselves bloody at night would absolve them from the sins of sexual desire they wallowed in during the day—the sin admitted by Augustine, by which he concluded that humans actually have no free will.

Those centuries were marked by ignorance, wars, and plagues. It was a tough time to be alive. Men died in disproportionate numbers, and women increasingly outnumbered them. With so many men lost to the Crusades, there weren't enough left behind to marry, and the convents had become elite institutions for noblewomen—the entrance fees to convent life were set high to keep out the riff-raff. The women of the time had no rights, either in marriage or in the Church. They had nowhere to go and no way to feed themselves. So outside the gates of many European cities and towns, destitute women began to gather and form little ramshackle but self-sufficient warrens—highly religious enclaves that were at first not taken seriously by the Church.

These communities of women came to be called the Beguines. They took no vows and were allowed to come and go freely, to marry, and even to leave permanently. They were generally skilled in the womanly trades, though some beguinages were made up of the poor. Some, such as one in Ghent, Netherlands, had thousands of women and formed entire communities, having their own churches, hospitals, cemetery, streets, and shops. The women sometimes acquired reputations for stigmata, as well as visions, trances, and extreme asceticism. Beguine communities in Germany were ministered to by the mystic Meister Eckhart, who spoke to the women as equals—unheard of in that day.

The Beguines taught, devoted themselves to prayer and good works, and counseled those who came for help. They were devoted to the Eucharist (the Christian bread ritual based on Jesus' Last Supper), and, like most Christian mystics, they emphasized love as the way to unity with the Divine. Their eventual demise was heralded by the fact that they wielded such a profound influence on the faithful of their day. Villagers and townsmen began coming to them for spiritual guidance, eventually favoring the women over the local priests and friars. This infuriated the church, so by the fourteenth century, they were gone except for a few beguinages that still survive in Europe today. (During this same period, men, called the Beghards, formed enclaves of their own. They consisted of old or injured tradesmen who could no longer work.[17]) Some famous Beguines were Mechthild of Magdeburg (1212–1282), the visionary Christine of Stommeln (1242–1312), and the Spirit experiencer and writer Marguerite Porete, who was burned at the stake in 1310 basically because she wouldn't shut up about it.

Mystics and Spirit-inspired communities continued to pop up throughout the Renaissance, a time in which Europe fell under a Christian empire ("Christendom") and a legacy of corrupt popes that begs to be compared to the ancient kings of Israel. For centuries people were unhappy with the oppression, and by the nineteenth century a whole new explosion of prophets had entered the scene, all trying to bring the Spirit back into the hearts and minds of the people.

THE SPIRIT OF 1830

After the Reformation, it seemed the cat of reform was forever out of the bag of orthodoxy. On one hand, the reformers seized from the Roman Church the sole authority of dispensing salvation, forgiving sins through confession, and ushering the queue of the faithful to God through the exclusive portal of the sacraments. The Reformers gave that authority to the individual to square himself with God. On the other hand, the individual remained a sinner, dependent upon grace from God through Christ for salvation. The Reformers placed special emphasis on the Spirit in this process. Through the death and resurrection of Christ, they believed, the individual is "as a Christ," automatically saved.[18]

In subsequent centuries, other Reformers came along who thought the original Protestant churches had created kind of a gloomy reaction to Catholicism by lashing everything to a literal interpretation of the Bible. No amount of merit could satisfy God, and one stood forever judged for one's failings. Even so, by their faith, they were saved by grace, which did not require a church authority to dispense it. The new priesthood was a "priesthood of all believers," like the awakening congregation described in chapter 6.

NEW HERETICS

The splits in the churches, in almost every case, were spawned by misunderstandings and the forgetting of genuine experience with the Spirit, as is common in the initial years of any new religion. This was the thrust of the Reformation. Subsequent Radical Protestants rebelled even against their Lutheran and Presbyterian forebears. These were the descendants of the Anabaptists, Mennonites, Moravians, and Brethren, but also Congregationalists and Friends (Quakers) and, later, Methodism and the Disciples of Christ who, like all those who had fought for the Spirit since the Ascension of Christ, hoped to set the Spirit free. Said another way, they freed the people to believe that the Spirit was available to them just for the asking and by following a couple of commonsense universal laws.

The Protestant emphasis on the Spirit must have had a lot to do with what happened during the nineteenth century, particularly between 1830 and 1844. Inspiration, visions, and dreams awakened dozens of new prophets spawning a number of new religions, most based on the Spirit of God, that are still with us today.

In 1830 came Joseph Smith and his angelic vision of gold tablets that gave birth to the Mormons. In the same year in France there began a series of apparitions of Mary, the mother of Jesus. Subsequent appearances would occur in 1846 in La Salette, in Lourdes in 1858, and Pontmain in 1871. Other appearances are noted in 1879 in Knock, Ireland, and in 1917 in Fatima, Portugal. The year 1836 saw the birth of Sri Ramakrishna, a powerful Hindu priest believed to have been an incarnation of the Hindu god Shiva. He is mentioned here because of his tremendous influence on Hindus and the modern yoga movement.

A number of events made 1844 auspicious for manifestations of the Spirit. Baptist William Miller predicted the Second Coming on October 22 of that year, based on Bible study. In the same year Baha'ullah was born, the one believed by the Baha'i faith (which he founded) to be the Promised One of all religions. It was also the beginning of the thirteenth Toltec era and the year predicted by the Aztecs for the return of Quetzalcoatl.

Movements in spiritualism and the occult also burgeoned, including the mediumship activities of the Fox sisters, beginning in 1848, and Theosophy, founded by Helena Petrovna Blavatsky in 1875. Messianic Judaism became formalized in 1850 by Dr. C. Schwartz, followed in 1867 by the formation of the Hebrew Christian Alliance.

In 1860, Ellen White emerged from the Millerite movement of 1844 to found the Seventh-day Adventists. In 1865 came William Booth, who founded the Salvation Army to help the poor. Charles Taze Russel, also of the Millerites, started the Jehovah's Witnesses in 1870, and in 1879 Mary Baker Eddy founded Christian Science, which emphasizes the power of the mind in healing.

THE RAPTURE ERROR

The year 1830 also gave rise to two Spirit-driven religious phenomena that became influential forces in Christianity throughout the Western Hemisphere—but with unexpected results.

That was the year John Darby founded his Brethren sect and introduced the term *Rapture*. Many fundamentalist Christians today believe that one day in the Rapture, Jesus will come to claim all believers and bring them bodily up into the air for eternity.

This erroneous concept was based on Paul's First Letter to the Thessalonians (4:16–17), in which he was speaking to those who were "alive in the Spirit." He wrote, in part, that when the Lord comes, those who are asleep or dead in Christ will rise first, and those who are alive in Christ "shall be caught up together with them in the clouds to meet the Lord in the air." Some interpret this to mean that even the bodies under ground will burst out of their caskets and rise up. (Few seem to notice that in this quotation, *everyone* will rise up by turn, not just some select group. The symbol of a rising in consciousness is overlooked.)

In the bestselling *Left Behind* books of Tim LaHaye and Jerry B. Jenkins, this is depicted literally. People who are driving cars or flying airplanes vanish on the appointed day, and their vehicles, still containing those left behind, will simply crash, killing anyone who's in the way. Way to go, God.

Like the Trinity, the term *rapture* appears nowhere in the Bible. It became popular in the United States because of Cyrus Scofield's *Scofield Reference Bible*, which was the King James Version annotated with Scofield's own comments promoting the literal interpretation. People came to equate Scofield's annotations with the actual word of God![19] Where misinterpreting the literal meaning of Scripture is concerned, it's always something.

Darby is a modern example of a prophet inspired by the Spirit to find a new way to get at the truth, but whose teaching becomes misconstrued and altered by equally well-meaning people. You can't blame the Spirit, but you can blame human error.

Some authors say that Darby got his idea from an Irish mystic, Margaret MacDonald, who in 1830 had a stunning vision of a great future tribulation. She was vilified as a heretic in her day, but her vision helped fuel a new phenomenon of the Spirit that in the early twentieth century would become the Pentecostal movement. It got its official start in 1901 in Topeka, Kansas, in a Bible school conducted by a Methodist pastor named Charles Fox Parham. Since World War II, Pentecostalism has been the fastest-growing religion in the world.

The gallery of prophets and heretics described showed me something very important in the off-road search: that the Spirit shines its Fire and Light through any mind and within the limitations or openness of the willing heart manifests a teaching that in some way draws the hearers ever toward the Source. The lesson is that the Spirit will shine through our hearts, too, to our individual capacity or to whatever extent we allow. As an individual you may never start a new religion of the Spirit, but you can certainly open a local chapter within you and take your place in the awakening congregation.

SLAIN IN THE SPIRIT

There is one main difference between the Pentecostal and Charismatic movements: the proof of baptism of the Holy Spirit. Charismatics look for the "fruit of the spirit" described in Galatians 5:22–25; the Pentecostals look for glossolalia (speaking in tongues), prophesying, and the other "gifts of the spirit" described in Acts 2:1–4.

In November 2005 I attended a Pentecostal service. What I witnessed was something I'd never seen in a church before: a family of families alive and thrilled, singing and calling out with the excitement of a crowd at a football game. The pastor was dynamic, loud, articulate, and organized. He preached up and down the aisles, sat with people, whirled about in a sermon performance that I thought was both entertaining and inspiring.

Oddly enough, my visit to the Pentecostal church reminded me of the synagogue. The friendship and love the congregants expressed for each other and for me, the stranger in their midst, and their pastor was genuine and infectious. Many people opened their palms heavenward and swayed in the rousing songs of friendship with God, surrender, and praise for Christ. Like at the synagogue, the air was alive with the Spirit of God.

I didn't observe speaking in tongues in the service I attended, but typically in such services people act out their feelings of the Spirit with dancing, singing, and a surrender to the Spirit that apparently displaces their personality and causes the person to vocalize in unrecognizable words. On the whole, the congregation becomes a cacophony of noise. It sounds like babble to the visitor's ear, but the many Pentecostals and charismatics will tell you they are one with God in these moments, so filled with the Spirit that they overflow with bliss.

Pennsylvania writer and former Catholic school teacher Carole Lazur described her experience with charismatic services:

I attribute a lot to the Holy Spirit. I've always felt that my dreams are inspired by the Spirit. I've seen the dove and light, and I've also had the experience of smelling roses. I guess I've been lucky to have had a lot of these different experiences.

I remember the first time I smelled roses. I had gone to a charismatic mass that my son and I attended, though he doesn't anymore. He was in junior high school at the time, and I wanted to see what he was into. A teacher introduced him to it, and I wanted to make sure this teacher was on the up and up. [Note: These charismatic services were held on Wednesday nights at her family Roman Catholic Church.]

In the middle of the Mass, you get up to go to Communion at the usual time, and you also go up later for a blessing, when you see people "slain in the Spirit," in which they fall backward into the arms of a "catcher" who lays them down on the floor. So, I got up to go to Communion, and I was standing in the aisle, when all of a sudden the smell of roses came at me from behind. I felt like somebody tapped me on the shoulder. I turned around but didn't see anyone. I just got this fragrance, almost like a wave coming over me of roses. And that was all that really happened. Another time, I did fall back, and they caught me. I saw light from that experience—when the priest touches you on the forehead—and I went backwards and saw great light. I don't know how long it lasted, maybe thirty seconds. Every time I've gone to charismatic services since then I had that experience. It's a very amazing thing.

One could suppose it possible that someone near her was wearing a rose scent; however, the smell of roses is well known to people who have spiritual experiences. When I was in Assisi, Italy, in June 2005, I and several of my fellow travelers smelled roses at the tomb of Francis of Assisi; several others there did not. One traveler continued to smell them in her hotel room; her husband did not. The mystic saint Thérèse of Lisieux not only smelled roses but, before her death, several witnesses testified that physical roses manifested in her lap.

I asked Carole why she thought this "slaying in the Spirit" happens in charismatic services, but not in standard services.

"It happens during the blessing, when you call down the Spirit to come and enter you."

She said she thought it had to do with the dynamic calling forth out loud and the expectation. I found it interesting that she, a mainstream Catholic, had had such an experience.

> Yeah, I even hesitated to raise my arms in singing like the charismatics do. I felt ridiculous, at first, but eventually I was able to do that. It took me a long time, though, even though I had smelled the roses, and even though all this happened to me. I was self-conscious. I didn't want to be like one of these "holy rollers." You don't want to think of yourself that way.

Carole expressed a deep love of the Catholic tradition, even though she doesn't always agree with its policies.

> I don't believe everything that the church says. I love the traditions. I'm very happy with it. It's home to me. It's just like when you're with your family. You don't agree with everything your family says, but you love them nevertheless. And you're there, and it's home. That's what I feel about the church.

Movements involving and inspired by the Spirit of God are emerging everywhere, even within the centuries-old traditions of the Catholic Church. Carole's experience proves the permeability of the Spirit through dogma, habit, belief system. It's just like the Spirit to find each of us, wherever we are in our beliefs and consciousness.

TEARS OF JOY

As far as anyone can tell, modern Pentecostal and charismatic services might vaguely resemble the early Spirit communities of the centuries before Constantine. Remember that the church expressly outlawed claims of such direct contact with the Spirit. Are these services something like the experiences of the early

Christians at the time of the messengers? In the fourteenth century, attending such a charismatic service could have gotten you burned alive. The charismatics and Pentecostals believe that during their services they are being filled with the Holy Spirit. Who's to say they're wrong?

The movements just described came through prophets who were inspired by the Spirit to reclaim and restore some aspect of Jesus' teachings that they perceived had been lost or forgotten. Likewise, one man's heresy is another man's truth.

History continues to reveal inspired heretics developing new or refined approaches to theology, each of which is a reaction against some perceived lack in prevailing teachings. Each one seeks to open a new door to the Spirit of God.

William James defined the role of heresy well:

> A genuine firsthand religious experience . . . is bound to be a heterodoxy [contrary to the accepted norm] to its witnesses, the prophet appearing as a mere lonely madman. If his doctrine proves contagious enough to spread to any others, it becomes a definite and labeled heresy. But if it then still proves contagious enough to triumph over persecution, it becomes itself an orthodoxy; and when a religion has become an orthodoxy, its day of inwardness is over: the spring is dry; the faithful live at second-hand exclusively and stone the prophets in their turn. The new church, in spite of whatever human goodness it may foster, can be henceforth counted on as a staunch ally in every attempt to stifle the spontaneous religious spirit, and to stop all later bubblings of the fountain from which in purer days it drew its own supply of inspiration.[20]

The bottom line is, it's hard to argue with tears of joy. In the happy state of the Spirit, the inspired, the prayerful, the "taken up," the charismatic, the Pentecostal, the saint, the mystic, and the sinner alike have joined in consciousness with the One God through contact with the Spirit, which was the promise of the Anointed One. It doesn't much matter whether we approve or whether their theology makes sense. They're having a ball with their Lord. Just for those moments, the oneness removes the belief in separation, absolves judgments against others, and dissolves the Big Illusion: dualism, the imaginary boundary between humankind and God.

A SHOWDOWN WITH DUALISM

For the People of the Book, gaining an understanding of the Spirit of God is a tough order, mainly because of the assumptions of dualism—an issue that has cropped up in previous chapters. Dualism is the belief in a fundamental separation between the human and the Divine, between the spiritual realm and the physical world. It's the belief that God is up there out of reach, and we are stuck down here without a working cell phone. Buddhists say that the apparent dichotomy is an illusion created by our limiting sense perceptions—most of us don't see God, but we can see the world. Duality has provided job security for the priests and ministers of every religion for millennia.

Discussions about God in the West are usually contained inside the box of dualism. This is because the arguments assume a barrier between matter and spirit, between God and humankind, as though they are bitter opponents on some battlefield. We can thank Aristotle for that, and wonder why Plato's idea of oneness—intrinsic in the "One God" religion of Abraham, espoused by Origen, and preached by Jesus—was rejected as heresy. (Neoplatonists have been trying to revive it ever since.)

INNER KNOWING

My off-road search led to a major contradiction between this dualistic concept of the separation between God and man and the unity revealed in the Library of the Spirit. Franklin Takei, Ph.D., the retired professor of Greek philosophy and world religions introduced in chapter 2, provided some insights into this contradiction:

As I understand it, the duality issue is fundamental to mainstream Christian perspective. There is God, who creates the heavens and the earth. God as Creator is fundamentally distinct from his creation. Thus, always, there is the distinction between the Creator and the created. This duality pervades the Hebrew Bible and the New Testament. It is presupposed in whatever relation that exists between God and humankind.

As long as an individual is within mainstream Christianity, there is no overcoming this duality. However, Christianity is also a spectrum in the sense that from the very beginning of the Christian faith, there was a diversity of thinking and understanding. There were Jewish Christians who looked upon Jesus as a prophet of God and who fulfilled the expectations of the Messiah. They believed that the message presented by Jesus was for Jews only. Interestingly enough, Peter was one of this persuasion. At the other end of the spectrum were those who denied that Jesus was ever human. He merely took on the "appearance" of a human being. Fundamentally, he was really a spiritual being sent by God.

Both the Gnostics and the mystics (and they are clearly related to each other) talked about "inner knowing." Both positions are "contrary" to the "official" duality, and present the sense of the "oneness" of God and man. Eckhart, for example, talks about how we are all the "begotten" of God.

Although theism (Judaism, Christianity, and Islam) presupposes the dualistic distinction between the Creator and the created, there are alternative Jewish Gnostic, the mystical perspectives of Kabbalah, and the Muslim Gnostic/mystical perspective of the Sufis [to counter it].

Dr. Takei emphasized that the statement "The Lord thy God is One" in itself reflects Eastern philosophy, signifying a unified (hence non-dual) vision of the relation between God and creation.

Before his passing from cancer, Rev. Kieth VonderOhe shared his comments on duality. He, too, saw dualism as an unnecessary hindrance to our direct experience with the Spirit of God.

The traditional viewpoint is that God is "out there," totally separate from creation; even though you have a relationship, God is totally separate. Human beings are down here on earth and we have these physical bodies. It is this duality—radical separation between God and the creation—that's the foundation of basic Judaism and Christianity.

How were they to bridge that gap? How did God speak to people, and how did people make this connection with God? When Jesus was here, people initially felt here is somebody with a special connection. But once he left, he realized that people weren't going to understand everything he was trying to say, so he said he would send another power to help people maintain this connectedness.

In my own life, I don't perceive that sense of disconnectedness with God. There are certainly different levels of consciousness, and I don't yet have that intimate close connection that Jesus had, but I believe it's a potential within all of us. It's like you have an ice cube down here and steam up here. They're still water. And I could be part of the ice cube and God is the steam, but it's all still H_2O. It's just that the ice cube hasn't made the connection totally with the steam yet.

I think as the twenty-first century progresses, as spirituality and human evolution progress, as far as spiritual understanding, we will find new terms, and we may be expressing all of this very differently years from now. But we're still with that dualistic language. We're in a bridge area of trying to help people see that there's a different way of viewing God.

FUNNY RELIGION

Does the Spirit of God really have to remain a mystery? Will it always be on the other side, over there, out of sight and out of reach? Is there nothing more we can do than try to live a good life and wait on the whim of God to throw a little grace our way or lay a whopper of a spiritual experience on us that we can tell our friends and neighbors about?

In terms of human sense perception, there is certainly a difference between what we can see and what we can't see. For example, I can see myself in the mirror, but I can't see God. However, if we were created in the Divine Image, like God, a part of us can never die: our immortal consciousness, the soul, the "I Am That I Am" (the awareness of being aware) lives forever. The separation, therefore, must be an illusion bound up in the ego, the amusing personalities that we use in the day-to-day—a leftover philosophy that was once useful by a less evolved humankind. Within ourselves, however, we can enjoy a non-dual oneness with the Divine—those of us who have tasted it know this in our hearts.

How can it be any other than the Spirit that dwells within? The encounters with the Spirit reported in this book, and many that you can read elsewhere, dissolve the illusions of separation. Duality vanishes into oneness. Perhaps if we simply stop believing in our sinfulness and separateness, direct contact with the Divine can increase dramatically.

The idea of dualism may seem natural from the point of view of a humanity that, for now, sees only physical objects, but the idea was accepted in the early days. Some of the best heretics accepted the Oneness of all things, but prelates who had a lot to lose apparently thought this was carrying the "Hear O Israel! The Lord thy God is One!" a little too far.

So, the People of the Book have a belief system based on dualism, by which Spirit is separate from matter, and humankind is separate from the Creator, in whose image we were created. It's a philosophy that we are cursed with Adam's sin from birth, chronically corrupted by the world, and lost forever unless we somehow earn salvation through blind faith.

At a conference on Christian philosophy, the Zen master D. T. Suzuki made the following comment on western religion, which seems to sum up our hit-or-miss relationship with the Spirit of God: "God against man. Man against God. Man against nature. Nature against man. Nature against God. God against nature. Very funny religion!"

GOD IS IN EVERYTHING

These conflicts in the Judeo-Christian traditions, however, may be changing. A series of articles in the April 2005 issue of *Science and Theology News* reports another growing trend in international religious thought called panentheism, which may well be another movement of the Spirit, finding the prophets, reformers, and individuals who can draw people back to the original and ever-present Source.

Pantheism is the belief that everything is God; panentheism is a belief that God is in everything, but that God is also greater than everything. This means that the laws of nature reflect the nature of God and the phenomena we observe are the effects of the Spirit. The view also holds that the image of God is within human beings, too—urging us to be at our best, asking our cooperation in healing and unity, and helping to improve the world for everyone. Evil is a result, not of God's creation, but of human misuse of the creative power inherent in the Divine Image. According to panentheism, God is the epitome of absolute love and goodness.

The articles suggest that it could also be the common ground on which the churches of the East and West can agree. It seems to me that this philosophy provides an all-purpose theology by which the tenets of all religions can sit side by side in the same pew.

The article also suggests that panentheism could well be the common ground on which both science and religion can agree. It turns out that the problems of dualism and oneness have become big issues in the sciences, too. Is it possible that science can tell us something about the Spirit and our direct experience with the Divine? Science actually has quite a lot to say about the Spirit. Scientists don't like to admit this, but it has all along.

Chapter 8

OF SCIENCE
and
SPIRIT

One of the goals of this book is to break down limiting beliefs and false assumptions that stand in the way of our direct experience with the Spirit of God. We've looked at the experiences of various traditions, specific individuals, and historical realities, and it seems clear that we humans experience the Spirit in many ways. The Spirit is universal and apparently available without limit. It's also inside every one of us, and the sciences are making impressive strides toward reading the handwriting on the wall. For all its pride in precision, science is often an unpredictable collision of hard work, genius, serendipity, and dumb luck. If the truth be told, the luminaries of science going back to Aristotle were quite nearly all trying to come up with a way of explaining God. Albert Einstein once said: "Science without religion is lame, religion without science is blind."[1]

So what can science tell us? It turns out that advanced research is being done in the fields of consciousness studies, quantum physics, biology, mathematics, and medicine, that explores the forces behind the forces of nature. They're actually coming up with models of universal reality, in both the mind and the universe, in which God just might feel at home. Movements within science may actually be outpacing theology in rendering God in understandable terms. This is ironic, because modern science began as a reaction against reliance upon the spiritual. And who could blame them? People even took gravity on faith. Debates over the Spirit have been causing schisms, distrust, and wars practically since the beginning. Scientists wanted something to measure—they wanted facts, and as everyone knows, the Spirit of God can't be measured, analyzed, or manipulated. Or can it?

In the summer of 2005, I wondered if I could find a scientist willing to openly talk about God in terms of science (or science in terms of God). I found several who were not only willing, but eager to do so.

SOUNDS LIKE THEOLOGY TO ME

It was in 1962 that MIT professor Thomas S. Kuhn coined the phrase "paradigm shift," which refers to those rare and marvelous moments when a new discovery dramatically changes some universally accepted belief. This isn't just about discovering that germs cause disease, although that was a biggie. It's when the entire foundation of how people understand themselves, their world, and the universe—including God—jazzes everyone with some new insight from the Spirit of Truth. Think about that dramatic moment when anthropologist Margaret Mead showed the New Guinea tribesmen the first flashlight they had ever seen. It changed forever what they had believed to be possible. If the Spirit inspires new truth, as Paul wrote, then wouldn't it be ironic if science has been guided by the Spirit all along?

GREAT SHIFTS

Examples from history's major paradigm shifts tell the tale. The ancient Ptolemaic Cosmology (earth-centered universe) was overturned by the Copernican (sun-centered). (We won't mention the fact that the Indians knew the world was a round planet orbiting the Sun a thousand years earlier.) Isaac Newton was seeking the truth about God when he united the separate elements of classical physics into a single physics. His laws defined mass, motion, energy, and light that always, he thought, behaved the same ways under various conditions. This was, to him, a Theory of Everything (TOE) that rendered the universe down to a clockwork mechanism of matter and motion.

Newton believed his mechanics to be the real proof of God's existence, and that all one needed in order to know God was scientific observation. He dedicated his life to driving the catchall phantom of "mystery" out of Christianity, which he believed was used by the Church to keep the ignorant masses under control.

It wasn't Newton's intention that science would become a religion in itself, but it did. It became the new religion based on empiricism (seeing is believing). But like any religion, its assumptions were destined to be challenged by the next new prophet bent on getting back to some original, unadorned, vibrant truth.

Philosopher Friedrich Nietzsche was also deeply concerned with God. His commonly misunderstood obituary, "God is dead," was no arrogant atheistic declaration as is commonly taught in school. He was lamenting what had been done against the true understanding of God in the names of both religion and science. Nietzsche wasn't promoting nihilism as a career choice. He had merely observed it in the world around him as a result of the loss of a meaningful relationship with God due to the new religion of science. He wrote:

> God is dead. God remains dead. And we have killed him. How shall we, murderers of all murderers, console ourselves? That which was the holiest and mightiest of all that the world has yet possessed has bled to death under our knives. Who will wipe this blood off us? With what water could we purify ourselves? What festivals of atonement,

what sacred games shall we need to invent? Is not the greatness of this deed too great for us? Must we not ourselves become gods simply to be worthy of it?[2]

"When people deny the existence of God today," wrote theologian Karen Armstrong, "they are often rejecting the God of Newton, the origin and sustainer of the universe whom scientists can no longer accommodate."[3]

Often omitted in the classrooms is the fact that in their lofty pursuits, Descartes, Newton, Leibnitz, Einstein, and many other original scientific thinkers were contemplating a true understanding of the Divine. In his quest to eliminate the "mystery" about God, Newton had raised an embarrassing question: Doesn't keeping God shrouded in mystery imply that God, despite five thousand years of holy books and prophets, has been incapable of expressing himself clearly?

DOING THE MATH (AND THE BIOLOGY)

Mathematics, too, is inching closer to a TOE through lofty mathematical theories such as Galois Extensions and the classic Riemann Hypothesis (both of which would require lengthy explanations beyond the scope of this book). Fibonacci discovered the order in spirals, and Mandelbrot, through his fractal geometry, even showed the order in chaos.[4] Like time and space, maybe numbers themselves will turn out to be an illusion with no beginning or end. At the turn of the eighteenth century, G. W. Leibnitz suggested that only ones and zeros matter—it's certainly true for computers, which operate on the binary number system. Perhaps that discovery will lead to a new math that captures the Spirit and the soul.

The life sciences are approaching the Spirit, too. For example, the New Biology seeks to understand the interrelation of the largest and most complex systems, making biology more fundamental, like physics, seeking to define the nature of reality. This new holistic approach to biology reasserts the importance of the whole organism—an entire individual or ecosystem—over the behavior of isolated genes.

Cell biologist and author Bruce H. Lipton, Ph.D., has contributed to the field of epigenetics, the study of changes in gene function that occur without initial changes in the DNA sequence. He has demonstrated that the cell membrane, rather than the long-held emphasis on the nucleus, controls the cell's behavior. Moreover, he showed that genes and DNA are controlled by signals from outside the cell, including messages in the energy emanating from our positive and negative thoughts and beliefs.

In his book *The Biology of Belief: Unleashing the Power of Consciousness, Matter and Miracles*, he writes that the New Biology "casts life as a cooperative journey among powerful individuals who can program themselves to create joy-filled lives." Once we understand this, he writes, "we will no longer fractiously debate the role of nurture and nature, because we will realize that the fully conscious mind trumps both nature and nurture."[5]

He explains, "The fact that science led me to spiritual insight is appropriate because the latest discoveries in physics and cell research are forging new links between the worlds of science and spirit. These realms were split apart in the days of Descartes centuries ago. However, I truly believe that only when Spirit and Science are reunited will we be afforded the means to create a better world."[6]

So, what does science have to do with the Spirit of God? Everything. The greatest scientist the world has known, Leonardo da Vinci, once said, "Where the spirit does not work with the hand, there is no art." In his day, he had to write his notebooks backward with the aid of a mirror in case the authorities started sniffing around.

If God knows all and exists everywhere, these new scientific paradigms, which were only hypotheses or theories a century ago, may well provide a Theory of Everything worthy of the name. As new discoveries replace old ones, science continues to uncover the interconnectedness of all things, and this sounds like theology to me.

As Newton dedicated himself to rooting out mystery from religion, some scientists today work on the frontier of eliminating mystery from the universe itself—bringing the "mysterious ways" of God into sharper focus. Let's look at that frontier as it is being explored in psychology.

THE SCIENCE OF CONSCIOUSNESS

Since its beginnings in the 1800s, psychology has expanded into branches specializing in consciousness studies, transpersonal psychology, and parapsychology. These studies examine what it is to have consciousness and awareness, both in terms of the brain and in terms of the mental and spiritual experiences that transcend physiology. In so doing, psychologists join what I like to call the "awakening sciences," which are galloping toward the study of the Spirit of God whether they realize it or not.

NEUROTHEOLOGY

A number of studies on meditation reveal clues about our ability to mentally transcend physical reality. They show that spiritual contemplation comes naturally to us, and that by disciplining the mind we can more easily access the Spirit.

For example, a number of neurologists have been testing Tibetan monks, the most disciplined meditators in the world, with startling results. Meditation is merely a training of the mind in which you, the I Am-observer of your thoughts, take control of your mind and subdue your emotions in order to free the mind from assumptions, prejudices, desires, and distractions. Tibetan Buddhists are masters of this discipline. (I'll discuss meditation in more depth in chapter 10.)

Richard Davidson, working at the University of Wisconsin's $10 million W. M. Keck Laboratory for Functional Brain Imaging and Behavior, is involved in an ongoing study that compares the brain activity (particularly gamma waves) of experienced Tibetan monks with that of novice meditators. In one experiment, published in the Proceedings of the National Academy of Sciences, Davidson had the two groups meditate on unconditional compassion, defined as the "unrestricted readiness and availability to help living beings." The focus was chosen because it was nonspecific and involved a transformed state of being. The subjects were monitored by 256 sensors about the head and body.

Soon after beginning meditation, the monks' gamma waves increased dramatically, while those of the novices showed little increase. The monks also demonstrated highly integrated, synergistic gamma activity throughout the brain, while the same waves in the novices were chaotic. Davidson believes the research shows that over long periods of time meditation actually restructures the way the brain functions.

Just so we don't think of meditation as an idiosyncrasy of the East, we must not overlook the research of Maria Beauregard, a (male) neuroscientist from the University of Montreal, who conducted research on the *unio mystica* or mystical experiences of a group of Carmelite nuns. When the nuns recalled these mystical experiences (most had had only one or two in their lifetime), functional MRI testing revealed an increase of activity in the center of their brains. The EEG results showed an increase of slow theta wave activity. Beauregard's work in "neurotheology" reveals that in people who have lived more tragic or abusive lives, the circuitry of the brain that perceives mystical experiences is never activated. He hopes to find ways to train the brain to become more receptive to spiritual experiences. (One might conclude that the abused—and there are many types of abuse— have the toughest time knowing the Spirit's gentle invitation to awaken.)

In 2001, Andrew B. Newberg, M.D., assistant professor of radiology at the University of Pennsylvania School of Medicine in Philadelphia, co-authored a book entitled *Why God Won't Go*

Away, in which he and his associates show that humans seek God because our brains are biologically programmed to do so. This falls into the realm of neurotheology, which maintains that the human brain is actually hardwired with an innate connection to the Divine. The conclusion, of course, comes as no surprise at this stage in the off-road search, but it is exciting to know that science may eventually uncover the reality of the Divine Image—the presence of God, the kingdom of heaven, and the Spirit within.

In 2001, Newberg and his associates published a study in *Psychiatry Research and Neuroimaging*, in which they, too, tested the brain activity of Tibetan Buddhists. Using a special x-ray procedure called SPECT, they noted increased activities in the brain during meditation. They saw activity in the area of the brain responsible for focused concentration, but also the brain region that keeps us oriented spatially. Newberg believes this may explain why meditators sometimes feel transported out of the physical body and into the alternative reality of the spiritual. Like Beauregard, Newberg also tested religious women—Franciscan nuns in the act of prayer—and noted similar brain patterns. Not only that, but Newberg noted decreases in heart rate and blood pressure and changes in hormone activity, which he says may even improve the immune system.

These experiments don't prove the existence of the Spirit by any means, but if I may interpret, they show our mental capacity to control the body, and a surefire method, meditation, by which we can free the mind to the open, receptive state that invites Spiritual experiences.

PSYCHOLOGY AND SPIRIT

Psychology's interest in religious experience goes back a long way, probably originating with William James, the philosopher who turned psychology into a physical science. James was the first to create a laboratory for the study of the mind, and religious and mystical experience were at the top of his interests.

The next heavy-hitter in psychology was Carl Jung, the son of a pastor. As a child he had many transcendent events, lucid dreams, and powerful experiences with God. He tried to communicate these experiences to his father, but without much success, as his father was losing his own faith in God.

A longtime collaborator with the founder of psychoanalysis, Sigmund Freud, Jung departed from Freud in 1912, disagreeing that neuroses were mostly based on sexuality. Jung differentiated four functions of the mind: thinking, feeling, sensation, and intuition. He later developed a theory based on his own transcendental experiences, putting forth for the first time in modern science (though it was well known in Eastern and ancient Western traditions) the concept of a universal mental realm called the "collective unconscious." He founded his analytic psychology as a reaction against Freud's psychoanalysis.

Like James, Jung spent much of his later life further developing his ideas, especially on the relationship between psychology and religion. He studied ancient texts, including those of the Hermetic tradition, and asserted that Christianity was actually a step in the historical development of consciousness. But he maintained that the religion failed to give expression to all the key aspects of the human mind. He worked quite a lot with middle-aged and elderly patients whose lives had lost their meaning. Most of these had also lost their religious belief.[7]

The "collective unconscious" opened the field of psychology to explore an unseen, unlimited non-dual reality, unbound by time or space, which would provide a model into which operations of a concept such as the Spirit could fit.

In *The Undiscovered Self*, Dr. Jung wrote, "The seat of faith . . . is not consciousness but spontaneous religious experience, which brings the individual's faith into immediate relation with God."

In the 1950s, parapsychology brought concepts such as intuition, precognition, and extrasensory perception (ESP) into the laboratory, and a scientific foundation was established for what is now known as Transpersonal Psychology (Jung was the first to use the term *transpersonal*).

This is the area within psychology that pursues consciousness studies, spiritual inquiry, body-mind relationships, and the dynamics of transformation. It was many years after Jung when this new science came into its own, and my off-road search for the Spirit of God led to two pioneers in this field—philosopher and author Ken Wilber and psychologist Charles T. Tart, Ph.D.

A prodigy who published his first book at age twenty-three, Ken Wilber is the author of over a dozen books in this field. Over the years, his work gradually revealed a progressive and comprehensive TOE, and his revolutionary Integral Psychology includes spirit and soul to create a virtually complete vision of the entire human being. In 1998 he founded the Integral Institute, a think-tank for studying science, society, and religion as a whole.

In his *The Marriage of Sense and Soul* Wilber expands the definition of empirical evidence, the requirement (and restriction) of science that relies strictly on five-sense observation. Explaining that science is only one way of "knowing," Wilber considers himself a staunch empiricist, meaning that although he demands evidence for what he believes, he doesn't limit such evidence to the five senses. He allows the possibility of sensory and mental evidence, of course, but also spiritual evidence—knowledge gained through mystical and spiritual experience.[8]

Wilber simplifies this idea by describing "the eye of flesh," "the eye of mind," and "the eye of contemplation," each of which peers into different levels of reality.[9] He goes on to say that "authentic spirituality is not the product of the eye of flesh and its sensory empiricism, nor the eye of mind and its rational empiricism, but only, finally the eye of contemplation and its spiritual empiricism (religious experience, spiritual illumination, or satori, by whatever name)." He suggests comparing the data of your spiritual experiences with others, "and in the verification of that transcendental data, the existence of Spirit will become radically clear—at least as clear as rocks are to the eye of flesh and geometry is to the eye of mind."[10]

In Integral Psychology, experiences with the Spirit of God are an admitted possibility that could one day be achieved and measured through various techniques.

THE PROMISE OF THE TRANSPERSONAL

Charles T. Tart, Ph.D., is currently a professor emeritus of psychology at the University of California, Davis, and a core faculty member of the Institute for Transpersonal Psychology. He pioneered the field of consciousness studies back in the 1970s. His classic best-selling anthology *Altered States of Consciousness* has been called one of the most important books on psychology of the twentieth century.

Tart is credited with legitimizing the study of altered states, including hypnosis, meditation, lucid dreaming, and drug-induced states. He initiated several important lines of research in parapsychology, including teaching ESP and out-of-body experiences. His resume lists more than 250 articles in leading scientific and professional journals including *Science and Nature*, and numerous well-known books. His *Transpersonal Psychologies*, for example, became the core text in the then-new field of transpersonal psychology.

Dr. Tart is also the creator of the TASTE website (The Archive of Scientists' Transcendent Experiences), first described in chapter 2, where scientists post their spiritual experiences.

Tart said,

> I think of myself as both a scientist and a spiritual seeker. That means there are parts of my personality that are interested in matters we call spiritualism. It's vital to me. But there's also a part of me that doesn't like to be fooled and that's very careful about trying to stick close to data instead of getting lost in speculations or abstractions or theories or beliefs. I like to get people talking about what they actually experienced and not get lost in the way they categorize it.

One of the proudest accomplishments of my life is helping to found the field of transpersonal psychology. Where you might say one of its main focuses is to try to get back to what are the actual experiences of spiritual things people have, before you get the particular belief system, the particular cultural overlay put on top of it, and kind of come up with a more universal understanding of what spirituality is for actual human beings. . . .

I go to consciousness conferences all the time where people proclaim that we finally understand consciousness, or we're on the verge of it, and it's all reducible to brain functioning. And I have to smile at the arrogance because these people are not being good scientists. They're ignoring all the data of parapsychology that don't fit into that physical framework at all, and yet they're very high-quality data.

From all my investigations of the mind over the years and that of many colleagues, the mind does things that brains can't do. And that means there are fundamental questions we have to investigate about the nature of the mind. And some of those things the mind does sounds like what we call "spiritual" things. For instance, every religion I know of gives an important place to prayer. From a materialistic viewpoint, what's prayer? It's "talking to yourself." But wait a minute, look at parapsychology, and the evidence we have for telepathy. If two human beings can sometimes communicate information when there's no physical way for it to happen, that sounds like a kind of mechanism by which prayer might work. To me that means we should really be investigating telepathy at much greater length and its prayer-like aspects and understanding it on its own terms, not assuming that someday it will be explained in terms of brain functioning.

I asked him if anybody was actually conducting that type of research.

In terms of applying science to questions about spirituality, which I think is vital, we're doing almost nothing. Let me elaborate on that. I don't think science is the answer to everything. I don't think anything is the answer to everything, but science applied to the physical world has clarified an awful lot of things and increased our understanding and ability. There are a lot of areas of the spiritual world and psychological world where, if science were applied directly to the phenomena, I think we could do a lot better.

I'm not happy with religions that essentially just tell people "be good or else." And I think that's one of the reasons there was such an interest in exotic Asian religions back in the sixties and seventies. We had our religious traditions, yet for a lot of people they didn't work. You were told to be good. You didn't have much success at it. You just felt guilty about it, and then you gave up. The Eastern religions that came along were saying, "You don't have to believe this but here are some methods you can try and see if they work for you. There's something specific you can do," and, inefficient as they are, they work for a lot of people. That changed the whole culture around.

KEN WILBER'S *THE EYE OF SPIRIT*

In *The Eye of Spirit*, Ken Wilber describes the "Great Search for Spirit," the activity and belief of most westerners that we are on a perpetual search for God. Explaining the non-dualistic traditions (such as Buddhism), Wilber calls this a symptom of the "separate-self." The non-dual traditions, therefore, undo the separate-self, the self that believes itself separate from the Divine. (The non-dual traditions believe that there is only Spirit, everywhere, all the time. This is not pantheism, which holds that everything is God, but panentheism, which holds that God is in everything.) Wilber writes,

> The Great Search for Spirit is simply that impulse, the final impulse which prevents the present realization of Spirit, and it does so for a simple reason: The Great Search presumes the loss of God. The Great Search reinforces the mistaken belief that God is not present and thus totally obscures the reality of God's ever-present Presence. The Great Search, which pretends to love God, is in fact the very mechanism of pushing God away; the mechanism of promising to find tomorrow that which exists only in the timeless now; the mechanism of watch-

ing the future so fervently that the present always passes it by—very quickly—and God's smiling face with it. . . .

We wish to get from our unenlightened state (of sin or delusion or duality) to an enlightened or more spiritual state. We wish to get from where Spirit is not, to where Spirit is. . . .

If Spirit cannot be found as a future product of the Great Search, then there is only one alternative: Spirit must be fully, totally, completely present right now—and you must be fully, totally, completely aware of it right now.[11]

This would cast my off-road search for the Spirit of God in a dubious light, except for the tremendous need for effective ways to break down the illusion of separateness. The off-road search seeks to do just that and, in the process, reveal the ever-present reality of the Spirit to anyone who doesn't already know it.

Wilber's psychology is an integral, holistic paradigm that includes the universal "I" awareness. Consciousness. To my mind, this is the "I Am" who spoke to Moses; who speaks to us all. The "I Am" is the clear singing flame that lives in our consciousness, far beyond or deep within our innermost thoughts. It is the Divine Image.

As the psychologists inch toward integrating the Spirit with the human psyche and collective unconscious, the physicists are meandering toward a similar end. The difference is that they are doing so through Relativity and Quantum Theory.

THE PHYSICS OF THE FIRE AND LIGHT

In an age of superstition and totalitarian authority, Isaac Newton's ideas were overdue on arrival, but did his mechanics answer all the questions? Newton was good, but he had overlooked something big.

IN PURSUIT OF THE LIGHT

Albert Einstein's revolutionary theory of relativity showed that Newtonian mechanics didn't explain quite everything. Quantum theory has shifted our understanding of time and space yet again, with implications that reach to our very relationship with "the One Who Is." When you break material objects down to the nth degree, you find that objects are merely light.

"And God said, 'Let there be light'; and there was light," reads Genesis 1:3. But only then did "I Am That I Am" create the physical world—the world we see, through the mechanism of the Spirit. If quantum theory is correct, God made the things we see by compacting light into super-dense masses. In the light of divine consciousness, "I Am That I Am" condensed light tightly into forms based on the sphere, a 3-D representation of the atom—the single most dimensionless point, the essence of God's own nature. God compacted light into stars, planets, and all objects that God conceived. At the level of light, there is no difference between objects. Unpack the light or energy of an object in just the right way, and you get a nuclear explosion. Unpack it in another way, and you get a sun.

Cambridge-educated physicist, author, and futurist Peter Russell is a fellow of the Institute of Noetic Sciences. After studying in India, he was the first researcher to formally study the psychology of meditation. I like how he summarizes the modern theories of relativity and quantum mechanics.

> Both relativity and quantum physics, the two great paradigm shifts of modern physics, started from anomalies in the behavior of light, and both led to radical new understandings of the nature of light. For example, in relativity theory, at the speed of light time comes to a stop—in effect, that means for light there is no time whatsoever. Furthermore, a photon can traverse the entire universe without using up any energy— in effect that means for light there is no space. In quantum theory, we find that light has zero mass and charge, which in effect means that it is immaterial. Light, therefore, seems to occupy a very special place in

the cosmic scheme; it is in some ways more fundamental than time, space, or matter. The same, I later discovered, was true of the inner light of consciousness.[12]

Albert Einstein avoided formalized religion in his adult life. Nevertheless, he was deeply concerned about the nature of God and the universe. He wrote, "There are only two ways to live your life: as though nothing is a miracle, or as though everything is a miracle."

He could not accept what he perceived to be the wrathful, vengeful God of the Judeo-Christian world. He referred to himself as agnostic in that respect, but he never stopped admiring or seeking to understand the central truth of a divine source. He explained it this way:

> My religion consists of a humble admiration of the illimitable superior Spirit who reveals himself in the slight details we are able to perceive with our frail and feeble minds. The deeply emotional conviction of the presence of a superior reasoning Power, which is revealed in the incomprehensible universe, forms my idea of God.[13]

Dr. Einstein spent many years pursuing one question: What is light? He thought that if he could understand light, he could understand God. With his famous $E=mc^2$, he finally found the answer. In 1905, while listening to two church bells toll from different sides of town, he had an epiphany in which it all became clear. His paper on general relativity was only three pages long, but that, along with other papers he published the same year, proved that light is energy in the form of an electromagnetic wave. Perhaps more important, he proved that light is part of a deeper unity, in which there is no difference whatsoever between energy and matter. So much for dualism. If energy and matter are the same, why should we believe there's a separation between us and the Spirit?

"A spirit is manifest in the laws of the universe," Einstein wrote, "a spirit vastly superior to that of man, and one in the face of which we with our modest powers must feel humble."

THE "BIG I"

San Francisco physicist and author Fred Alan Wolf, Ph.D., has brought a new physics of consciousness onto the radar screen of public awareness. His books establish a scientific ground in which Spirit doesn't need a license to operate.

Dr. Wolf's work successfully explains the visible and invisible universe along with a paradigm for the concept of the Spirit. I began my interview with a question about miracles: did he have an explanation for the miracles of Jesus, the Hasidic rabbis, and the siddhis of the yogis.

"No," he said. "These are unexplainable. What I try to do, and what anybody doing research on consciousness is trying to do, is to find specific ways of understanding what is a conscious experience, and the clue that there is some relationship between brain and mind, or between the physical and the mental, that comes from what is called the 'Observer Effect' in quantum physics."

In quantum theory the Observer Effect states that a phenomenon cannot occur without an observer to perceive or conceive it. This means that a preexisting observer is required for everything—the physical universe is the direct result of consciousness—an overarching consciousness that reminds me of Jung's collective unconscious, or the mind of God. Human consciousness itself, therefore, is also observed by God, and, going back to the Platonists, the observer can be no other than a universal consciousness or the mind of God—the "I Am That I Am." I asked Dr. Wolf for his thoughts on this.

It has to do with how our present viewpoint of the material world has been changed drastically by quantum physics. What it has predicted about this thing we call "the material world" is that it is not a material world at all, but a possibility field of possible material worlds overlapping, which can be revealed or unveiled by the observer effect, whereby the observer chooses to look at reality from one point of view rather than another, and, as a result, reality pops into existence in a distribution of possibilities aligned with whatever it is the person is looking for.

According to quantum physics, then, the observer (you, me, God, or the collective consciousness) creates the reality it chooses to see—nothing exists that is not being observed. I brought up the idea of non-local reality, a realm of universal reality that doesn't bother with time and space—it's everywhere, everything, and it's always now. One way to conceive it is realizing that the thoughts you are thinking aren't taking place inside your cranium, but bloom into being beyond the boundaries of your physical body. The validity of non-local reality has been proved through research in quantum theory, in which two particles can be shown to exist in two places at the same time. It has also been proved in remote viewing experiments, in which a person can describe a scene from a remote location with amazing accuracy. I asked Dr. Wolf if such research can help us understand the God consciousness described in various religious traditions, which seems to be the awareness of awareness. He explained,

> The basic idea, in kind of a mechanistic way, is that the mind of God is a "field of all possibility" and it represents what we call spirit. It's unbounded, unlimited, beyond space and time. So it fits in with any of the basic doctrinaire things that you'd find in Indian philosophy, such as those in the Bhagavad Gita—the Lord Krishna, the realm of Brahma, and others. Also the concept in Kabbalah of the great void out of which everything eventually appears. In Buddhism as well, there is the unborn, unformed, uncreated, unoriginated. All these point to a realm of existence that is both existent and nonexistent, paradoxical at the same time, out of which everything arises. I don't know of a single one of the many spiritual orders that I've investigated—including

Australian Aboriginal, as well as Hindu, Buddhist, Muslim, Jewish, Catholic, and so forth—that don't all point to this one realm.

So we begin there. I call it the realm of spirit. And in trying to make a model of it, I said that this realm is inherently vibratory. What is it vibrating around? It's vibrating between coming into existence and not coming into existence. It's in a constant state of what you might call flux. So in a way the mind of God is highly unstable, likely to pop into anything. And that's what it's like from a quantum physics point of view.

Dr. Wolf explained one possibility of the Spirit's presence in what is called the Big Bang theory of creation, and how the individual souls emerged from the All. (Regarding the evolution versus creationism—or more recently, intelligent design—debate, it's no problem for me that God burst forth with love in a big bang that uses evolution as a tool to express divine will.)

But there's a will or an intent, beyond any description that appears, and how that appears, and what it does, we don't know, but according to the physical world picture, there has been a big bang, where the universe, and possibly even multi-universes, came into being. And as this bang proceeded, what happened was that the mind, the spirit, got enraptured, fell in love with, or was narcissistically involved with itself. What seems to transpire is that a reflective process takes place.

The spirit gets trapped as the universe begins to expand. Particles of matter, which are trapped forms of spirit, self-reflect and form basically unconscious elements. Then as the universe continues to expand, another form of spirit gets trapped and it becomes what we call the universal soul—the one mind—the big "G" that we normally call the living God experience. And that is still very much part of the mind of God, but it's now been caught up in boundary conditions. It's been caught in the big bang and the two conditions are the initial impetus, which is the big bang and the final impetus, which is either the big crunch, or accelerating expansion—all expressed forever. Most likely it's going to be a big crunch, but the current thinking is it's going to expand forever.

Its history depends on a boundary condition, and what that does is it causes these spiritual waves to reflect from either boundary, like when you flick a jump rope that's attached to a wall. The wave bounces back and forth. It's the same for the spiritual waves, which reflect backward and forward through time. And this produces a pattern of consciousness which might be called the big "I." Part of that appears as matter. What that pattern of consciousness does is that it begins to seek or desire a reflection of itself and wants to know itself because it suddenly feels apart or alone. It's kind of like the old traditions talk about the fall of man, about fallen angels, or fallen beings.

So, the trapped mind of God, if you will, begins to want to see itself. It feels the trap of time and wants to get out. Before, it was neither immortal nor mortal, but it has now become immortal. It lives forever in time, meaning from the beginning to ending of time. That's what's called forever. And there is an ending of time coming as there was a beginning of time. It's the same for space and matter and everything else.

In my limited understanding of physics, Dr. Wolf's explanation of the Big Bang meshed with the creation myths of many cultures. They are told in story form, whereas he tells his in terms of quantum physics. Here we had the formless, the "Spirit brooding over the waters" (of unconsciousness), and light (awareness) is allowed to be. As with many creation narratives, the Ultimate Reality bursts forth with pure love and wants to multiply itself. Consciousness forms the "I Am That I Am" (Elohim, Creator God), which throws off Divine Sparks of itself—mini-I Ams, or souls who are awake like itself.

Wolf continues,

What we're experiencing in the universe is the embodiment of intelligence into matter, and we are only part of that process. The transformation of the human mind into matter is only a part of it. Animal mind into matter is also a part of it. There are many different ways in which this can happen.

Indeed, the human mind is trapped in the physical body. Around itself, it builds boundaries, and the mind either evolves back to its original God Consciousness, or focuses on the body in which it lives.

Christians believe in transcending the world by being "saved"; Buddhists believe they can save themselves through achieving bodhi, becoming enlightened. I mentioned how other traditions, too, talk of escape from the entrapment of consciousness in the physical body and asked if these mental and disciplinary efforts are able to release them from these cycles within the physical body. Wolf responded,

> There are recognitions which are always present that the mind is not contained within the body. There are recognitions of the universality of and the desire for salvation, or saving, or whatever. This really cannot be denied because you are already saved. You are already part of that whether you like it or not, so you don't have to really worry about it. The only thing you have to concern yourself with is adhering to a picture of yourself.

I asked him what this picture should be, and he said it was recognizing our essential nature. Who we really are. To me (and the Kabbalists) we are all chips off the Old Block—spiritual points of divine consciousness who choose to muck about in the fun-filled Earth.

Dr. Wolf summarized the goal of his work and his concept of the Spirit:

> My basic goal is one of trying to achieve a state of being in which we truly understand both our sacred and physical natures without dismissing one for the other. I believe that once that understanding sets in, needless conflict will diminish.
>
> Basically the Spirit means a unity. It is a whole thing of itself, but it's beyond space and time and matter and energy. And it is a vibrational

pattern of the mind of God, if you will, and it vibrates because it's constantly dealing with the dilemma of "to be or not to be."

In his scientific concept of a "spiritual universe," Dr. Wolf is not alone, but one of a growing number of scientists working toward a unified theory that includes consciousness. Dr. Amit Goswami, University of Oregon professor of physics and author of *The Self-Aware Universe: How Consciousness Creates the Material World*, believes that physics has the tools to prove that consciousness creates the material universe and thereby the existence of God. He supports the concept of the Observer Effect, believing that the universe exists because a sentient being is aware of it. He cites research in cognitive psychology, biology, parapsychology, and quantum physics, as well as certain ancient mystical traditions, for a new paradigm he calls "monistic idealism," in which consciousness, not matter, is the foundation of everything that exists.

MEDICINE AND THE FIRE OF THE SPIRIT

In the ancient reference to the Spirit of God as Fire and Light, we've stated that fire is "the fire of change and transformation" and light is the "light of consciousness and understanding." So far, the discussion of science and the Spirit has focused on the nature of light. But what about fire?

Chemistry is involved with the transformative symbol of fire—combining chemicals to produce reactions that create new forms and substances. In clinical psychology, the fire can be found in the healing of a troubled psyche through psychotherapy; in biology, through cloning, manipulation of DNA and genes, and genetics; in physics, the fire of the Spirit can be seen in nuclear reactions. But as far as benefits to human beings are concerned, it seems that the fire aspect of the Spirit is most exalted in medicine. We will know it as the fire of healing, however healing takes place, whether from medicines, surgery, or even the spiritual ingredient. In particular, a lot of medical research has been done in the area of energy medicine and the effects of prayer on treating illness.

The interplay between the body and the mind has long been known in the field of medicine, and in recent decades holism has become a respected point of view. Although many alternative healing practices await the verdict of proper research for acceptance in allopathic medicine, enlightened physicians today know that the entire person should be treated for illness, rather than merely firing a pharmaceutical bullet at a specific symptom.

Distinguishing themselves in this area are a host of medical doctors who have written books about their pioneering new practices and discoveries. They include Judith Orloff, M.D. (a psychiatrist and a practicing intuitive); Andrew Weil, M.D. (a pioneer in integrative medicine); Carolyn Myss, Ph.D. (a medical intuitive and an authority in energy medicine); Christiane Northrup, M.D. (a gynecologist who considers alternative therapies); and many more.

Energy medicine borrows from the medicine of the East. Researcher William Collinge, Ph.D., in his book *Subtle Energy* explains how the earth is one enormous energy field and that the human body is a microcosm of "interacting and interpenetrating energy fields."

"The world's spiritual traditions share the understanding that energy and spirit are intimately intertwined. Energy is the 'raw material' of which Spirit is continually forming our physical reality. Energy is the medium in which Spirit moves through our world, the bridge between Spirit and matter."[14] Medical researchers, too, have been exploring the relationship between energy, spirit, and healing.

Physician and author Larry Dossey, M.D., was the first to explore the application of non-local reality in medicine. He advanced the concept of how both physician and patient can benefit by using this knowledge. He also paved the way for the scientific study of prayer and the soul in healing. His many books include *Recovering the Soul, Healing Words,* and *Reinventing Medicine.*

He writes, "I used to believe that we must choose between science and reason on one hand, and spirituality on the other, in how we lead our lives. Now I consider this a false choice. We can recover the sense of sacredness, not just in science, but in perhaps every area of life."

Before the publication of his 1993 book *Healing Words*, only three U.S. medical schools offered courses that explored the role of religion and prayer in health. As of 2006, nearly eighty schools offer such courses, often using Dr. Dossey's books as texts.

When I contacted Dr. Dossey he was on a camping trip in Montana; he spoke with me by phone during a brief stay at a motel there. He was very enthusiastic about my project.

> This entire topic has caused extreme theological indigestion over millennia. Wars have been fought over it, I'm sure you know, and people have taken this extremely seriously and have killed over the theological descriptions about how to understand the Trinity, the Father, the Son, and the Holy Spirit. So, this has not gone down easily, or without controversy in the history of western theology. I grew up in a fundamentalist Christian Protestant background, and preachers were always trying to make the Holy Spirit understandable, and I remember as a kid thinking this is the most mysterious thing I've ever heard in my life. What is the Holy Spirit? And the term in Baptist churches, growing up, also was the Holy Ghost. And that didn't help things. Ghost . . . and how is a ghost holy? The whole thing was wrapped up in mystery for me growing up.

> I later just gave up my formal interest in Protestant religion through the course of college and medical school, and came out at the end with

an eclectic version of spirituality that didn't resemble at all what I grew up with. Just to be specific, I don't subscribe to any formal religion at this point in my life. And I don't belong to any religious organization, so I'm not pushing any sort of religious agenda, either.

I think the term *spirit* deserves some attention. It's related to the word *spiritus* meaning to breathe. Spirit refers to the breath, which actually says a lot for me about how to understand the Holy Spirit. It suggests that it's an internal, intrinsic part of who we are. Just as our own breath is who we are, which we cannot do without. So, this is a necessary intrinsic component to who we are, and I think the term *indwelling divinity* captures my understanding of what the Holy Spirit is. I do not believe it's something extrinsic out there that we need to acquire or somehow take on. But it is part of our being, and it seems to me that the eternal spiritual goal is to understand that and to live that and to have that be real for us. I have had a decades-long interest in the nature of human consciousness and in 1989 wrote a book about it called *Recovering the Soul*. In that book I coined the term *non-local mind* to try to capture the way consciousness manifests in the world. And this picture of consciousness is one in which consciousness is not confined to any specific point in space or time, but [is] non-local.

I don't mean to imply that consciousness itself is physical in the sense of anything material. I think it certainly is not that, although it can have physical manifestations of course and operate through the brain and body, but in its behavior it violates all constraints of space and time. For me that really says a lot about what spirit is. And again, our goal, it seems to me, is to acquire that kind of understanding that lets that be real for us. Because if we don't, we pay a huge price. There are some huge dividends for understanding this aspect of consciousness— such as, for example, immortality. Anything that's non-local in time is eternal. And immortal. So one of the consolations of understanding this aspect of who we are is the assurance of immortality, and I think the stakes are pretty high, in terms of understanding that it's real.

As with most of the people I interviewed for this book, I asked Dr. Dossey if he could remember any particular experience he had with the Spirit.

I thought about that, and I cannot point to any epiphanies or any specific world-class Olympic-type experiences. I have an indwelling abiding sense of spiritual presence almost all the time. And it doesn't come in huge doses for me. It's an awareness that is almost constant in my life and it has been such for a great many years. And it's the little things that are most meaningful to me when it comes to Spirit.

For example, I think that I'm most in touch with Spirit when I'm immersed in natural environments. And it's coincidental that we're having this conversation now because my wife Barbara and I are in Montana. We've just come out of the Wind River Mountains in Wyoming where we spent two weeks atop the Continental Divide. Being in nature—this is a retreat for us. Annually, we just disappear into the wilderness. It's a ritual that is so restorative and fulfilling. It puts us in touch with what I refer to as Spirit. It's a way we have of finding fulfillment and recharging our batteries to last us the rest of the year until we do it again next year. And there's something about being immersed in that kind of environment that's rugged which is completely divorced from any kind of human contract in terms of electronics, telephones, faxes, and pagers. We are just simply out of touch [with all that], and the world comes alive, and your senses become much more acute.

The whole tenor of life gets ratcheted up, it seems, after an immersion like that. And then after coming out of the wilderness in Wyoming, we came to Montana, where I'm fly-fishing in some of the great fabled rivers in southwest Montana. We're on the banks of the Madison River, one of the great trout streams of the world. So I spend my days right now, standing knee-deep in crystal clear water and communicating with fish. So I hope you get my point. Immersion in nature is for me a way of venturing into the domains where Spirit comes alive. And it's as necessary for me as breathing to have this experience six weeks each year. So I wish I could give you some specific experience that just knocks one's socks off, but that's not what it's like for me.

I asked him about his work with the Spirit and medicine, asking if it wasn't pretty risky broaching the subject in the medical and scientific communities. I asked him why he decided to pursue it in the first place.

I think if you keep your eyes and ears open, any physician comes across certain kinds of healings from time to time that are just impossible to explain without introducing some sort of spiritual influence. These examples captivated me over the years, and I really felt that I had to enter this area to make peace with my own position as a doctor. For example, the role of spiritual meaning in people's lives is just absolutely profound when it comes to healing, and it's no exaggeration to say it's a matter of life and death for some people.

The sense of being connected to a higher source or power, if you will, is healing for a great many people. I have a file drawer of letters that patients have sent me documenting these sorts of experiences in their lives. I've written extensively about this. I was taught to dismiss this as just pure anecdote, as people's silly stories in medical school, and to pay no attention to them, but that really didn't satisfy my curiosity. In the mid-1980s people began to do something I never conceived possible, which was to do controlled randomized clinical trials looking at the role of prayer in healing. And there have been, to date, about nine or ten human studies looking at the role of prayer and healing where people do not know they're being prayed for, and easily half of these studies show statistically significant results. So something is going on here.

I was so intrigued by this, I've written three books looking at the role of prayer in medicine, and trying to sort through all of this and answer some questions about it, such as what it means, how it works, and how to use it. So this is an avenue in medical research that takes us into the domain of spirituality and Spirit. I don't know any way to ignore this data. It's congruent with how people think healing happens. It's doctors mainly who have enormous trouble with this intellectually. But easily 90 percent of the public believes that these effects are real in their lives and contribute to health and illness. So there you are. I don't think there's any way for us to back away from this if we're going to be intellectually honest.

It's not correct any longer in terms of scientific evidence to say that science can't approach this. It clearly can. It has already. Currently of the nation's 125 medical schools, around 80 have developed courses looking at the role of spirituality and health. And I think this speaks volumes to how legitimate this area of research is. So, in a sense, your book is extremely timely, because spirituality is coming back big-time in medicine and your book is cresting on that wave it seems to me, because this is not an issue that is going to go away. It's becoming academically respectable.

Medical doctor, author, and spiritual advisor Deepak Chopra believes humankind is gradually becoming more spiritually aware. In a 2006 interview with Kevin J. Todeschi in *Venture Inward* magazine, Chopra said:

I think the most significant development in the last twenty years has been our understanding of the deepest realms of what we call existence—consciousness, or what the layperson calls spirit. Today we know that beyond the physical and the quantum levels of existence, beyond material levels, beyond energy, and beyond information, there's an underlying field of intelligence or consciousness or spirit. This field exists beyond space-time—that is, it is transcendent. In this field there is infinite organizing, infinite correlation, non-locality—communication that is instantaneous and faster than the speed of light. The field conceives and constructs and becomes and governs everything we call reality. By understanding human consciousness we can understand what we call everyday reality. That includes biology, which includes social interactions; that includes our behavior, which includes our personal relationships; that includes our social interactions; that includes what we call the environment; and ultimately, also the forces of nature.

So there's nothing more important than attempting to understand the consciousness of spirit, and we are in a very good place right now to do just that and to achieve well-being in all aspects of our life. There are only two really important things in life: One is good health, which includes physical, emotional, and spiritual well-being. The second is the authentic experience of love. We can achieve both these things if we understand our deepest nature.[15]

I sometimes wonder if the psychologists will achieve their Theory of Everything before the physicists do. I asked Dr. Tart this question, and he wondered if there is some kind of competition going on. I told him that if there isn't, I would like to start one.

One thing is certain: there's only one circumstance in which we'll know that either of these disciplines got it right because they will have arrived at the same exact conclusion. They will have conceived a paradigm that unifies the sciences as instruments of the divine and harmonizes them with the Library of the Spirit. Newton's pendulum of rationality, that had swung so far away from mystery, will come to rest at the still point of spiritual awareness burnished in the Fire and Light of "I Am That I Am."

When that day comes, perhaps both science and religion will merge into some new spiritualized empiricism that will ascend to the throne of both faith and reason and finally guide humankind with the Spirit of Truth. The unity of science and religion will be the jackpot of paradigm shifts, because the former consciousness of war, fanaticism, and wysiwyg will dissolve, finally coming to rest in the ecstatic swoon where the mystics have always known the speed of light.

Chapter 9

THE BEAUTY
of the
BELOVED

The human tribe drifts in and out of contact with the Spirit, feeling its occasional lift, its flicker of light, a familiar tingle, flush of energy, or birth of new truth. Once touched, our minds and hearts open in wonder and relief, and the energy field of the Spirit floods like a bright corona into the dark spaces of the psyche. The Spirit cuddles up so intimately. It's like a hug from an old friend, and the synthetic little self melts, even if only for a moment, into the Ultimate Reality. The Spirit of God invites the Spirit within you to recognize itself in "I Am That I Am," the original glory of the Fire and Light. We are consumed, lifted into ecstasy above and beyond the body, above the illusions into unity, and into the higher understanding for which we thirst.

In those moments, the Spirit within us resonates, thinking constantly: love, unification, wholeness, joining, forgiveness, and reconciliation in the endless eternal now. Align your heart and mind with those same qualities, and you will know the Spirit in your life just like the prophets and mystics once did.

In *Holy Spirit: The Boundless Energy of God*, Ron Roth, a priest for twenty-five years and founder of the Celebrating

Life Institute, wrote, "People talk frequently about 'the human spirit,' yet I'm not so sure that there is such a thing. Rather, it is the Spirit of God appearing within us in various frequencies depending on our thought patterns. If that spirit is not allowed to manifest in an appropriate format, it will seek to express itself any way it can."

Thinner than the air, the Spirit flows without regard to resistance, filling the sky of consciousness like a diamond vapor as it drifts, gusts, blasts, surges, rushes, or races, according to our capacity to perceive it. When our experiences with the Spirit occur, when our thoughts are loving thoughts, our actions helpful, our motives other-centered, the Spirit in turn raises the viability of our nation, community, family, and us as individuals.

With all the analysis complete, the examples listed, and the secret histories unveiled, the Spirit's performance may best be known to us on the stage of feeling. Those who don't already know wonder what it feels like when the Spirit wakes you for a reality check. What's it like when the Spirit bubbles up from inside you, unencumbered by your human muck, personality quirks, attachments, and distractions? Muhammad wrote "God is beautiful, and He loves beauty."[1] In knowing beauty, perhaps we will find the most vivacious experience of knowing God face to face. My off-road search, therefore, next led me to the playground of the mystics.

THE PROXIMITY OF ECSTASY

Your assignment is this: describe for me Dvorak's *New World Symphony* in words that will give me the experience of listening to it. You might try words like *dramatic, quiet, loud, sublime, thrilling, warm, mellow*, and so on, but let us agree that no matter how eloquent you are, a verbal description will never give me the experience of listening to the actual music.

The same must be true for the Library of the Spirit and its many varied descriptions of the Spirit of God. The knowing and the feeling will be in the direct experience of it, and proof will belong only to the one who knows it firsthand. As with the symphony, no two experiences will be quite the same, but the proof in the heart is identical. Sometimes the Spirit intervenes, comforts, or guides. Other times it inspires with bliss and raises people from all walks of life into the realm of mystical experience.

THE FEELING OF THE SPIRIT

Consider Carol Sue Janes, a Seattle lawyer who is also a professional singer. She says the Spirit has operated both in her singing career as well as in the practice of law. She was raised Unitarian, but her family wasn't especially active in the church. She received no particular religious training as a child. As an adult, she adopted a practice of meditation and prayer, and this seems to be typical for many people who experience God directly. When she's singing, she enters what she calls "the zone," which she describes as a sense of suspension of time or elasticity.

> I used to sing with the San Francisco Unitarian Church choir. I wasn't a soloist but they were putting on a big end-of-the-season production in a beautiful cathedral, and I had learned all the soloist parts. It was a Mozart Mass—in Latin. I had been the one to sing the soprano solo parts in rehearsal. But then for the actual concert, they brought in a paid soloist, and I thought *Oh fine. I hadn't been asked.*

When Carol arrived at the church the Sunday morning before the performance, however, she was told that the soloist had gotten sick, and that Carol would have to solo.

> Within less than an hour we were performing, but I remember at the end of the concert, a sort of feeling like I hadn't been there. It was like I channeled the whole performance, like I checked out and someone else sang it for me. Everyone was very complimentary about it afterwards, but I just remember this feeling of some other power taking over to do what I needed to do.

Carol relates a similar experience, in which she had a small part in Gilbert and Sullivan's operetta *Princess Ida*, and then found out she had to sing the lead—with only a few hours preparation. Again, the lead singer had gotten sick, but though she knew the show, Carol had not understudied the part.

I got to the theater about 11 A.M. and was onstage by 2. What was fascinating was that I actually was "present" on this occasion, it was me doing the singing, but for me the intervention of the Spirit was that I was able to do it. Something geared up in me that was able to memorize the whole part in the two hours before I got to the theater, but also that I was the recipient of so many acts of thoughtfulness and kindness of people helping the show go on. . . . The support and love sent my way onstage and offstage were just so miraculous. I felt at ease and had this sense of confidence that it was all going to work, because so many people believed in me—a sort of openness to the possibility that Spirit could make it happen.

I asked her to explain her understanding of the Spirit of God.

I guess at one level I think of the Spirit as being like light or electricity or some sort of force that is all-pervasive throughout the universe. But I would say at the same time that I put an intelligence to it—and love. And then when I start putting love to it, I can't think of love being something that doesn't have a face and so for me it then helps to think of a loved one or something that I love. I also think of the Spirit as a sense of connectedness. I don't know quite how to describe it, but a sense of intelligence or a higher consciousness. Interconnectedness to others and, I guess, to my higher self, and also to the universal intelligence and guidance of love that's available, or God, without putting labels on it.

I think of it as basically an amorphous force, but if I think about it too much that way, then it becomes too abstract, so it helps if I can imagine something that gives me a sense of a loving feeling, and that helps me understand the feeling of the Spirit.

SHORTENING THE DISTANCE

Some people feel the presence of the Spirit all the time, so I asked Carol if that was true for her or if such experiences were intermittent.

Over time, as I've worked on my spiritual life, I feel as if it's a shorter distance in connecting the dots. Sometimes you feel like you're awake and loving and conscious of your opportunities to be of service in the world, and of God's presence in the moment, and sometimes when I look at my life as a whole, I look at the valleys, because there were longer periods in between those moments and when there are good times in my life, it's when there were shorter times in between those moments. When you can make those times shorter and shorter and have it happen several times a day rather than months or weeks, then I feel like I'm more in tune and look for opportunities to be of service and to be present with the Spirit.

For Francis [her husband] and me, we had a challenging year last year. It just wound up being our year of living with death because we had several loved ones pass away, most significant of which was Francis's father, a year ago January [2004]. It was the only time I was present when someone passed away, and we just felt the Spirit so much in that process. There was a series of events that helped us through that process but also helped us help his mom through it.

She was in denial about it, and it was hard for Francis to get her to the hospital. The father had hung on for five days with no reason to—no water, no life, no food, nothing. We wondered why this was taking so long. And finally one day I was inspired and just said to her, "I'm taking you there. You need to come with me."

It was 9 A.M. on a Sunday morning, and she finally got it that this was the end. There was no fuel in his gas tank, and he turned his head toward where she was sitting, and almost said her name, and he was gone within minutes. She was able to have the feelings of closure with him dying. We felt so comforted that we had been able to be a part of the process. We felt that the intervention of the Spirit was in the circumstances that allowed that to happen. It was an expression of grief and a good-bye that needed to happen.

Because Carol had such dramatic experiences in music, I wondered if she was aware of the Spirit helping her in her law practice. She said she was grateful to have the opportunity to bridge both worlds spiritually, because she often receives intervention and inspiration.

There are things that happen on a daily basis. Like having the intervention to say the right things to someone at the right time or finding the right argument to make in a brief, or whatever it is. I'm grateful, and I think that it's there for anyone who opens themselves to it and looks for it. For example, I just had a long brief to write and to be able to figure out an impossible argument and find that right piece of evidence or documentation to put forth [my] position or be able to draw out of it when I need to or find the right page to cite to—I feel like that happens almost too many times to think of examples.

My last question was how she would advise people to have more direct experiences with God.

Be open-minded. Be open to the possibility that God can speak directly in your life. Tune in, whether that's through meditation or some other centering experience that works for you. Harvest the stories of your own experiences with the Spirit and of other people who have them. It's so easy to go through life and not do that. Recollect and reflect on them, and it increases the possibility that they will happen again.

The variety of ways in which we encounter the Spirit of God is vast and varied. However, when considered together, they form a fragrant garden of experience that is, by definition, mystical. In my off-road search, I wanted to demystify mysticism itself and find out just what constitutes a mystical experience.

WHAT IS A MYSTIC?

The Spirit has never ceased to find sympathetic minds and eager voices, turning ordinary men and women into mystics and prophets. Such a person—anyone—who experiences the Divine directly is by definition a mystic. The experiences of these people are mystical. The founders of most of the world's religions therefore were mystics. Jesus was a mystic because he experienced God directly, the Spirit in particular. Paul was a mystic. The prophets were mystics. Many people alive today who practice a disciplined, spiritual life of various faiths are mystics, too.

Some people rear up at the word *mystical*, but that may be because they confuse *mystical* with *supernatural*, a word they equate with crystal balls and séances. But the definition of *mystical* refers to any direct, subjective experience with God. It can also mean an event or experience that possesses a deep or profound spiritual meaning that's not apparent to the senses or intellect. Those who more deliberately pursue the disciplines, thoughts, and behaviors of a spiritual life, however, tend to experience the Spirit of God more often and more intensely.

William James wrote, "In persons deep in the religious life . . . the door into this region seems unusually wide open; at any rate, experiences making their entrance through that door have had emphatic influence in shaping religious history."[2]

The Spirit is known throughout the world, and it is well that we survey the universal sweetness of mystical experience. Poet and author Kahlil Gibran wrote:

> I love you when you bow in your mosque, kneel in your temple, pray in your church. For you and I are sons of one religion, and it is the Spirit.

THEY WORE WOOL

Some of the most awesome descriptions of the beauty of spiritual experience can be found in the literature of the Sufis. Their poetry conveys the beauty of mystical reality much more closely than any I've seen—words that come close to conveying the experience of a symphony.

The Spirit opened many hearts among the early Muslims. In the pattern of reformers about five hundred years after the Prophet lived, the Spirit opened the eyes of a small group of Muslims who didn't like how the caliphs and kings were living. As a reaction to the rulers' riches and fineries, these Muslims wore "suf"—wool. The Sufis preserved what they believed to be the original spirit of Muhammad's Qur'an and became well known in Persia and the Arabian Peninsula. It's a familiar story: the Sufis held that the mainstream Muslims had forsaken the true teachings by becoming materialistic and warlike. The Sufis—the mystics of Islam—wanted to honor the water, it was said, rather than the vessel that contains it.

Sufis can be either Sunni, Shiite, both, or neither. Love is their central principle, along with the belief that all religion is one and that everyone can experience God directly. They believe that God desires beauty and sees its own divinity mirrored in nature. The great thirteenth-century Persian Sufi poet Mahmud Shabistari wrote:

> "I" and "you" are the veil between heaven and earth;
> Lift this veil and you will see
> No longer the bonds of sects and creeds.
> When "I" and "you" do not exist,
> What is mosque, what is synagogue?
> What is the Temple of Fire?
>
> —from "Rose Garden of Mystery"[3]

Another Persian poet, the venerated Rumi, wrote of the intense Sufi passion to know God directly:

Listen! Open a window to God and begin to delight yourself by gazing upon Him through the opening. The business of love is to make that window in the heart, for the breast is illumined by the beauty of the Beloved. Gaze incessantly on the face of the Beloved! Listen, this is in your power, my friend![4]

Sufi initiates are the white-robed "dervishes" who slowly twirl in ecstatic dance, a meditation of movement that fills them with the Spirit and joins them to oneness with God. A prophetic saying (Hadith) of the Qur'an has God explaining why the world was created:

"I was a hidden treasure and I wanted to be known: That is why I created the world."[5]

Mystical experience—direct experience with the Spirit of God—isn't the sole property of one religion or another. Religion doesn't have a lot to do with it, except to keep us inside our moral and ethical fences, and in the same county as the Spirit, conceptually speaking. Meeting the Spirit is about the chemistry between your heart and the heart of God, so give yourself permission to be a mystic and enable yourself to experience the Spirit in your life. Why not start now?

"GOD-ING"

The ecstasy of contact with the Divine is also known by the Jewish mystics, the Hasidim and other Kabbalists. Jewish mysticism goes back to the beginning of western religion, first appearing in references to the priesthoods of Melchizzedek and Aaron, in which direct experience with God was as everyday as sunshine. (At the time there was no need for a word such as *mystic* because the prophets and children of Israel were technically all mystics.)

As mentioned earlier, out of Judaism came three concepts of the Spirit, *ruach, shekinah,* and *kaddosh,* terms for different experiences of the Spirit and the presence of God. Rabbi David

A. Cooper, in his book *God Is a Verb*, writes, "Jewish mysticism is a profoundly sensual, nature-connected spiritual practice that openly discusses angels and demons, souls' journeys after death, reincarnation, resurrection, and the goal of achieving messianic consciousness."[6]

Referring to an idea developed by Rabbi Zalman Schachter-Shalomi, Rabbi Cooper explains how the best understanding of God is as a verb, rather than a noun.

"The closest we can come to thinking about God is as a process rather than a being. We can think of it as a 'be-ing,' as verb rather than noun. Perhaps we would understand this concept better if we renamed God. We might call it God-ing, a process, rather than God, which suggests a noun."[7]

We are made in the image of God, so we ourselves are processes rather than things. Rabbi Cooper writes about the relationship between a "David-ing," or a "Jon-ing" and the "God-ing."

For me, this concept accelerates my understanding of God—another process or "gift" of the Spirit, to gain a feel for the Spirit of God as a perpetual motion-process taking place in the permanent now. God is a process, but the Spirit within you is also the process of *you*.

Rabbi Cooper writes eloquently about experiencing God directly:

> The true discovery of the intimacy of our ongoing relationship with the Divine can dramatically change our lives. It often happens spontaneously, without a reason. Some call this experience "grace." It arises out of nowhere. You could be sitting on a beach, walking in the woods, caring for someone who is dying, even driving on the freeway, and suddenly you are overwhelmed by a strange light that penetrates your consciousness and you are never again the same. We read accounts of such transformations and conversion experiences that have changed the world.[8]

I encountered a number of these in my off-road search.

IN THE DIRECTION OF GOOD

Author, pastor, and linguist Richard Henry Drummond, Ph.D., a longtime professor at the University of Dubuque Theological Seminary, has taught and led congregations all over the world, particularly in Japan, where he was a professor of Christian studies and classical languages. An ordained Presbyterian minister, he is also an expert on Buddhism and Islam. I asked him to comment on his own experiences with the Spirit, and on the Spirit in Buddhism and Islam.

> I do have many experiences of the guidance of God. Even that God in his Spirit has spoken to me, briefly. My own experience of the guidance of God is that God does not chatter. That is to say, my experience of God speaking to me is that he does so very briefly, in very short sentences, or just phrases, but it's very often. Many times every day to concrete situations. More often than not at my request for guidance. So that in my experience, like some of the evangelicals, I can say "God has spoken to me," and I believe it is through his Spirit. Over the years, you learn very quickly what is the quality of that guidance. You learn that as Muhammad himself [did]—and this is one of the main themes of Muhammad's teachings, which [are] so similar to that of Jesus—namely, that God leads us unto goodness. If your experience of the Spirit of God is along those lines, that God does lead us on to goodness, you come to having increasing confidence in the fact that it is of God because the quality is so consistently in the direction of good.

As a professor of comparative religion, Drummond seeks the differences and similarities among faiths. The Qur'an came out of an intense spiritual experience on the part of Muhammad, who delivered to the idolatrous and rapacious Arabia of his day a code of laws under the unity of the One God—the same God worshipped by Jews and Christians. He said that Muhammad insisted that God reveals Himself through both prophetic messengers and the inner life of every human being.

Muslims, of course, have accepted Jesus as an authentic prophet before Muhammad, and in fact Muhammad himself, as we get from the Qur'an, thought of Jesus as the greatest of the prophets before him. In fact as the very bearer of the Spirit of God and the word of God. And therefore Muhammad had a very high view of Jesus as a prophet. Not as the Son of God but as an authentic prophet of God. And the greatest of them all.

Islam, Buddhism, and Christianity share a belief in transcendence: that we can transcend the misery of earthly life through salvation and redemption.

One must remember that because another language does not use the word *God*, the English word of Germanic origin, doesn't mean they don't have some understanding of whom we call God. There are a number of western scholars who speak of Buddhism as a nontheistic religion, in effect almost to say it's atheistic, but that's nonsense. The vast majority of Buddhists in Asia, for example, and across the centuries China, Japan, Korea, as well as India and Southeast Asia, these people are religious people. They believe in a transcendent reality. And that's absolutely basic. They all believe in a transcendent reality, and Buddhism's historically negative view of this world is all the more indication that they believe in a transcendent reality.

Dr. Drummond explains Buddha's view of the Spirit in Buddhist terms, dharma and karma. Dharma is divine law, the basic principles of cosmic and individual existence, and one's duty fulfilled by observance of one's faith. Karma is the law of cause and effect, akin to "whatever a man sows, that he will also reap";[9] your own actions determine your future, to be sure; what goes around comes around. For Buddhists and Hindus, karma is the force of your actions that keep you incarnating on the earth.

Now dharma for the Buddha was in a sense a force, a supreme transcendent force that makes for righteousness that leads to goodness and this is at the very heart of his teaching. He felt that the very basis of the religious life was intimacy or friendship with the "lovely." The heart of the religious life was intimacy or friendship with the lovely. And for him the lovely is a term for dharma. And it's a term that implies not only beauty but above all, goodness. For the Buddha, this is at the heart of his faith. The Supreme Transcendent Reality depends upon who will be able to lead the religious life and also will be able to escape the bonds of karma so that he didn't have to be reborn into this life. See, early Buddhism looked forward to a transcendent life no longer under the compulsion to return to this world. They have a more negative view of this world than either Judaism or Christianity.

According to my experience and studies, the Buddha did not speak of divine revelation in a verbal sense. I don't recall any specific statement of that kind. But that is not divine revelation in a verbal sense, but divine force at work leading in the direction of beauty and goodness. That is most emphatically what he was about. And in his periods of meditation, the tendency of some western scholars is to see it as sort of contemplating his own navel, but that's not so. The heart of the matter was it was friendship and intimacy, a spiritual relationship with the most high that was the heart of his meditation. It was a life giving an encouraging thing of beauty and love, but it was friendship and a personal relationship that was at the heart of the matter, not lonely meditation. Not too many Westerners understand that, but Easterners do.

THE CHRISTIAN MYSTICS

One of the first Christian mystics, Paul, wrote of the "hidden wisdom, which God ordained *before the world*." (1 Cor 2:7) [italics added] The hidden wisdom is revealed by the Spirit in bits and parts, in dribbles or even floods to prophets, mystics, and ordinary folks like us.

The persons and events that define Christian faith are in themselves mystical. Think about it: a virgin conceives by the Spirit; a prophet is filled by the Spirit at the River Jordan and then heals the sick, raises the dead, and rebukes the devil; after he is killed, he lives and continues to teach, before ultimately transmuting himself, body and all, into light; then he ascends. Catholics believe their sacraments to be mystical. In the Eucharist, for example, they believe that the bread and wine transform into the body and blood of Christ. The Gospel of John is mystical, beginning with 1:1, and, as mentioned before, it was nearly omitted from the Bible for this reason.

So, whether they realize it or not, Christians are by definition mystics, though most are mystics asleep, because they don't realize that they have a direct pipeline to the Spirit—the promise and gift of the Christos, Christ Consciousness, and the Spirit that their prophet handed to them on a silver platter. From an unsung mystic of the nineteenth century comes the following quote:

> For what is Mysticism? Is it not the attempt to draw near to God, not by rites or ceremonies, but by inward disposition? Is it not merely a hard word for "The kingdom of heaven is within"? Heaven is neither a place nor a time.

This statement was made by the "Lady with the Lamp," Florence Nightingale, who founded modern-day nursing.

The roster of Christian mystics begins with Jesus himself, of course. The direct experience of the Divine can't be plainer than in the one who was on a first-name basis with his Father in heaven. He performed miracles. He overcame the tempter in the desert and was transformed into shimmering energy on the mountain with Moses and Elijah. (Mt 17:1–3) He appeared to his messengers after the destruction of his physical body and ascended—whoosh—out of sight into the Shekinah glory like Enoch and Elijah before him. Then, as he promised, he sent the Spirit to all those who ask—and sends them still, it is written, even now.

Paul had a stunning experience with the Spirit on the road to Damascus. He was struck blind as though by lightning—an encounter with the Spirit that we can be thankful doesn't happen every day, perhaps especially on the road to Damascus. Paul, a trained rabbi who originally worked against the Christians for the Romans, was filled with the Spirit. For the rest of his days he interpreted the life and teachings of Jesus, and his writings overflow with the evidence of his inspiration by the Spirit and his love of Christ.

The list of Christian mystics since Paul would be long indeed. It would include Origen, Clement of Alexandria, Augustine, Gregory I, St. Anselm, and scores of others. And very many women: Mechtild of Magdeburg, Catherine of Siena, Julian of Norwich, and Thérèse of Lisieux, just to name a few. Add to the list Jakob Boehme, Thomas Aquinas, Emanuel Swedenborg, and William Blake. In more modern times, we find Thomas Merton, Padre Pio, Mother Seton, and even Pope John Paul II, who had many mystical experiences in his lifetime.

Many of these transcendent experiences are stunning and inspiring, but this book allows space for only two. I've chosen Hildegard of Bingen and Meister Eckhart, Germans involved with the Beguine movement (see chapter 7) who emerged in an extraordinary upsurge of mystics in the early centuries of the second millennium. They are important because they exemplify courage in allowing the Spirit to shine through during the darkest time of authoritarian control over the Spirit. The stories are important for us as we seek the comfort and guidance of the Spirit, because until their transforming events, these mystics were ordinary people like you and me.

HILDEGARD'S FIRE

The astounding visions of Hildegard von Bingen (1098–1179) began in her childhood. She kept them to herself, however, until she was forty-two, when she was told in a vision to share them with the world.

"When I was forty-two years and seven months old," she wrote, "a burning light of tremendous brightness coming from heaven poured into my entire mind. Like a flame that does not burn but enkindles, it inflated my entire heart and my entire breast, just like the sun that warms an object with its rays."

This is how she described her "awakening," enveloped, one could say, in the Shekinah, the glory of the Lord, the presence of God—the Spirit.

"All of a sudden, I was able to taste of the understanding of the narration of books. I saw the Psalter clearly and the evangelists and other catholic books of the Old and New Testaments."

Overwhelmed by this infusion of light and understanding, Hildegard grew sick and went to bed, where she remained until one day when she picked up a pen to write. At that moment, she was filled with renewed strength and spent the next ten years writing her first book, a theology entitled *Scivias* ("Know the Ways"), from which these quotations come.[10]

One can think of Hildegard as the first Leonardo. She preached, taught, organized, established monasteries, reformed the established church, composed music, painted, healed, studied, and prophesied. We still have 145 letters that she wrote to popes, emperors, bishops, and nobles, often chastising them for some of their lamebrain practices. She wrote seventy-nine songs, including the first opera, creating a unique musical idiom centuries ahead of its time. She wrote over seventy poems and nine books, including biographies and books on medicine and theology. And all this in the age when even male troublemakers hid their mystical experiences in fear.

Hildegard's visions (called "Illuminations") continued for years, and she credited them to the "Holy Spirit," which she wrote "alighted" upon her like the tongues of fire on Pentecost—parted tongues of fire. She, in fact, pictured the Spirit as fire, writing:

> Oh fire of the Holy Spirit,
> Life of the life of every creature,
> Holy are you in giving life to forms.

She wrote, "Who is the Holy Spirit? The Holy Spirit is a Burning Spirit. It kindles the hearts of humankind. Like tympanum and lyre, it plays them, gathering volumes in the temple of the soul. . . . The Holy Sprit resurrects and awakens everything that is."

The tenth century was a time like that of the cousins, John and Jesus. The populace was thirsty for something genuine in their religion, and found no small number of street-corner prophets to bend their ears. Hildegard emerged with startling things to say. It just so happened that her love for the church also earned the approval of the pope for her books.

Hildegard was the first medieval woman to write about the state of women and their spirituality. She also wrote of "God as Mother" and stated that "all science comes from God." She was a self-described "female prophet," and her contemporaries compared her to Deborah and Jeremiah. She thought of God as "the living light and the obscured illumination," and believed she had been called upon to teach. She wanted to "rescue the human heart" by restoring the direct experience of God for all people.

Hildegard wanted people to awaken and take responsibility for their own spiritual lives. "God has illuminated me in both my eyes," she wrote. "By them I behold the splendor of light in the darkness. Through them I can choose the path I am to travel, whether I wish to be sighed or blind by recognizing what guide to call upon by day or by night." (*Scivias*)

She said that people who pursue the ways of wisdom "will themselves become a fountain gushing from the waters of life. . . . For these waters—that is, the believers—are a spring that can never be exhausted or run dry. No one will ever have too much of them . . . the waters through which we have been reborn to life have been sprinkled by the Holy Spirit." (*Scivias*) She also wrote, "The Holy Spirit is like a fire, not one that can be extinguished, which suddenly bursts out in flames, and just as suddenly darkens."[11]

Eighty-one years after Hildegard's passing, the Church was still open to the words of the occasional inspired mystic, if he or she could manage it without embarrassing the authorities. Not many would get past the menacing eye of Pope John XXII, and Meister Eckhart was one of the last ones who did—at least until just after the mystic's death.

ECKHART'S "INNER EYE"

Meister Eckhart (1260–1327) was a Dominican priest and philosopher who had kept alive some of the tenets of Origen and the concept of gnosis—knowing the truth within—in a peculiar mix that included the Trinity, which he interpreted mystically.

Eckhart taught that Divine Reason (= Logos = Word) could be born in the soul by stripping the mind of all active thought and images—emptying it to make room for the mystical experience—the direct experience with the Divine. (This concept was well known in Eastern religions.) He taught that "God" and the "Godhead" were as different as heaven and earth; that the Godhead was "an eternal silent undifferentiated One-ness."[12] The Godhead is the formless "All," the Ultimate Reality, the Vedantic Brahman, the Kabbalistic Ein Soph, the impersonal God of the universe that corresponds to the higher Self in humankind. In contrast, God is the personalized Creator, Elohim, that conceptualized the earth and human beings. Most people cannot apprehend the entirety of God, and the Godhead is that grandest broad "observer" of everything that is beyond human comprehension, just as a child cannot apprehend the entirety of his own parents. These concepts were known since before Plato, in early Judaism, as well as the Gnostic and other schools of early Christianity. The difference between Godhead and God can be explained by the Observer Effect in physics: Godhead acquires desire to create, observes the Creator within, and proceeds to observe the created.

"Godhead and God are realities as distinct as heaven and earth," Eckhart wrote. "God appears when all creatures speak of

Him. All creatures do speak of God. Why do they not then speak of the Godhead? Because all that is in the Godhead is unity, and one can say nothing of it. God operates; the Godhead does not."[13] In Taoism, it is written, "He who says, does not know; he who knows, does not say."

Bringing this concept down to earth, Eckhart wrote, "The contemplation of the Holy Spirit purifies the soul of all fault in such a way that it forgets itself and all things else. Then, what it receives from the Godhead is the eternal Wisdom of the Father, the knowledge and understanding of all things. In this way, the soul is no longer reduced to appearance, to conjecture, to faith— for it has arrived at the Truth."[14]

This is a difficult concept for the intellect to dissect, but easy for the soul to see once the inner eye is opened by the Spirit.

Like Hildegard, Eckhart wrote of an "inner eye," the eye of the soul, freed by the Spirit of Truth: "The soul has two eyes— one looking inwards and the other outwards. It is the inner eye of the soul that looks into essence and takes being directly from God." He also wrote, "The eye by which I see God is the same as the eye by which God sees me. My eye and God's eye are one and the same."[15] Also like Hildegard, Eckhart's mysticism included the feminine. He often referred to God as "Her" in his sermons. He taught nuns in several convents and spoke to them as equals, which outraged the patriarchy of the day.

Eckhart held many high appointments in the Church. His writings and sermons had been approved by the pope, but when the authorities got wind of Eckhart's concept that any man or woman can become one with God without help from the church,[16] he was arrested and investigated. He had been a poet, it seems, and some of his metaphors were unfortunately taken literally. For example, he wrote, "I pray God to rid me of God." (A student once asked Buddha what he should do if he saw Buddha by the side of the road. Buddha answered, "Kill him." This is about when the idea of God becomes more important than God.) After Eckhart's death, twenty-eight of his propositions were deemed heretical. Church paperwork shows that before he died he recanted, but there were no apparent independent witnesses.

Hildegard and Meister Eckhart lucked out with their new/old ideas of the Spirit. Their writings and teachings actually led to much-needed reforms in the friaries, convents, and monasteries. They, and other medieval mystics, had something else in common: they both endorsed the idea of the divine feminine. In chapter 6, we looked at the masculine and feminine elements of the Divine Image. Although you have to dig to find this in the Bible, we find in the writings of the mystics repeated emphasis on the importance of the divine feminine. Find the masculine and feminine in yourself, and you grow closer still to a true communion with the Spirit.

A HUG FROM THE DIVINE MOTHER

Women have a receptive intuitive nature that's naturally loving, so it may be fair to say that there have always been more female mystics than male. Their natural inclination to love their babies and families over and above their own personal desires and fears affiliates them with the electromagnetic field of the Spirit, which is also feminine in nature. In women, the connection seems to be built in. Their experiences with the Spirit are part of the day-to-day life, whether they realize it or not. (Perhaps women assumed the roles of the oracles and sibyls of ancient times for this reason. The story of the Beguines in chapter 6 is a case in point.)

Modern theologians and writers have begun to incorporate the feminine in new approaches to theology. Episcopal priest and author Matthew Fox identifies the Spirit with the feminine aspect of God as he takes an aggressive stand against the Catholic Church—in particular, Pope Benedict XVI, who defrocked him and a number of other progressive-thinking priests in the 1980s. Recognizing the Divine Feminine is one of the points of his proposed New Reformation of the Catholic Church.

On June 8, 2005, the audacious Fox was in Wittenberg, Germany, surrounded by a cheering crowd. He stood at the door to Wittenberg Cathedral and nailed his own ninety-five theses to the door, just as Martin Luther did in 1517. His book *A New Reformation: Creation Spirituality and the Transformation of Christianity* calls for the same, and his list of theses, or "faith observations," begins with the assertion that God is both mother and father.

The idea of God as mother was well known in the towns and villages and even in some pulpits of medieval Europe. The beguine Mechtild of Magdeburg (1210–1285) wrote: "God is not only fatherly, God is also mother who lifts her mother's cloak wherein the child finds a home and lays its head on the maternal breast." Meister Eckhart also described God as mother: "From all eternity God lies on a maternity bed giving birth. . . . What does God do all day long? God gives birth."

SHOWINGS

Let's flash back to May 13, 1373, when a thirty-year-old English woman lay on her deathbed wracked in pain and eager to die. But instead of dying, she found her pain miraculously lifted. After recovering completely from her illness, she experienced a series of sixteen mystical visions that she would later call "Showings," in which she believed that God, Christ, and Mary, the mother of Jesus, spoke to her. Her spiritual experiences are among the most elegant ever recorded.

Considered the first lady of English letters and England's greatest mystic, her true name is unknown. Her Revelations of Divine Love, in which she described the Showings, is considered one of the most extraordinary and beautiful expressions of sacred experience. Her manuscripts are widely read to this day. She became an anchoress—sealed for life, after a formal funeral service, in a tiny stone room attached to the side of Saint Julian's Church, Norwich, England, dispensing advice to people who approached a tiny hole in the wall. Her real name is lost to posterity, and she is now remembered only as Julian of Norwich.

Like the mystics mentioned earlier, Julian spoke of the opening of an "inner eye," the eye of the soul referred to by Augustine, Catherine of Siena, and Meister Eckhart, Grandfather Black Elk, and dozens of other mystics from a variety of wisdom traditions. She wrote:

> And then our Lord opened my spiritual eye and shewed me my soul in the midst of my heart. I saw the Soul so large as it were an endless world, and as it were a blissful kingdom. And by the conditions that I saw therein I understood that it is a worshipful City. In the midst of that City sitteth our Lord.[17]

Julian's revelations overflow with poetic descriptions of God's love and contain many unique perspectives on the most profound Christian mysteries. For example, she wrote that we are not a product of original sin, but a product of divine creation from the very beginning. She wrote that God is both father and mother. She was a lover of God and found goodness everywhere, writing that body and spirit are One, meaning that the body in and of itself is not sinful. Unless the body is used to our detriment, even our sensuality should be praised as having a unique relationship with God. (The tantrics, Taoists, and Hasidim know this well.) She wrote that body and soul are united in a "glorious union." Modern history would be quite different if the Church fathers had maintained Julian's view instead of that of Augustine, who declared that "the soul makes war with the body." It seems clear that, for many, it does—it certainly did for him. But it does not have to be so.

During one of her Showings, Julian asked God why he created the world, and God answered,

You want to know your Lord's meaning in what I have done? Know it well, love was his meaning. Who reveals it to you? Love. What did he reveal to you? Love. Why does he reveal it to you? For love.

Julian wrote that we don't know God until we first know clearly our own soul, a theme found everywhere in Neoplatonic and Gnostic sources—"know thyself." She offered definitions of the soul that did not exclude our sensual nature, but acknowledged it as part of the way we were created:

Both our Substance and Sensuality together may rightly be called our Soul. That is because they are both *oned* in God. [italics added]

Julian often used the word "one" as a verb, as in, "God 'oned' me into an understanding of it." She made many other statements in her "Showings" characterizing God as Mother:

Just as God is truly our Father, so also is God truly our Mother . . .

The deep Wisdom of the Trinity is our Mother. In her we are all enclosed . . .

And Jesus is our true Mother in whom we are endlessly carried and out of whom we will never come . . .

God is the true Father and Mother of Nature, and all natures that are made to flow out of God to work the divine will be restored and brought again into God. God feels great delight to be our Mother.

The Feminine Gift

If the Spirit manifests as the feminine Shekinah and the feminine gift of wisdom that inspires men and women alike, why can't the Spirit manifest in womanly form? We have every reason to include the Spirit's role in the Marian apparitions—claims of appearances by Mary, the mother of Jesus, which have been reported hundreds of times over the past two thousand years, several modern ones of which have been documented on film.

Because God communicates to human beings through the Spirit, such communication in the form of a lady of heaven cannot be rejected out of hand unless you reject all forms.

Here are a few such appearances that are well respected and trusted by millions the world over:

- In 1531 a poor Indian saw a "Lady from Heaven" at Tepeyac, a hill northwest of Mexico City. She told him she was the "Mother of the True God," and instructed him to have the bishop build a temple on the site. Her image was emblazoned on an article of clothing he was wearing. The image is still there on display, and Pope John Paul II visited there four times.

- Mary appeared to a poor fourteen-year-old girl, Bernadette Soubiroux, in Lourdes, France, between February and July 1858. There were eighteen appearances in all, during which Bernadette often fell into ecstasy. The lady was "lovelier than I have ever seen," she said.

- A vision of Mary appeared six times to three shepherd children near Fatima, Portugal, between May and October 1917, warning of wars to come.

- The lady appeared to four girls in Garabandal, Spain, many times from 1961 to 1965, with warnings to pray for peace, and, as with many of the appearances elsewhere, she warned the priests and bishops to mend their ways. However, in the light of the recent molestation scandals plaguing the Roman Catholic priesthood, those warnings went unheeded.

- Mary appeared often since 1981 in Medjugorje, in the former Yugoslavia, warning of the destruction of the nation a few years before that very thing happened.

When I viewed the videos of the children in the Garabandal appearances, it was very difficult to dismiss the astounding, metaphysical, mystical events shared simultaneously by the children. They were clearly seized and filled by the Spirit as I imagine were the prophets of old. I'd be less able to accept the possibility at face value, if I hadn't experienced her myself one day in 1988 while visiting a retreat center in Atlanta, Georgia.

THE LADY'S PRESENCE

It was a sunny morning. I was sitting by myself on the floor of a sanctuary, surrounded by sacred art objects. Among them was a painting of Mary, one in which she was depicted as a teenage girl, which Mary was when the Spirit appeared to her. I was staring at the painting, when all of a sudden the image came to life, lifting slightly off the canvas. Her face glowed brightly and her eyes came alive. Her smile and compassionate dewy eyes melted my heart and healed a personal conflict I'd been experiencing, giving me understanding that solved the problem. There is no question in my mind that I saw what I saw.

Let the jury continue to deliberate on the feminine nature of God, the feminine orientation of the Spirit, and the appearances of Mary, but pay heed to the firsthand experience with the divine mother by a woman who is not only non-Catholic, but who had no formal religious training whatever.

Tish Kronen-Gluck and her husband, a real-estate developer, live in San Francisco. In June 2005 she was touring France with her Aunt Olga, when she had an experience with the Spirit that changed her life.

Although Olga, who was in her seventies, had been Catholic all her life, Tish grew up in a household in which religious training was optional. She had only attended a few religious services as a small child, and like Dani Vedros she had never been indoctrinated into a religious tradition. She attributes her contacts with the Holy Spirit to the persona of Mary during her visits to Lourdes, France, and Garabandal, Spain. She described her experiences in July 2005 after her return from Europe.

It was so amazingly powerful. I've been thinking about it continuously, and yet I don't quite know if I could do it any justice in mere words. As soon as we got to the area of the basilica, the magic started transporting me to the higher realms, and from then on, I was floating in an ethereal dream that is unforgettable.

We decided to join the candlelight Marian procession. We bought candles and joined thousands of people, all carrying candles, and chanting prayers to the Virgin Mary, and singing. I can't begin to describe how powerful it was. This lasted several hours. The procession wound its way to the front of the Basilica of the Immaculate Conception. Then there was a ceremony of some kind, and a song, "Salve Regina," the final tribute to the Holy Mother. I don't really know what these prayers were, exactly, as I am not Catholic, but the Spirit was undeniable. And universal.

When the procession was finished, people dispersed. Many headed for the Grotto, where Bernadette [one of the children who witnessed the apparition in 1917] saw the Lady—they touch the rocks, they sit and reflect, pray, meditate, soak in the Spirit. Everyone is high from it all. They're all there for the light.

The next morning they headed for the baths, or the *piscine*, as the French call it, which means "pool." Attendants help pilgrims into the waters there where they are briefly immersed—a cleansing ritual in which many people claim to have spiritual experiences. As thousands prayed the rosary, Tish and Olga waited their turn.

The chanting, the orderliness, and repetition created almost a trancelike atmosphere. So that by the time I reached the bath, I was truly receptive; in a state of contemplation and spirit. And yet I was unprepared for the overwhelming emotion that engulfed me.

We were escorted first to a bench outside the baths, then to a bench inside the bathhouse. When our time finally arrived, some angelic women volunteers sweetly guided us to remove our clothing, while they held a cloth up in front of us, for modesty, then they wrapped the large cloth around us. By this point I felt very emotional. One woman, who could see this, smiled and told me not to be afraid. They then guided us to a rectangular sunken tub with steps descending into it. First they told me to close my eyes and pray silently, and to focus on my intentions. Then I was guided down the steps into the tub and to the far end to a crucifix that had the figure of Mary at its center. I was instructed to kiss it, while continuing to focus on my intentions.

Then I was to bend my knees as though sitting on an invisible chair. At this point I was gently lowered backwards into the water, which bathed me completely, except for my head. The water was cold, yet it did not matter. I felt like I had been baptized—on many levels. I felt cleansed in my very soul. Emotion overwhelmed me. I cried. And I hugged the ladies and thanked them. Somehow I dressed. We were never given a towel, and yet we seemed to dry immediately. The water is meant to stay with us. The experience definitely does.

Since then the Lady seems so present for me. I had a truly spiritual experience. My aunt Olga, who also was greatly affected by the bath experience, and I, bonded on a very spiritual level. We hugged. We cried. We soared. We stayed in Lourdes for about three days.

The travelers had heard about another place, Garabandal, in Spain, where Mary appeared to four village children from 1961 to 1965. The event was well documented on film, and most of those children are still alive today. Though the Church never officially sanctioned or recognized the phenomenon, the children received many messages.

Hoping to keep the spiritual experience alive, Tish and Olga drove nearly eight hours to the remote village in the Cantabria Mountains of northern Spain. They secured a room with a local couple who also gave them dinner.

"Garabandal was the opposite of Lourdes in appearance," Tish said, "yet the Lady's presence was undeniably there also."

Tish and Olga visited the spots in the village the children had seen in the 1960s. On their final day in Garabandal, Tish brought Olga up the steep, rocky hill to "the Pines," one of the sites associated with the children's experiences, where she made a request of her aunt "that was completely outside of my background."

There was a bench near the trees. We sat down. Looked at the view. Caught our breath. Felt the presence of the Lady. Then I pulled out a simple wooden rosary that I had bought at the shop while she was out packing her things into the car, and I told her that I had brought her up there to ask her to teach me the rosary.

This must have surprised her, because she knows I'm not Catholic. We sat together on that bench and she taught me the rosary, which we said in its entirety. When we finished, I closed my eyes and had a very intense meditation. Tears streamed from my eyes the whole time. The presence was never closer or more intimate. I was one with it. All was one. I truly reached an altered state. A state of grace, I think. I was amazed at how close the Lady's presence could be felt. I truly feel she is with me now in a way that she never was before. I feel like I've been baptized by the Lady, herself.

SWEET SONGS AND SILENT UNITY

William James once observed, "The whole array of Christian saints and heresiarchs, including the greatest, the Bernards, the Loyolas, the Luthers, the Foxes, the Wesleys, had their visions, voices, rapt conditions, guiding impressions, and 'openings.'"[18]

The eighteenth and nineteenth centuries knew scores of these "openings," some of which led to the formation of Spirit-inspired utopian societies and communes in England, Europe, and the Americas. I wanted to know more about them so I might have more openings myself.

What I wanted was to follow the advice of the "belle of Amherst," the mystical poet, Emily Dickinson:

The soul should always stand ajar,
ready to welcome
the ecstatic experience.

SHAKERS AND QUAKERS

Though few would admit it, the entire charismatic and Pentecostal movements in Christianity are mystical. One can regard Mormonism as highly mystical, too, with their angels and visions of future paradise. But my off-road search found mystical experience alive among the least visible of the faithful: The Plain Folk. The Religious Society of Friends. The Quakers.

In 2000, I attended a Friends meeting, which had convened to honor the passing of one of its members, an acquaintance of mine. The meetinghouse had no steeple and no apparent symbols of Christianity. After some stirring songs, I waited expectantly for the "service" to begin, but the congregation just sat in silence. It made me nervous. After a while someone stood, hat in hand, spoke briefly about the departed, and sat down again. Three more silent minutes passed, then another stood and spoke. I didn't know it then, but the plain folk around me were waiting for the Spirit of God to move them to speak.

Quakerism grew out of the profound spiritual revelations of George Fox (1624–1691) in seventeenth-century England. In 1646, Fox had a series of inner experiences in which he discovered the Christ within himself. It was his "opening," in which he came to believe that Christianity wasn't an outer activity, but an experience of the inner light by which Christ illumines the soul within. He believed that all Christians were saved because of their belief, rendering rituals unnecessary, and that the only qualification for ministry was the Holy Spirit, meaning that any man or woman had the right to minister, as long as the Spirit was guiding them. Finally, he believed that he saw how God dwells in the hearts of obedient people, and that religious experience didn't require a church, but could be enjoyed anywhere.

The Quaker experience is buoyed on this silent contemplation that anticipates the awakening of the inner light within. In the contemplation, some seek to know Jesus; others seek to know God; still others are holding someone in the light, mentally envisioning someone in the presence of God. (Not all Quakers believe in Jesus. In fact, not all Quakers are Christians, though the vast majority are.)

Called "mystical Christianity" by Quaker scholar Howard Brinton, Quakerism is concerned with life in this world rather than the next. It has no theology of heaven and hell. Within Quakerism there are a variety of practices and beliefs. There are pastoral Quakers (which do use some programmed services), independents, conservatives, and even evangelical branches. Quakers generally do not believe in a fixed creed or dogma, but seek the leadings of God within oneself. They value feelings over Scripture as the best way to test doctrine. Many believe that the scriptures of all people are valid, and that everyone is lit by the light of Christ within. Their pacifism and conscientious objection to war are well known.

The Spirit was known among the other "plain folk" sects as well, including the Harmonists, the Jansonists, the Monastics, and a peculiar offshoot of the Quakers called the Shakers, or the "shaking Quakers," who trembled as they sang and danced in the blissful energy of the Spirit.

In Shaker communes, men and women resided in separate buildings. They believed in total celibacy, and practiced it so effectively that they died out through attrition. They believed that abstinence from sex, along with their 24/7 abiding in the presence of the Lord, had led them to paradise on earth in the form of first-person spiritual experiences. As they worked their handicrafts and operated their farms, they believed their practices would lead them to paradise in the afterlife as well. Of course, they're now gone, but who's to say they were wrong?

UNITY

The Spirit seems never far away from any initiative that unifies, cleanses, and inspires. Modern mystics have also made their marks, and the most successful of them did their work in quiet ways. One can find the pattern repeated in the story of Unity, founded in 1889 by Charles and Myrtle Fillmore, after the latter was healed through intense prayer and affirmations. What began as small prayer circles in people's homes became a worldwide movement that today has over nine hundred churches.

Unity describes itself as promoting a positive, practical Christianity that teaches the application of truth as taught by Jesus and a way of life that promotes health, prosperity, and peace of mind. Unity is inclusive of everybody, believes sin to be merely anything that separates you from God, and believes in the inherent basic goodness of all people because the Spirit of God lives inside each person.

Charles R. Fillmore, grandson of the founder and chairman emeritus of the board of directors, wrote, "Unity says that true religious growth is a 'do-it-yourself' project. . . . One might describe Unity as a religious philosophy with an 'open end,' seeking to find God's truth in all life."

The movement practices baptism and communion, but only as symbols of spiritual truth. They believe that understanding the Bible brings it alive and that cleansing the consciousness allows the entry of the Spirit. Baptism is seen as a mental and spiritual phenomenon that occurs when an individual aligns himself with the Spirit of God. In the off-road search, I found Unity services welcomingly open, with a nonjudgmental sweetness that opened my heart the way it always opens when I'm among people seeking the Spirit.

Rev. Albert Wingate has served as a Unity pastor. He was most recently cominister of Unity of Naples (Florida) Church. Prior to that he was with Atlanta Unity Church, where he served for nine years as senior minister to a congregation of five hundred. He said,

> I've never been "overtaken" by the Spirit, or spoken in tongues. I've seen it more as an experience of the events and the people that are around me. I've seen that presence expressing through the events and through the people in my life. And so it has never been something that came in and took me over.

There is a great deal of fear suffocating the planet. When people are faced with fear they want certainty, they want answers and assurances. In truth, the message of Jesus offers us none of that. Fundamentalism does. You no longer have to think, you just accept. If you have been "washed in the blood and believe Jesus as your Savior," then the next life, the hereafter, will be wonderful for you. And that is true even though you may be faced with difficulties now. I believe Jesus called us to live a life where the Kingdom of God is experienced here and now. We find it in sharing life with the outcasts, the sick, the destitute, the oppressed. It is possible we may see nothing from that sharing except our having been there. That is frightening to many people and contributes to the rise and attraction of fundamentalism.

If it's not a call to life and wholeness, it's not the Spirit of God but the expression of the human personality. As has often been written, we are spiritual beings having a human experience. When anger and cruelty prevail, there is a forgetting of that Spirit, which we are.

Albert referred to the writings of John Shelby Spong, the revolutionary bishop from New Jersey who was censured around the same time as Matthew Fox. "He asks if the event is life-affirming. Does it bring life, affirm life? Does it bring wholeness? If not, then it's probably not of the spirit. And that has been a real good test for me. And so when I see people living in fear of life rather than living life, then my sense is that what they're doing is not life-affirming."

The idea of testing the validity of spiritual information originated with Jesus, who said in Matthew 7:20, "By their fruits you will know them." Paul had urged "do not quench the Spirit but test all things and hold fast to what is good." (1 Thes 5:19–21)

Albert continued,

The Spirit of God moves in the world as the call toward life and wholeness. It is that indefinable something that expresses through us as love, as caring, as the desire to nurture one another. It is the synergy that is created when two or more gather in furtherance of life, love, caring, and compassion, and there is something greater than the sum of those who come together. The Spirit of God is that which is beyond the definition that I can create or the vision that I can hold. If I can define or envision it, then the Spirit of God is always greater.

In chapter 6, we looked at the question of whether Jesus was God, and Albert offered the following comments:

Those who wrote the Scripture experienced something in the life of this person called Jesus that caused them to feel and experience the presence of God. Over the centuries that something has been argued by some to be God. For me Jesus wasn't God, but was an embodiment of that which changed people's lives and called them into living as if the Spirit were expressing itself through them.

Albert went on to explain his experience of the beauty of God, a topic few people bring up.

Beauty is knowing that the presence of God is active and seeing that presence. Wherever I see a call to life, wholeness, and oneness with each other, there is beauty. While it may not be on a planetary level, there are incidents of it occurring. Those instances, though they may be small and fleeting, are beauty. Those of us who are trying to live as if the Spirit of God is expressing through us must keep our eyes open to see those moments of beauty wherever they may occur.

When asked what we can do to bring the Spirit's influence into our lives, he responded, "Be the love that we desire, be the peace that we desire, be willing to die, but not to kill in order to bring that about."

TAIZÉ

Modern ecumenical movements intrigue me because of the absence of judgments and condemnation of others. I've found nurture in services where doctrine makes way for the direct experience of God in the moment at hand, that energetic feeling of the Spirit rising within. I found it again in the service of a movement begun in 1940 in Taizé, France, by the Lutheran brother Roger Schutz, a Swiss-born monk who provided refuge for those fleeing the war. Taizé (pronounced tiz-AY) isn't a denomination or type of church, but a style of Christian worship that has quietly become loved throughout the world.

The spiritual community in Taizé, located in the South of Burgundy, is made up of an international community of over a hundred brothers from both Catholic and various Protestant churches representing over twenty-five nations. It is a community of men who engage in prayer, silent meditation, and simple songs, of candlelight and reflection, and communion with the Spirit. (The nuns of a nearby convent also participate in the services.) Since the 1950s, thousands of young people from all over the world have traveled to Taizé for the weekly meetings.

Brother Roger once said, "Right at the depth of the human condition, lies the longing for a presence, the silent desire for a communion. Let us never forget that this simple desire for God is already the beginning of faith."

The Taizé meetings are held in churches here and there in towns and cities everywhere. They may be sponsored by a Catholic church or an Episcopal, or other, are normally on a weekday evening, and meditative singing holds sway, without being led by a priest and in which a sermon is optional. The service consists of chants, music, readings from the Bible associated with a chosen theme, "intercessions," prayers for specific needs either kept to oneself or anonymously read aloud, and then silence.

One such meeting is held in Norfolk, Virginia, on the third Sunday of each month. Founded in 1998 and led by Connie Faivre, it is sponsored by Taizé of Tidewater.

Connie grew up in the Methodist Church in Indianapolis, Indiana, and she discovered Taizé one night when, upset over the treatment of her mother in a hospital, she dashed into a church across the street where a Taizé service was in progress.

The leader, a woman, saw her crying and comforted her. She welcomed her to the service, and that changed Connie's life.

Connie, also the founder and president of Tidewater Humane, Inc., an animal welfare organization, says she has had many experiences with the Spirit.

> There are times when I don't really know the difference between Spirit and grace. It's sort of the same thing. It's that all-encompassing veil that I feel God puts on all of us whether we're awake enough to realize it's there. It just tells us where we are in our spiritual journey.
>
> The most visible signs of the Spirit for me have been in dealing with the deaths of my parents and also the animals who live in my home. In them, I see the true meaning of God's love, which is unconditional love.

Connie's mother died of lung cancer not long after that first Taizé service, and only two short years later, her father was given the same diagnosis. Connie said the contemplative quiet of the service and the chanting were the only ways she got through her parents' deaths.

> The only way you can do that is feeling enveloped by the Spirit. Listening to God's voice, calming me down, and the Taizé experience really gave me the courage and strength to be there for my father.
>
> Part of what is really wonderful in Taizé is that it will help to center you and focus you and bring you back to that place where you can find God again when you think that everything is in chaos. You can quiet yourself, hear the music, you don't even need the words, you can hear the music and you can feel God's presence again.
>
> I think what Taizé does for the greater community at large is to basically fulfill what Brother Roger wanted to do when he founded it in the early 1940s, and that was to bring in people who feel marginalized or separated from God for some reason; who may feel ostracized from the greater church community, whatever denomination that might be.

I've had people say to me, "This is the only service where I felt like I was worthy to come." I guess they feel like they're being judged at other places or the other denominations say we don't want you because you've done this or that. The Taizé service transcends all that, and that's exactly what Brother Roger's dream was. It's a place of reconciliation. It's a place of peace and acceptance no matter what. We don't see it as strongly here, but I was reading about someone's experience at the Taizé, France, who said it's probably the only time where you will see a Serbian child and a Croatian child sitting next to each other praying together. And really that's what it's about. It's about no boundaries, no borders, and it's very Christian. It's not Buddhist, it's not anything else—it's a very Christian service. But beyond that there is no delineation.

I asked her if she thought the Taizé service was mystical.

Well, that depends on how you define mystical. If you define it as something to do with the occult, then no, it's absolutely not. But St. Hildegard of Bingen was a mystic. St. Theresa of Avila was a mystic. If you're talking about mysticism in terms of a direct connection to God and the free-flow of thought and energy back and forth, then maybe somebody would consider it mystical. I tend to stay away from that word because it has so many strange connotations. To me it is a very transcendent service because it puts the worshiper in a place where it is just them and God. You're not going through an intermediary to pray. The songs are the prayer, and you're participating in the songs.

The September service in Norfolk was called the "Service of Light." Connie explained that the churches who sponsor Taizé services can choose their own themes—there's no rigid format. I asked her to explain "light" relative to their service.

You can take it on several different levels. Of course, Jesus is called the light of the world. And a Taizé service is nothing more than a mechanism to preach the good news of Christ in the world. Our introductory sentences all have to do with light and the first hymn is "Come and Fill." The second level [of meaning] is that the whole church is lit with candlelight. The third level is that the Spirit, when it fills you, it's not just the light that fills you, it also fills you with warmth, and that's the third aspect of the light—that you receive the warmth of the Spirit, the light of the Spirit. You're seeing the visual Spirit, but again, Jesus is the light of the world and that's what that refers to, so it operates on several different levels.

Brother Roger was murdered at age ninety-one on August 16, 2005, by a deranged, knife-wielding woman who stabbed him in the throat during a service before a crowd of 2,500 people. It barely made the news. The Taizé theme of "reconciliation" was apparent at Brother Roger's funeral, because the first prayer was to forgive the woman who killed him.

At the end of each year, Taizé convenes a large meeting in a major European city. Thousands of young adults from all over the world attend. Part of an ongoing Taizé "pilgrimage of trust on earth" program, the meeting at the end of December 2005 in Milan, Italy, drew fifty thousand. Think of it: fifty thousand souls of many religions, attuned to the Spirit of God, gathered for the purpose of peace and reconciliation, and with no political agenda whatsoever. The Taizé movement shows that the Spirit never ceases to seek expression in an individual, a group, or a crowd. The Library of the Spirit says the Spirit will persist until we have all become One with it.

The mystics of the world's traditions don't quibble over whether God is experienced through Spirit, whether the Spirit is a "He," or whether it is earned by entering the doors of a church or synagogue. They spend their time, as much as possible, in the actual experience itself.

"Every truth without exception—and whoever may utter it— is from the Holy Spirit," wrote the thirteenth-century theologian Thomas Aquinas. "The old pagan virtues were from God. Revelation has been made to many pagans."[19]

Author, philosopher, and theologian Howard Thurman, in his *The Creative Encounter*, wrote, "It is my belief that in the Presence of God there is neither male nor female, white nor black, gentile nor Jew, Protestant nor Catholic, Hindu, Buddhist, nor Moslem, but a human spirit stripped to the literal substance of itself before God."[20]

Experiences with the Holy Spirit seem to occur when individuals display those qualities. Attunements occur. Openings. The perception of reality shifts into high gear. The blazing fire of the mind of God flows in, pours freely one into the other because they are the same. The Spirit within, the primordial fire of the soul is electrically charged at the same frequency, inspires the mind to the grand ideas toward which the character of Spirit always points. Desire is transformed. The heart knows its oneness with love, whenever the will expresses it.

The Spirit of God has never ceased brooding over the waters of the soul. The Spirit forever breathes life into the nostrils of awareness, compassion, and consciousness, and makes thoughts and feelings brand new. It can be as personal as you make it, for it waits in eternity, outside the artificial spheres of space-time, for each of the billions of points of consciousness fueled by it.

How does one invite the Spirit in? Bring the Spirit out? How can one cultivate more direct experiences with God? Is there anything one can do to bring the Spirit to bear on our daily life, our problems, our growth, our potential? Find some of the answers to these questions in chapter 10.

Chapter 10

TO
EXPERIENCE
the FIRE
AND LIGHT

According to all that's holy, the Spirit of God is everywhere, in everyone, all the time, since the beginning. It's in the air, earth, ethers, plants, and animals. The Spirit is in subspace. The Spirit may even be subspace. The Spirit is the Ultimate Reality, the active principle of Divine Unity. The Spirit is a most simple intelligence that wants one thing all the time: the oneness of all in eternal loving bliss. The Spirit never ceases to breathe its influence into the human mind, and we can awaken to the Spirit within us any time we want.

Imagine if everyone lived with open awareness of the Spirit of Elohim. We'd exercise wisdom and be more loving. We'd be able to take more guff and be more forgiving, because we'd realize that if it's not of the Spirit, none of it matters, whatever it is. We'd be able to guide ourselves and our families sensibly through life, even when things go wrong. We'd realize that everything we have is really on loan and that the transition to the next life is no big deal. We'd be healthier, because the Spirit of Wisdom would guide us on how to live better. We'd be able to understand the scripture of any faith and call out, "Wow, I finally get it!"

In *The Left Hand of God*, Adolf Holl wrote, "Only rarely does the heavenly light let itself be perceived on earth, and in such cases it seems at best a small, capricious, unpredictable spark in the depths of the soul. But to anyone who has seen that light, even if only once, all earthly light seems dim."[1]

Just how do we draw, attract, reveal, access, release, become one with, or awaken the unifying power of the Supreme Creative Force? How do we *one* ourselves (Hildegard) with *God*-ing (Rabbi Cooper)? This should be a piece of cake. So why isn't it?

The world's wisdom traditions provide a variety of ways by which we can align ourselves with the Spirit and have a more direct experience with God. Whole books have been written about this, but here are five tips that I hope will be easy to understand and use. In this chapter, we're going to look at how to:

- be more like the Spirit by understanding what attracts and repels it,
- live "at the speed of light" with some simple rules for living,
- make less of the little self and more of the "divine Self,"
- talk to the Spirit and listen for the answers, and
- keep real your contact with the Divine.

If the Spirit is everywhere, including inside us, how do we realize our innate oneness with it?

ONEING WITH THE SPIRIT

In my off-road search, I talked with many people of deep religious faith who shared their stories, from Jews to Christians, Catholics to Baptists, fundamentalists to people who reinterpret Christian philosophy, as well as mystics and atheists. We've also heard from people who left the churches of their youth and later returned. They are engineers, doctors and lawyers, artists and musicians, psychologists, clerics, teachers, and many others who have had contact with the Spirit that seems to well up inside them or descend over them. People describe their experiences using a variety of words and phrases, but in their essence, the experiences share an intrinsic similarity. We own the "I Am" presence within us, for we are a bucketful of the ocean that is God. We are the first sons and daughters of the Fire and Light.

So, what are you doing with your share of "I Am That I Am"? Most of us are busy using it for other things just now, thank you very much. There's pressure at work, the kids have the flu, hubby or missus might be seeing someone on the side, the bills, income tax, a bad check, an empty feeling inside, fear and doubt, worry, the relentless TV, and every cell screaming for a rest—yeah, a good long rest. Heck, if I only had a rest, I could give more time to my spiritual life. There are also our precious careers, big tests (or parties) at school, relationships to cultivate or ruin, the f-a-m-i-l-y, and good God, don't you know there's a war on? There must be a reason why we aren't walking on air all the time, buoyed in ecstasy with every breath, blissful in the great Comforter, one with the Creator who breathed the illusion of the world into existence. Part of the reason is our habits and training and prejudices, along with an ingrained belief that we are unworthy or unalterably separate from God.

Do you feel close to the Spirit of God yet? Maybe you really do, but you're too busy with other things to realize it. Maybe the Spirit is actually humming softly beneath all the other radio stations playing in your head. The point is, if you think the way the Spirit thinks and do the things the Spirit does, you can achieve symbiosis between the part of you that's the Spirit and the part of the Spirit that is you. That's all there is to increasing the consciousness of God in your life. It's easy.

The Divine Breath, the *ruach*, the Spirit of God is always seeking to make everything like it, as it was in the beginning. If you want more of the fire of transformation in your life, then draw on the light of understanding.

Exactly how do you go about that?

The Library of the Spirit offers plenty of advice on how to become one with the Spirit. The idea is to get rid of everything in your mind and feelings that inhibits or repels the Spirit. If oneing with the Spirit of God is our goal, as Hildegard wrote, then missing that mark must indeed be the lollapalooza of mortal sins—missing the only target that really matters. If you don't feel the Spirit yet, then become a vigilant reformer of yourself. Free the Spirit trapped inside the tired old dogma of your self-limiting beliefs. Start a new church inside your own heart and join the awakening congregation that transcends the boundaries of institutions.

What we need is a new attitude in which we claim God as our own, God as a part of us, and us as a part of God. With the fabulous potential of "I Am That I Am," we really can reshape ourselves into anything we wish. We actually do this every day.

THE DIVINE IMAGE REVISITED

We have forgotten some fundamental principles about our innate divinity that, if remembered, can help us know the Fire and Light. These principles include the seven elements of the Divine Image—the Image of God in which we were made, discussed in chapter 6. In that chapter, we also looked at the three unsung steps of the creation of man, and the fact that we were spiritual beings before we took on physical bodies and lived on the earth. Our souls are immortal, so immortality was listed as the first element of the Divine Image.

Let's revisit the components of the Divine Image:

- Immortality—though our bodies die, our consciousness never dies
- "I Am That I Am"—the state of "awareness of awareness" that we share with God
- Spirit Within—the Spirit of God lives within us, with all the potential of the Christ, the Buddha, or the Prophet

- Free Will—we freely make our choices every day between the unifying and the separating
- Love—God is love, so when we express love and compassion, we are expressing God within
- Masculine and Feminine—embrace gender and its many expressions in humankind and in yourself
- Creativity—as co-creators, we create in the world just as God created the world

To me, these elements of the Divine Image aren't mere theoretical possibilities. They are First Principles in understanding the primary questions of existence and the manifestation of the Spirit in our lives. They define those aspects of God in which we share very intimately. If this is true, and I believe it is, then we can draw closer to the Spirit of God simply by realizing the truth of them and remembering them.

So incorporate these seven into your daily thinking. List them for yourself. Put them on a bookmark or card and refer to the card several times a day, so you remember how much of God is in you. Let the Image of God shine on your face as it did on the face of Moses. Let the Spirit fit more comfortably inside you and inspire you to be aware of your unlimited potential. And in that knowledge, be very, very happy.

LIKE ATTRACTS LIKE

In considering the attraction and repulsion of the Spirit, it's important to know that this isn't about moralizing. It's more like physics: our behaviors, thoughts, and actions are forces that shape our personalities through habit.

What attracts the Spirit of God? The Library of the Spirit says universally that God is unconditional love—with no subdivisions, redistricting, footnotes, exceptions, or fine print. Love is the most important act that makes human beings most like the Spirit.

Like attracts like, so a new attitude should include relaxing into a loving point of view.

Love is such an abused word. Above all, love is unity, wholeness, and oneness with the Divine. It's creative, blooming, healing, gleeful beneficence, and kindness to all life. It's unselfconscious ecstasy, bliss, and nourishment forever in the here and now. The Christian mystic Paul wrote, "Love does no wrong to a neighbor; therefore love is the fulfilling of the law." (Romans 13:10)

The scriptures of other religions speak as eloquently of love—the great attracting and unifying force. As a vital element of the Image of God, it should be easy. All we have to do is remove the dissuaders from our thinking and attitude, and it should come quite naturally.

The Spirit blazes forth like the Sun from the blinding central furnace of the Mind of Elohim, the still point where all mind meets. Unconditional love consumes all points, proceeds from all points, recedes from all points; fills all points; empties all points; expands and collapses to and from all points, in every direction, dimensions within dimensions, expressing the all, at the speed of light, forever. Physics may one day recognize love as a universal force, though it will likely give it some technical name.

So, make love your only thought and you magnetize yourself to that great Allness and its Divine Breath. Fill yourself with the Fire and Light, and become a deliberate, corrosion-free electrode of the Spirit by knowing the truth, loving Love, and loving others.

Attracting the Spirit is all about motivation, attitude, and practice. Compassion in the heart is a welcome mat for the Spirit. We've seen it in the founders of the religions and in the mystics. The Dalai Lama Tenzin Gyatso says, "This is my simple religion. There is no need for temples; no need for complicated philosophy. Our own brain, our own heart is our temple; the philosophy is kindness."

Compassionate service will one day become the natural state of an awakened, evolved humankind. Living as an instrument of compassion. Teaching. Healing. It doesn't have to be any more complicated than that, every day, wherever you work, wherever you live. Permit yourself to be like the Ruach Elohim that created the world and you will find the Spirit within you. If we emulate it, we can know it. We can know it inside us by accepting the truth of the seven points of the Divine Image, the greatest of which is love. This is gnosis—knowledge within.

We can begin to build a compassionate attitude through intent and practice, beginning with getting out of bed in the morning. Grace descends. We accumulate merit, as the Buddhists teach, and store up "a treasure in heaven." (Mt 19:21) Buddhist priest Shigeru Kanai once shared a Japanese phrase that helps me often during the day: *Gigo gitoku*, which means, "One's actions determine one's situation." Merit and grace accumulate in the soul—the immortal part of the Divine Image in us that lives forever—and magnifies the Spirit within ourselves and others.

And what of the forces that repel the Spirit? One of the most difficult conditions that impedes closeness to the Spirit is the belief in an innate sinfulness and separation from God. For many Christians, Jews, and Muslims, this is learned from birth. Why? Because experiencing the Spirit of God directly has everything to do with an accepting and deserving inner attitude. Remove the forces that repel the nature of the Spirit, and you can achieve what Mahatma Gandhi referred to as "when what you think, what you say, and what you do are in harmony."

Certain attitudes, behaviors, beliefs, thoughts, speech, and actions repel the Spirit, because their very nature runs contrary to the Spirit's physics. Think of how two magnets push each other away. That is an artificial state between human will and divine will, when human will thinks only of the little self and lets the divine self rise out of reach. As the little self builds its stingy little empire, we turn away from the Spirit. Love also vanishes in moments—or over a lifetime—of unfulfilled desire, desperation, and fear.

People like me have always rebelled at the "thou shalt nots," but the principles of right action are found in every major religion. They, too, have to do with the physics of a loving God, not the anger of a punishing god. Unlike the rest of the universe, including the animal kingdom, we alone have the will to choose thought patterns, beliefs, attitudes, and desires that attract or repel the Spirit. Imagine that.

Obvious dissuaders of the Spirit include habits of greed, anger, envy, hate, and lust. The moralists aren't wrong about these, you know. Why? Because misusing "I Am That I Am" to flatter and admire the little self places a fragile glass crown high upon its head.

With the help of the light, we can know and find and understand the truth. The Big Truth and the little truths, about ourselves, where we might be going wrong, missing our mark (the ancient archery reference for *sin*), and a clear path to follow— information we've stored within us since birth, but lost track of when adulthood turned us from good kids to naughty kids.

To access the fire of change, we have to work on attitude. Make ourselves more like the Spirit, and the Spirit will give us a boost, like the breath of a breeze at your back, whenever you aspire to change. Change can also come when you least expect it. Sometimes, while you're on the road, lightning strikes. We can have unexpected epiphanies. Eureka, Aha! moments. Complete conversions of thought, belief, and understanding, the dissolving of prejudices, reform of motivations, and stunning revelations in the magnificent and unbearable oneness.

The Spirit of God can do this. Hedge your bet by becoming the best, highest-quality *you* that you can be. If you're looking for a partner, the best *you* will attract the best mate. If you have aspirations, then make a plan that includes the Spirit of God. If you have faults, make a plan. If you have addictions, get help today—and make a plan. Have faith, and the Spirit will do the rest. Add love, and you already know the kingdom of heaven within you.

LIVING IN A SEA OF LIGHT

It's easy to see the value of attitude in attracting and oneing yourself with the Spirit. You can also see these principles in the Four Noble Truths of Buddhism, in the Tao, in the lovely poetry of the Sufis, in the Upanishads, and in the teachings of Jesus. Absorption into God, or oneing yourself with the mind of God, is precisely what the Buddha, the Nazorean, and the founders of other religions did. They also taught something called the Golden Rule. Regardless of the outer differences between the religions of the world, it's a credit to the Spirit that this message found its way into every faith:

> *Islam:* "Do to all men as you would wish to have done unto you; and reject for others what you would reject for yourselves." (Hadith)
>
> *Hinduism:* "Do not to others what you do not wish done to yourself; and wish for others too what you desire and long for, for yourself—this is the whole of dharma, heed it well." (Mahabharata)
>
> *Native American:* "Humankind has not woven the web of life. We are but one thread within it. Whatever we do to the web, we do to ourselves." (Chief Seattle)
>
> *Christianity:* "Judge not, and you will not be judged; condemn not, and you will not be condemned; forgive, and you will be forgiven. . . ." (Jesus, Luke 6:37)
>
> *Buddhism:* "All men shrink from suffering and all love life; remember that you too are like them; make your own self the measure of others, and so abstain from causing hurt to them." (Dhammapada)
>
> *Judaism:* "What is hateful to you, do not to your fellow man; that is the entire law; all the rest of it is commentary." (Hillel)
>
> *Taoism:* "Regard your neighbor's gain as your own gain and regard your neighbor's loss as your own loss." (Common saying)

Jainism: "In happiness and suffering, in joy and grief, we should regard all creatures as we regard our own self." (Lord Mahavir, Twenty-Fourth Tirthankara)

Shinto: "Be charitable to all beings. Love is the representation of God." (Ko-Ji-Ki, Hachiman Kasuga)

Sikhism: "Don't create enmity with anyone, as God is within everyone." (Guru Arjan Devji, 259. Guru Granth Sahib)

Confucianism: "Do not unto others what you would not have them do unto you. You need this law alone. It is the foundation of all the rest." (Analects)

That's the Library of the Spirit for you. The Spirit of God infusing common sense into the Scriptures of all people for all time. And observing the Golden Rule is so like the Spirit. It draws the Spirit down and brings the Spirit forth. It calls out the two commandments of the New Testament: "You shall love the Lord your God with all your heart, and with all your soul, and with all your mind. This is the great and first commandment. And a second is like it; you shall love your neighbor as yourself. On these two commandments depend all the law and the prophets." (Mt 22:37–40)

Most of us aren't thieves or murderers. Some of us may hate our parents, but we don't worship golden calves. Well, maybe a little. (And let's not talk about the embarrassing business of coveting.) But the fact is, most of us are good decent people who naturally practice compassion, which, at face value, is pretty easy to understand. However, in other religions, I found some details that have been very helpful in my off-road search. Whether you are a Christian, Jew, Buddhist, or atheist, studying and practicing these principles will help you achieve your life goals because they will tune you in to the frequency of the Spirit.

The Yoga Sutras of Patanjali provide some nuances to Moses' Big Ten, with hints of techniques that can actually help us hit our targets. The eight limbs of yoga include these six: posture, breath control, sense withdrawal, concentration, meditation, and absorption into Universal Consciousness—the mind of God. A study of any of these can help you live a more spiritual life. But the two remaining limbs are especially helpful in refining our attitudes and behaviors enough to feel the presence of God in our lives. These are the Abstinences (Yamas) and the Observances (Niyamas). They're going to look familiar, but instead of telling you what not to do, they tell you what to do:

The Abstinences (Yamas)
1. Nonviolence (cause no pain or death to any creatures)
2. Nonlying (always speak the truth)
3. Nonstealing (includes goods, ideas, honor, credit, emotions)
4. Continence (sexual self-restraint; self-control)
5. Nongreed (generosity)

The Observances (Niyamas)
1. Purity (of thought and motive)
2. Contentment (needing what you have and having what you need)
3. Accepting but not causing pain (own what you create, but leave others alone)
4. Study of Scripture (I recommend the Library of the Spirit)
5. Worship of God (surrendering self to the Spirit and its principles: hey, it's in you!)

In Buddhism, we find additional principles, such as practicing right mindfulness and right speech. They are two parts of the Noble Eightfold Path that Buddha gave the world. Here is the complete list:

1. Right View: seeing and understanding things as they really are

2. Right Intention: good will, resisting negative desires, avoiding anger
3. Right Speech: being friendly, speaking gently, speaking when necessary
4. Right Action: creating a wholesome state of mind through wholesome actions
5. Right Livelihood: earning your living in a righteous way; earning wealth honestly
6. Right Effort: maintaining good thoughts, conquering evil thoughts
7. Right Mindfulness: thinking in a perfected way; living in the "now"
8. Right Concentration: directing mental faculties toward one wholesome purpose at a time

People will tell you that right and wrong are relative, but the Library of the Spirit is pretty clear. Define it by the Spirit, and "right" always becomes that which engenders love for your self, for your neighbor, and for the pervading, never-ending, loving, healing, inspiring, ennobling, compassionate Spirit of God. "Right" is knowing what God is and making your little self more like your "divine Self." Accept your deservingness of a divine self-identity, let go of the "unknowable mystery," and you might just find yourself aswim in the Fire and Light.

This may sound like a cliché, but you can increase direct experiences of the Spirit by reading inspired literature. This includes the Bible, both New and Old Testaments. The Sufi poets. The Torah and Talmud. The *Baghavad Gita*. The *Tao Teh Ching*. The Teachings of Buddha. The Zend Avesta. And the list goes on. If it has a Dewey Decimal number in the Library of the Spirit, then the teaching will deepen you, help you understand, and show you ways to apply wisdom in your life.

You can also learn from holy people. Whenever possible, try to talk with those who have studied and practiced all of the above. The Spirit rubs off on those who spend time with it. They tend to have more love, compassion, and wisdom than average blokes. You'll know them by how they speak and act, and these you can learn from. Attend their lectures. Speak conversationally with a rabbi, minister, imam, priest, shaman, sunyatsen, monk, swami, brother, sister, or nun—anyone who has devoted their life to spiritual discipline and study and consistently walks the talk. They learn a lot by doing so. Don't be afraid to learn all you can.

You don't have to live like a monk to discover the Spirit of God in your life, but there's quite a lot you can do to bring the Presence alive. The point is, if you practice the principles and avoid the errors, you can attract from within yourself the experiences of whichever path you follow religiously. As pointed out at the end of chapter 2, if you practice Buddhism, you will experience the Spirit as a Buddhist does; practice Vedanta, and you will experience the Spirit as a Hindu does; dance like the Sufis, and you'll experience the Spirit like a Sufi. Practice Judaism, and you will experience the Spirit the way a Jew does. Practice the teachings of Jesus, and you will experience the Spirit like a Christian. Practice atheism, and you will experience the Spirit like an atheist. The Spirit doesn't have a religion. The Spirit contains all religion. Expand your knowledge of the Spirit, and your divine experience will expand. You'll be living at the speed of light.

WISDOM OF THE EMPTY SELF

The aim is to create less of "me" and more of "I." It's the difference between your divine self (the Higher Self corresponding to the Divine Image within you) and the little self (the imperfect character you have created through your thoughts, words, circumstances, environment, choices, and inner urges). The concept is ancient. It was known to the Greeks, particularly Plato, and the Neoplatonists, Gnostics, Manichaeans, Zoroastrians, and early church theologians such as Origen. The distinction is very handy in understanding the Divine Image and how the personality draws toward or away from the Spirit.

You can create less of "me" and more of "I" by combining the ethical and moral practices described in the preceding sections with a technique known as "emptying the self." This idea is everywhere in the Library of the Spirit and in the writings of those who practiced it. It was first mentioned in chapter 3 in describing the mighty "wind" of the Spirit that seized the prophets of old, filling them with numinous ecstasy. Self-emptying always seems present in spiritual experiences. If you want to make room for the Spirit of God in your life, you have to empty out some of your "little self," the synthetic you that loves the illusions of the world and is unpracticed in knowing the Spirit of God. A Buddhist *bhikkhu* empties self in the charnel ground (burial ground). Before he began to teach, Jesus spent forty days emptying self in the desert. Muhammad surely emptied self in the cave.

The "empty self" is known in a variety of wisdom traditions. In the Psalms we find, "Create in me a clean heart, O God, and put a new and right spirit within me. Cast me not away from your presence, and take not your Holy Spirit from me. Restore to me the joy of your salvation, and uphold me with a willing Spirit." (Ps 51:10–12) In Matthew, we find "Blessed are the pure in heart, for they shall see God." (Mt 5:8)

What does this emptying of self really mean? Check out the beautiful language of the Sufi poets. Rumi explains it well:

> If you could get rid of yourself just once,
> The secret of secrets would open to you.
> The face of the unknown, hidden beyond the universe
> Would appear on the mirror of your perception.

The poet Mahmud Shabistari gives us a clue as to how you go about doing this:

> Go sweep out the chamber of your heart.
> Make it ready to be the dwelling place of the Beloved.

When you depart out, He will enter it.

In you, void of yourself, will He display His beauties.[2]

—from "The Rose Garden of Mystery"

In my own life, I notice that the more I keep my monkey-like mind and desires out of the way, or at least under control, the more aware I am of my "Self," the me that knows the truth and senses the presence of the Spirit. The more I conscientiously do what I know to be helpful to others, the more brightly the Light shines and the Fire transforms. This occurs during periods in which I deliberately try to do right by people and intentionally cultivate kindness in my day-to-day life. The feeling occurs when I'm in the habit of regular prayer. It occurs when I discipline my mind through meditation. (See "Talking and Listening to the Divine," which follows.)

When I interviewed theologian Franklin Takei, Ph.D., on this topic, he said,

I think it's important that a person has a shift from the source of information being "out there" to "in here." This is the principle of "gnosis," that inner knowing that then allows one to be in touch with that which one is—the Spirit.

In Eastern thought there is no fundamental distinction between spirit and matter. All is considered "one" however one chooses to interpret the one. Thus, the Spirit is not some entity that comes and goes (as in the Bible) but is the very essence of our existence. Hence, the Spirit is our given reality. All we need to do is allow it to manifest itself in our lives.

The practice of meditation discipline is partly the endeavor to "shut down" the cognitive processes in order to allow the insights to come from the Spirit. This is not to say that the cognitive process is an obstacle. In point of fact, cognition is a kind of manifestation of Spirit, but it needs to be rightly used in its appropriate context. . . .

The Spirit is of the essence of our very existence. One needs to develop that inward vision, to have that "inner knowing." Now, how does one get that? To a great extent, it's by understanding that [the Spirit] is already the very heart of your personal existence. A lot of times, it is simply a matter of accepting it as a fact. However, this is often very difficult for Christians because of the doctrine of original sin, and hence the belief that "no good thing can possibly come out of me." By overcoming this kind of ideology and reconstructing our lives with a more positive vision of our own existence, we make possible the manifestations of the Spirit.

IN THE ZONE

There is no way to predict an influx of the Spirit, yet when I'm open to it, it comes. When I'm deliberately "in the zone," spiritually speaking, over the long run, there's a pervading sense of the good company of the Spirit. It's the "every day" presence described by Scott Walker, Richard Drummond, Albert Wingate, and others in previous chapters. It's a good feeling within, a confidence, and a clarity of thought. It's a relief. I find I'm inspired by the right idea at the right time, inspired to do a loving thing when ordinarily I would not.

When I'm feeling in sync with divine love and have been thinking clearly, focused on helping other people, and keeping my desires under control, I invite the Spirit, and it comes. It's not "ask a favor, get a favor." It's more like a pervading assistance over many days and weeks of "good behavior." It's grace. It's like the Buddhist concept of merit, through relieving the suffering of others and abstaining from selfish acts—something like a bank account or trickle-charging a battery.

In those times, I am often shown the correct choice, direction, opportunity, and attitude. I'll see a door open, or find the right book, or meet the right person, seemingly out of nowhere. You could call this coincidence or synchronicity, but it increases when I clean up my inner act and feel more like my Self. It can manifest as any of the "gifts" enumerated by Paul and elsewhere in the Bible (see list in chapter 4). At other times, it's just a sense of contentment, peace, love, and loveliness within me that tells me that I'm in touch, and that I'm OK.

Sometimes we find the influence, appearance, or intercession of the Spirit when we're at our lowest ebb, in desperation, or without hope. This doesn't mean God waited until we cried "uncle" to help. What happens is that the little self has, for the moment, given up—you've become empty of resistance to the Spirit. Your mind and heart are finally attuned to the help you've been seeking all along. Recovering alcoholics and drug addicts know this experience well after they hit rock bottom and finally give themselves over to the "higher power." It's also called "the dark night of the soul."

COMPASSION AS A SPIRITUAL PATH

We don't have to hit Skid Row, emotionally or otherwise, to feel the Spirit's influence. The best way I've found to empty self is with a kick-start through compassion, activism, or performing any service on behalf of others. In his book *Ethics for the New Millennium*, the Dalai Lama wrote, "Thus spiritual practice . . . involves, on the one hand, acting out of concern for others' well-being. On the other, it entails transforming ourselves so that we become more readily disposed to do so. To speak of spiritual practice in any terms other than these is meaningless."[3]

Compassion is a great way to "empty the self." (It cures depression, too.) In a 2005 interview with BeliefNet.com, religion editor Laura Sheahen asked actress Susan Sarandon to discuss activism as a spiritual path. Sarandon answered,

> I think I'm an actor because I have very strong imagination and empathy. I never studied acting, but those two qualities are exactly the qualities that make for an activist.
>
> When you start to develop your powers of empathy and imagination, the whole world opens up to you. As my little guy said when he first learned about the origins of man, he said, "So Mom, I guess there really isn't such a thing as a stranger, is there?"

It's a spirituality that's empowering and inclusive and gives you a world that's so large and full of possibilities and so full of rewards. That's joyful. . . . If you walk down the street and see someone in a box, you have a choice. That person is either the other and you're fearful of them, or that person is an extension of your family. And that makes you at home in that world and not fearful.

Later in the interview, Sarandon said, ". . . Jesus' life was a very hands-on spirituality. It wasn't about excluding people. It was exactly the opposite. He was a shepherd to those who had been excluded already from the mainstream and who were needy."

After the 1980 murder of four nuns in El Salvador, former nun Elaine Hruska, introduced in chapter 2, expressed her compassion by becoming a political activist. Psychotherapist Santi Meunier applies compassion with her clients, as do the other counselors interviewed for this book. Connie Faivre, who voluntarily started and maintains regular Taizé services at her church, devotes her business life to helping animals through Tidewater Humane Society of Virginia Beach, Virginia, which she also founded. Compassion toward animals and the environment helps build a better world for everyone. Helping people in developing nations, through agriculture, education, and fighting unfair monetary practices are the only ways some people know the Spirit of God. They may be practicing the ideals of the Spirit without realizing it, and would balk at the suggestion that what they do has anything to do with religion.

Whenever we express compassion, the Spirit always moves us higher than where we were before. Sangeeta Kumar has a master's degree in education and works in the education department of the internationally recognized animal rights organization, PETA, People for the Ethical Treatment of Animals. She's engaged in the fire of transformation by living activism as a spiritual path.

GOD DOESN'T CREATE CRUELTY

Sangeeta grew up in a Hindu household, but by age twelve felt she wasn't getting the answers she needed. She joined the Hare Krishna movement, where she remained for four years until she discovered activism as a whole new way to express her spirituality. She said that becoming a vegan was a spiritual experience. (Vegans are people who eat no meat, fish, fowl, or any animal-derived products.)

I became an activist when I was sixteen years old, and that's when my whole world opened up. I had read a book about veganism, and for the first time I realized what a huge thing this is. I just had this feeling in me that I had to tell the world. I remember the day when I went vegetarian. It was like something went "click" and I knew that eating animals was wrong.

The writings of Mahatma Gandhi actually steered her onto the path of activism.

The segue from Krishna to activism was inspired by Gandhi. He is a wonderful example of melding spirit with activism. His Satyagraha movement is founded upon the soul force. It is the search for truth or the path of truth. The activists were called satyagrahis, meaning "those who are searching for truth."

Gandhi said two things that changed Sangeeta's life.

He said "my life is my message," and I thought how beautiful to live your life so it's a message for the world. I think, *are my actions right now an example for the world?* It doesn't matter to me whether the world knows what I'm doing or not. But it matters that I do it. And I feel like that gives me strength, spiritually speaking. Another thing he said was that we must "become the change we wish to see in this world." Again, the idea of responsibility. You can become the change, not just wish or hope for it. You can't just free yourself of all the problems of the world like it's nothing to do with you, because we are all connected, and we need to live in a way that we can make the world better.

Sangeeta believes the cruelty in the world is caused not by God, but by human beings. I asked her if she considered activism a religion.

If a religion is dharma, then this is certainly my path. It's a spiritual path for sure. But I'd say that I'm openly agnostic because I don't know, and I don't profess to know, what is out there. However, if there is an afterlife, if there is coming back and so on, I will happily keep coming back until there is no more suffering in the world. It's deep in my soul that our spirituality demands that we become active in some way. I feel like if God were to speak to us today he would say "Get up and do something." In the search for truth, in the quest to make the world better, you become better. It's not just sitting and reading. It's in action that enlightenment is found.

TALKING AND LISTENING
TO THE DIVINE

The best "how to's" I ever learned for emptying the self and opening the heart to the Spirit are active speaking (prayer) and deliberate listening (meditation) to the Grand Intelligence that birthed the universe. Together, they become the two-way radio that transcends duality and all the illusions that we are separate from God. They are the give and take that equalize the push and pull of the Presence of the Spirit.

Give some time to a spiritual practice every day, not as an obligation, but because it will take you ever closer to that which you love above all things (whether you realize it or not): the Spirit of God. Discipline your mind and body. Eat nourishing, fresh food. Watch what you eat with your eyes and ears as well. (What kind of diet do you "eat" from movies, TV, and your stereo speakers?)

PRAYER

The power of prayer is an aid in bringing more direct contact with the Spirit of God, because it helps declare your intent and gradually convinces your subconscious mind that you mean what you say. The Higher Self (the Spirit within you) eventually expands beyond the precious problems of the little self. You become a better you.

When I was a child, I repeated the prayers that I had been taught. I still recite some of them. But prayer can be more than just counting repetitions. It's applying the mind to a request, a petition, a confession, to express gratitude, to send help (transmit a good thought through non-local reality to another person or condition), or to praise the beauty of the One God.

Jesus of Nazareth had a lot to say about how to pray. Reminding people that they, too, are spirit, he said, "God is spirit, and those who worship him must worship him in spirit and truth." (Jn 4:23–24) He also said: "Whenever you pray, go to your room, close the door and pray to your Father in private." (Mt 6:6)

Prayer is the part where you talk to God. If you don't like the word *prayer* then call it something you like: decreeing, declaring, calling, declaiming, complaining, or proclaiming. Whenever you pray, however, remember that it's a two-party call, because the Spirit within you is also on the line; it's the Christ Consciousness potential, which in most people has low mileage because it's usually parked in the garage.

For crying out loud—why not pray aloud? Proclaim your prayers passionately with your heart and mind full to the brim with the meaning of the prayer. Prayer broadcasts thought through subspace. Once released, it's everywhere for all time. Let prayer be benevolent for yourself and others. Become a beacon of love and compassion and responsibility. Write your own prayers. Use carefully worded prayers freely, the tried and true, from the Library of the Spirit.

If you don't see it, ask for it. Jesus said that to have the Spirit, all you have to do is ask. Ask the Christos. Ask the Divine Mother.

Ask the Father. What better place to pray than before, during, or after meditation, when the mind is clear and the heart filled with love? Plan your prayers in advance. Boldly acknowledge the presence of the Spirit. Brazenly decree for what you need, and always pay it forward to someone else, somehow, every day. Be accepting if the answer is something unexpected, or even if the answer is "No."

Author and physician Larry Dossey, M.D., introduced in chapter 8, is a pioneer in applying prayer and meditation techniques in health and healing. He commented that finding the Spirit is easier than people make it out to be.

> The Spirit is not "out there." It's not that you have to go out and acquire it or find it. I think that many great spiritual traditions have been extremely helpful through the ages in helping people understand that this is an indwelling quality. That's something to be not acquired, but realized. So the goal is to allow it to surface and to become real and there certainly have been methods through the ages that helped people do this. If you want to boil down the wisdom of any of these traditions you would simply say what we need to do is to sit down, be quiet, shut up, and let it happen. And a lot of the meditative techniques and the techniques that emphasize quiet and prayer are simply ways of tuning in to something that is innate. I think this is why most people need a spiritual path that is disciplined and is a regular steady immersion in these activities that allow this to become real for us.
>
> The idea that this is something that we have to make happen and to acquire from an external source is a true barrier for realizing the power of Spirit to transform our lives. So, I think that people simply need to be creative and experimental in finding the way that feels natural and right for them. I don't think that there is a "one size that fits everybody" here. There's a smorgasbord of techniques out there these days that help people get in touch with Spirit and their own inner divinity, and I think it's difficult to prescribe for people how to do this. One simply has to inquire within and find out what seems right for them. My own personal source of nourishment, which is immersion

in nature—I couldn't do without that. That really is a path that's been really crucial for me for all of my life. I grew up on my farm and still have dirt under my fingernails and I just can't imagine not having a regular exposure to nature.

MEDITATION

If prayer is the part where you talk, then meditation is the part that most people neglect, the part where you listen. The Spirit imparts understanding, so in meditation you tune into higher knowledge, and "turn on the lights" of inspiration. Meditation is stilling the mind, freeing it from uncontrolled thoughts and feelings, and spending time in the silence. How else are you going to make room for an expanding Spirit within you? How else will you clear the jammed human circuits and amp up the divine transformer? The undisciplined mind is like a puppy. Meditation provides the leash.

The adepts of every religion study and discipline the mind and know that inner peace is achieved through contemplation, achieving the quiet stillness in which the mind stops entertaining itself and rests comfortably. It is what my friend, Virginia artist Richard Stodart, calls finding "the gaps"—the spaces in between your busy thought events. You can widen these gaps through practice, to the point where you create within your own mind a sanctuary of peace and communion with "I Am That I Am" and the Spirit.

Within those gaps, we spend time in the eternal now. Within those widening gaps, we can increase our awareness of awareness, augment our closeness to God, and, in fact, increase our transcendent experiences.

Effective meditation practices can be found in a variety of sources, but they nearly always begin with the principle of being "mindful" and "in the now." Being mindful is being present in the moment, and this requires practice of clearing the mind and resisting the lure of interesting thoughts. (When you think about it, "now" is all that really exists anyway.)

You can add to the practice as much as you wish and custom fit it for your needs. Start with this simple method. Let the words of renowned religion expert Huston Smith be your guide: "The brain breathes mind like the lungs breathe air." As consciousness itself is the open floodgate to the mind of the Creator, I submit that in like manner the soul breathes Spirit—the Divine Breath.

Achieving a controlled, peaceful meditative state requires five basic steps:

1. Sit upright in a comfortable chair. You want to be comfortable, but not so comfortable that you fall asleep. Whenever possible, meditate in the same place, perhaps a special chair. You need to be comfortable sitting in silence for ten or fifteen minutes every day. After a while, you'll understand how important meditation is. Expect the Spirit to enter your life, but don't look for profound experiences. Don't look for rewards. Be patient. Expect the gradual peace to come as you gradually become more peaceful.

2. Use your breath. As the breath of God created the world and filled man's nostrils, your breath is part of the Divine Image. Cherish it and respect it. Once you are comfortable, close your eyes and inhale deeply through the nose. Exhale slowly through the mouth. Use visualization: bring in the Spirit while expelling negative thinking, stray thoughts, all that is not Spirit in your consciousness. You can move past doubts and distractions by concentrating on the rhythm of your breath. Breathe in this manner nine times as you prepare to enter your place of inner peace.

3. Seek the silence. When your thoughts intrude, be the observer, but don't let the thoughts engage you. Let them, as well as any outside distractions or noises, pass like clouds in the sky. Each time you practice this, return

to the peaceful place within. The lovely gaps between ordinary thoughts will increase and last longer. Work toward sustaining this peaceful space for two to three minutes. Imagine that as you release ordinary thoughts and feelings and spend time in the silence, you are entering the non-local, universal realm of "I Am That I Am." Let your heart glow with compassion and love. What have you got to lose by trying?

4. Focus the mind. Once you establish your center of peace and can return to it regularly, you can either simply enjoy the calm and quiet or you can give your meditation a focus. For example, you can choose a "seed thought," some quotation from the Library of the Spirit. Ask for the Spirit to reveal understanding—ask out loud. The response will match the Spirit you are manifesting in your heart, day to day. Once you are in meditation, focus on the passage for five minutes. Seek the understanding, and it will come.

Another example is to meditate on the Divine Image within you, as listed in chapter 6. Meditate on the connection between your awareness of being alive to "I Am That I Am"—on your immortality. Meditate on the divine implications of free will; on your masculine and feminine nature; on the power of the Spirit within you to show you more of the Spirit: love, compassion. Ask to see the blind sides of your personality and the true spiritual identity that you share with others.

You can spend as much time with any one of these as you like—months, if you wish. The sanctuary of a disciplined mind is your meeting place with God.

5. Feel unconditionally loved. The "I Am That I Am" is total love and unity forever. It is in you. It sustains and contains you. It is the love you feel when others love you. Awaken to the oneness of universal love. Know it is possible and that you can find it within yourself.

Make a daily discipline of meditation, and in a few weeks you will find yourself eager for this time apart in the secret chamber of your heart.

Whatever meditation technique you use, it can help you to better follow your own belief system; maintaining a regular practice is the key. It will help you develop a positive new attitude, in which you can confidently decree, "I used to believe myself separate from the Divine, but I now know that the Divine is within me."

Meditation is your time to "one" yourself with the Spirit of God. To enter the kingdom of heaven within you. To open your mind to the truth as only the Spirit can reveal it. Finding the still and peaceful center, you establish a home base within you that becomes easier and easier to achieve the more you practice. Soon, you look forward to finding that inner peace. Meditate on the truths of the Library of the Spirit, and the Spirit opens the gift of interpretation and understanding. Guaranteed. Enjoy!

KEEPING IT REAL

Not everyone who experiences the Spirit is dramatically changed forever. Sometimes it occurs in a singular moment that never returns. Other times it lasts an hour or a day or a week. This is all dependent upon the individual. But we don't want to make the mistake of fourteenth-century English mystic Richard Rolle, who some say placed too much emphasis on peak experiences—on the phenomena of it. For most of us, our experience with the Spirit will be subtle; for others, a powerful conversion experience to a new way of thinking, living, or serving in the world. When you deliberately seek the Spirit and practice its principles, you tend to have more direct experiences with the Divine. The more you practice, however, the dramatic events grow fewer and in fact appear less dramatic.

DON'T FORGET TO LAUGH

Rev. R. Scott Walker explained that he has had few dramatic experiences with the Spirit.

> I think I experience the Holy Spirit on a continuous type of process versus a series of dramatic episodes. I think all of us begin to understand when we kind of simply know that God's spirit is working amidst something or we see something. And there's no way we can prove it, we just simply know it.

Scott described an experience while he was in South Carolina on vacation, in which he was having a tough time unwinding. He prayed to God, conversationally, simply to help him relax.

> Just at that moment, I looked off to my right and there was this big beautiful stallion with some other horses who—all of a sudden, I've never seen a horse do this—he just plopped down on his side, rolled over on his back, kicking his legs up in the air, scratching his back, rolling from side to side, just having the greatest time and then he rolled all the way over and stayed on the ground on his side. And I started laughing. Now that could have just been a coincidence, but there was a sense in which I could glimpse the presence of God, or God as Spirit in my life. Life is filled with hundreds of those, if you develop the vision to see it. I personally think anyone's life can be this way. It's where you try to become spiritually sensitive to see it. The older traditions would call it centering in or focusing or listening. But it's learning to see the presence of God in everyday life.

I asked him if this was the same as developing one's intuition.

> It's more than intuition. We all come to faith in the four basic ways: First, is the tradition that we're born in. For example, if you are a Christian, you're going to look at the world through a Christian viewpoint. Second is reason. Third is emotion. And the fourth is intuition. God as

Holy Spirit works through all of those. But that intuitive area is one that people tend to move towards when they're talking about God as Holy Spirit.

I'm a person who believes God is known as much by his apparent absence as by his presence. And many times when I just really need to have that kind of glimpse, it's not there. And I'm comfortable with that, knowing that this is not something that you get on demand. It is something that either comes when you're ready, or sensitive, or the interaction of events in your life. At the same time, in the more profound moments, I know that the presence of God is close when my eyes fill with tears just for a moment. And I've just learned to trust that. Sometimes you can be in a conversation, just a normal conversation. It may be with a stranger, it may be with someone you've known for years, and all of a sudden you get this keen sense that there are more than two people in the conversation. That there's another presence there.

THE UNION OF SPIRIT WITH SPIRIT

We don't have to adopt an ascetic lifestyle to be more aware of the Fire and Light. In *The New American Spirituality*, Elizabeth Lesser writes, "Another misconceived notion about spirituality that alienates the modern seeker is the association of sacredness with saintliness. It is erroneous to separate spirituality from everyday life. To equate holiness only with celibacy, or solitude, or poverty is to deny most of us a spiritual life."[4]

The Spirit gives vitality to our understanding and enthusiasm for our beliefs because we find the proof of it within ourselves. Spirit is the live connection to that which we cannot see. It is the meeting place between God and humankind. The Spirit is a function of our brains or education. This is the part of inspired awareness that unites the abstract with the practical. The Spirit lifts us above the ordinary to empower us to do great things, perform great acts of service or wisdom, or choose new directions in life. It can help us become aware of great realities and bring profound spiritual awakening.

Paul wrote,

Now there are varieties of gifts, but the same Spirit; and there are varieties of service, but the same Lord; and there are varieties of working, but it is the same God who inspires them all in every one.

To each is given the manifestation of the Spirit for the common good.

To one is given through the Spirit the utterance of wisdom, and to another the utterance of knowledge according to the same Spirit, to another faith by the same Spirit, to another gifts of healing by the one Spirit, to another the working of miracles, to another prophecy, to another the ability to distinguish between spirits, to another various kinds of tongues, to another the interpretation of tongues.

All these are inspired by one and the same Spirit, who apportions to each one individually as he wills.[5]

The Spirit never ceases to express itself through human beings who, whether by design or inner urging, demonstrate its virtues. The history of the Spirit through the evolution of human consciousness makes that clear. Beginning with Abraham, the Spirit guided a Chosen People to establish a bastion of belief in the One God. It became more intimate through the teachings of Jesus of Nazareth. After attempts to control it by the Roman Church, the Spirit emerged in "heretical" prophets and groups, and today it seems clear that the Spirit is working within individuals—the responsibility to lead people to the full realization of "I Am That I Am" no longer falls on institutions. It falls on you and me to do it for ourselves.

Like water, the Spirit flows along the path of least resistance, filling every tributary open to it. It flows in drops, rivulets, gushes, or floods, apparently according to our attunement and capacity. Our experiences with the Spirit occur through loving thoughts and actions that set Spirit-awareness within us resonating with the original source of all consciousness. When I raise my vibration through "will in action" to the character and quality of the Spirit, the Spirit in turn raises me higher. This applies to everyone, regardless of belief system.

Knowing the Spirit brings grace, rewards merit, and gives freedom from the erroneous habits of despising oneself and feeling unworthy. It's achieving genuine spiritual goals—anything that demonstrates true goodness, growth for self and for everyone you touch. One could leave it at that—practicing what the Good Book says, avoiding sin, and saying your prayers is just as legitimate a path as any. But it can be more than that. It's psychology. It's physics: "Love the Lord thy God and love your neighbor as yourself" creates an electromagnetic field that harmonizes with the Spirit alive in every human being, in "the light that lights every man who comes into the world." The Spirit is always nudging us to do so. When we are attuned, we experience the Spirit firsthand and touch the higher realities that the Spirit has always known. Tears flow. The soul sings.

When the Spirit reveals itself within you, it allows ordinary individuals to think extraordinary thoughts, to make wiser choices in life. At that most personal level, the same Spirit of God that brooded upon the waters broods ever upon the waters of the soul. It breathes life into the nostrils of your awareness, compassion, consciousness, and makes your thoughts and feelings brand new. The Spirit is as personal as you make it. It waits in eternity, outside the artificial spheres of space-time, for each of the billions of points of consciousness that access it, impersonally or personally, according to our capacity to love. It waits. It knows you will find it eventually.

To know the Fire and Light in your life, consider these steps:

1. Know that you are always one with the Spirit, not separate, sinful, and solitary.
2. Believe that you deserve the Spirit, because it is with you, in you, and all around you.
3. Live the universal law of love through compassion for all life. Treat others as you would have them treat you.
4. Ask for the Spirit out loud, in the full knowledge that God freely gives it.

5. Change your attitude toward yourself and others: we are spiritual beings having a human experience, not human beings having a spiritual experience.
6. Spend an hour each week reading in the Library of the Spirit.
7. Discipline your body through exercise and right diet.
8. Use moderation in fulfilling your desires and appetites.
9. Stop feeding self-destructive habits—cut them off now, and never look back. Ask the Spirit to help.
10. Discipline your mind through meditation and prayer.
11. Reconnect with nature as often as possible, far from human society.
12. God is love, so love God with all your heart.

As Ken Wilber wrote in *The Eye of Spirit*, the search for God in itself is an instrument of separation. "If Spirit cannot be found as a future product of the Great Search," he wrote, "then there is only one alternative: Spirit must be fully, totally, completely present right now—and you must be fully, totally, completely aware of it right now."[6]

Amen.

The Spirit is as personal or impersonal with us as we choose to be with the Spirit. It is intimate with us as we attune ourselves to love and service to others. When we open our minds and hearts to love, we become filled with the Spirit—we become enlightened. We know "I Am That I Am" firsthand. The Spirit is God in action that thinks love, unification, wholeness, forgiveness, and ecstasy forever. And the Fire and Light is everywhere. It is present in all of us, on and off the well-traveled road, and it never stops inviting us to find our way home.

Endnotes

Chapter One

1 Klepp, Susan E. Professor of History, Rider University. From Encarta Online Encyclopedia.

2 From "Mix-And-Match Religion," www.cbsnews.com, June 29, 2005.

3 Klepp, from Encarta Online Encyclopedia.

4 The authors of the *American Sociological Review* study that exposed how the data on church attendance are skewed by pollsters were Mark Chaves, Kirk Hadaway, and Penny Marler of Stamford University.

5 From an Associated Press article by Cheryl Wittenauer that appeared in the December 26, 2005, issue of *The Washington Post*.

6 See *Strong's Concordance of the Bible*.

7 Gn 2:7.

8 Ps 104:30.

9 Isa 32:15.

10 Ez 11:19, ff.

11 Is 32:15.

12 Jl 2:28–29.

13 www.zaadz.com/quotes/authors/mevlana_rumi/ Rumi, Mevlana. Persian Sufi mystic, 1207–1273.

14 Gaskell, *Dictionary of All Scriptures and Myths*, p. 365.

Chapter Two

1 Weatherhead, *The Christian Agnostic*, p. 87.

2 Acts 17:28.

3 Saint Thérèse of Lisieux, *Story of a Soul: The Autobiography of St. Thérèse of Lisieux*.

4 Crim, general editor, *Abingdon Dictionary of Living Religions*, p. 613.

5 Wach, p. 32-33.

6 James, *Varieties of Religious Experience*, p. 398.

7 Ibid., p. 31.

8 Ibid., p. 58.

9 Bucke, *Cosmic Consciousness*, related in an introduction by George Moreby Acklom in the 1969 Dutton edition.

10 Ball, *Modern Saints*, p. 101.

11 Buber, *Ecstatic Confessions*, p. xxxii.

12 Ibid., pp. 119–120.

13 Ibid., p. 147.

14 Smith, *The Religions of Man*, p. 191. Adapted from K. L. Reichelt's translation.

Chapter Three

1 Cohen, *Everyman's Talmud*, p. 45.

2 Gn 6:1–7.

3 Israel: 928 B.C.E. to 722 B.C.E.; Judah: 928 B.C.E. to 587 B.C.E.

4 Talmud J: Sukka, 5.1, c. 400.

5 1 Sam 20:23–24; 1 Sam 16:14.

6 See Ex 15:20; Jdg 4:4.

7 2 Ki 2:11–16.

8 Van Dusen, *Spirit, Son, and Father*, p. 36.

9 Dt 34:9; Num 27:18–20.

10 Num 11:16–17.

11 Jdg 3:10; 6:34.

12 Jdg 11:29; 14:5–6.

13 Gn 41:1, ff.

14 Dn 4:8; 5:11–14; 6:3.

15 1 Sam 3–16.

16 1 Ki 17:17–24; 2 Ki 4:18–37, 13:20–21.

17 1 Ki 17:12–16; 2 Ki 4:1–7.

18 1 Sam 16:13.

19 Midrash Eccl. Rabbah 12:7 ". . . and the spirit returns to God who gave it."

20 Gn 6:3.

21 Dt 34:10.

22 Talmud, Yoma 21b.

23 Dt xii. 11; xiv. 23; xvi. 6, 11; xxvi. 2; Neh i. 9.

24 Ez xliii.

25 Targ. Onk. To Dt xii. 5; Ps xlix. 15, cviii. 8.

26 Zeb 8a [0].

27 Shab. 31a; Sanh. 96a.

28 Gaskell, *Dictionary of All Scriptures and Myths*, p. 274.

29 1 Sam 10:10; 19:20.

30 1 Sam 9:19–20.

31 Smith, *The Religions of Man*, p. 242.

32 1 Sam 10:10.

33 Ex 15:20–21 (KJV).

Chapter Four

1 Lk 1:32–33.

2 1 Kgs 19:12.

3 See Eliade, *The HarperCollins Concise Guide to World Religions*, p. 168.

4 See *Encyclopedia Britannica* under history of Judea, 63 **B.C.E.**

5 The "Sicarii"; see *Encyclopedia Britannica and Armstrong, A History of God*.

6 See Horsley, *Bandits, Prophets, and Messiahs*, appendix timeline and *Encyclopedia Britannica* under Hellenistic Judaism: Roman Period.

7 Lk 1:15 RSV.

8 See Lk 2:9, the Shekinah glory around the shepherds when angel appeared to them.

9 Mt 3:10.

10 Jn 1:7.

11 Lk 3:16.

12 Lk 3:22.

13 See Hg 15a; Targ. to Cant. Ii. 12; Rashi to Gen. i. 2; compare Sanh. 108b.

14 Mt 13:57 and Lk 4:24.

15 Lk 4:14.

16 Lk 4:16–21.

17 Jn 1:9 (KJV).

18 Jn 14:10–11.

19 See also Mk 12:35–37.

20 Lk 1:80; 2:40.

21 Cooper, *God Is a Verb*, p. 1.

22 Lk 11:11–13.

23 Mt 19:16–17.

24 Jn 15:10.

25 Mt 22:37–40.

26 Mt 12:32.

27 Van Dusen, *Spirit, Son, and Father*, p. 55.

28 Lk 17:21.

29 Jn 20:11. Mary is wrongly believed to have been a prostitute. Scripture indicates serious mental illness, which Jesus cured by spiritual means.

30 Jn 20:22.

31 Mt 28:19–20.

32 Jn 14:20–21.

33 Mk 13:11.

34 Jn 14:12.

35 Jn 3:3. The King James Version uses "born again" (see Jn 3:3, 3:7, and 1 Pt 1:23). Nowadays the phrase is often used to challenge and segregate people.

36 Mk 16:17–18.

37 Lk 24:49.

38 Armstrong, *A History of God*, p. 86.

39 Van Dusen, *Spirit, Son, and Father*, p. 66.

40 II Cor 3:17–18.

41 Ps 127:3, Ez 11:19.

42 Isaiah 11:1–5.

43 1 Cor 7:7.

44 Jn 14:16–17.

45 1 Cor 3:16.

46 Van Dusen, *Spirit, Son, and Father*, p. 66.

47 Referred to by Peter in Acts 2:17–21.

48 Van Dusen, *Spirit, Son, and Father*, p. 59.

Chapter Five

1 1 Cor 12–13.

2 See www.bibletexts.com/glossary/prophet.htm.

3 Acts 11:27; 31;1; 15:32; Eph 2:20; 3:5; 4:11; James 5:10; 1 Pet. 1:10; Rev 22:6–9.

4 Epiphanius, "Hær.," xlviii, 11.

5 Holl, *The Left Hand of God*, p. 128.

6 Ibid., p. 68.

7 Armstrong, *The History of God*, p. 88, referencing Rom 5:12–18.

8 Ehrman, *Lost Christianities*, p. 3.

9 Ehrman, *Lost Christianities*, p. 154.

10 See http://students.cua.edu/16kalvesmaki/lxx/.

11 Armstrong, *A History of God*, p. 110.

12 Ibid., p. 112.

13 Ibid., p. 115.

14 John and others refer to baptizing in the "name of the Father, Son, and Holy Spirit," and identified them as three witnesses. They are not, however, identified in the Bible as a divine trinity.

15 Weatherhead, *The Christian Agnostic*, p. 67.

16 This quote is cited in *Time* magazine, Dec. 16, 1946, p. 64.

17 Douglas-Klotz, *Prayers of the Cosmos*, p. 3.

18 Van Dusen, *Spirit, Son, and Father*, p. 16.

19 Ibid., p. 92.

20 2 Cor 3:6.

21 Smith, *The Religions of Man*, pp. 121–123.

22 Van Dusen, *Spirit, Son, and Father*, p. 90.

23 Weatherhead, *The Christian Agnostic*, p. 27.

Chapter Six

1 Jn 3:8.

2 1 Pt 2:9.

3 Come, *Human Spirit and Holy Spirit*, p. 7.

4 Satchidananda, *The Golden Present*.

5 1 Jn 4:16.

6 Gn 2:18–23.

7 Pagels, *The Gnostic Gospels*, p. 68.

8 See also Mt 19:4.

9 See also Is 66:13 and Hosea 11:1–9.

10 Fox, *Creation Spirituality*, p. iv.

Chapter Seven

1 Pagels, *The Gnostic Gospels*, p. xxiv.

2 Ibid., p. xxxviii.

3 Ehrman, *Lost Christianities*, p. 155.

4 Pagels, *The Gnostic Gospels*, p. xx.

5 Armstrong, *A History of God*, pp. 99–100.

6 Küng, *Great Christian Thinkers*, p. 67.

7 Ibid., p. 71, ff.

8 St. Augustine, *Trinity* (399-422 C.E.), I, iii, 5.

9 Küng, *Great Christian Thinkers*, p. 82, ff.

10 Pagels, *Adam, Eve, and the Serpent*, p. xix.

11 Armstrong, *A History of God*, p. 124.

12 Ibid.

13 See James McDonald's website, www.languedoc-france. info/12011001_consolementum. htm.

14 See www.languedoc-france. info/1204_origins.htm.

15 See www.languedoc-france. info/12_cathars.htm.

16 Armstrong, *A History of God*, p. 252.

17 See "The Beguines," by Elizabeth T. Knuth, December 1992, www.users.csbsju.edu/~eknuth/ xpxx/beguines.html.

18 *Encyclopedia Britannica*: Radical Protestantism.

19 A. Robert Smith, "The Rapture: The Gospel (of Darby)," *Venture Inward*, Nov./Dec. 2005.

20 James, *Varieties of Religious Experience*, pp. 330–331.

Chapter Eight

1 Einstein, *Ideas and Opinions*, p. 46.

2 Nietzsche, from *The Gay Science*.

3 Armstrong, *A History of God*, p. 304.

4 Lipton, *The Biology of Belief*, p. 196.

5 Ibid., p. 29.

6 Ibid., p. 185.

7 *Encyclopedia Britannica*: Carl Jung.

8 Wilber, *The Marriage of Sense and Soul*, p. 152.

9 Ibid., p. 167.

10 Ibid., p. 173.

11 Wilber, *The Eye of Spirit*, p. 282.

12 Peter Russell, "Mysterious Light: A Scientist's Odyssey," *Noetic Sciences Review*, no. 50, pp. 8–13, 44–47.

13 Barnett, *The Universe and Einstein*, p. 109.

14 Collinge, *Subtle Energy*, p. 3.

15 Interviewed by Kevin J. Todeschi for the July/August 2006 issue of *Venture Inward* magazine, p. 43.

Chapter Nine

1 Perry, *A Treasury of Traditional Wisdom*, p. 664.

2 James, *Varieties of Religious Experience*, p. 484.

3 Florence Lederer, *The Secret Rose Garden of Shabistari*.

4 From Rumi's poem "Mathnawi," translated by Kabir and Camille Helminski in their book *Jewels of Remembrance*.

5 Andrew Harvey, *The Essential Mystics*, p. 143.

6 Cooper, *God Is a Verb*, p. viii.

7 Ibid., p. 69.

8   Ibid., p. 70.

9   Gal 6:7. See also Lk 6:38: "For
    the measure you give will be the
    measure you get back."

10 From *Scivias*, quoted from
    Matthew Fox's *Hildegard
    von Bingen's Book of Divine
    Works*, translated by Robert
    Cunningham from the German
    text by Heinrich Schipperges.

11 This was from a letter to Bishop
    Eberhard II of Bamberg.

12 O'Brien, *Varieties of Mystic
    Experience*, p. 124.

13 Eckhart, from *Nolite timere*.

14 Eckhart, from *Expedit vobis*.

15 Perry, *A Treasury of Traditional
    Wisdom*, pp. 817–818.

16 Armstrong, *A History of God*,
    p. 254.

17 Julian of Norwich, quoted by
    Perry, *A Treasury of Traditional
    Wisdom*, p. 819.

18 James, *Varieties of Religious
    Experience*, p. 478.

19 From the *Summa Theologica*.

20 Thurman, p. 152.

Chapter Ten

1   Holl, *The Left Hand of God*,
    p. 78.

2   From Mahmud Shabistara's
    thirteenth-century poem "The
    Rose Garden of Mystery."

3   Gyatso, Tenzin. *Ethics for the
    New Millennium*, p. 23.

4   Lesser, *The New American
    Spirituality*, p. 29.

5   1 Cor 12:4–11.

6   Wilber, *Eye of the Spirit*, p. 282.

Select Bibliography

Armstrong, Karen. *A History of God: The 4,000-Year Quest of Judaism, Christianity, and Islam*. New York: Ballantine Books, 1993.

Augustine, Saint, Bishop of Hippo. *Trinity*. Hyde Park, NY: New City Press, 1998.

Ball, Ann. *Modern Saints*. Rockford, IL: Tan Books & Publishers, 1983.

Barnette, Lincoln. *The Universe and Einstein*. New York: Mentor Editions, 1963.

Baumann, T. Lee, M.D. *God at the Speed of Light*. Virginia Beach, VA: A.R.E. Press, 2002.

Beane, Wendell C., Ph.D. *The Truth Within You*. Virginia Beach, VA: A.R.E. Press, 1998.

Besserman, Perle. *Kabbalah and Jewish Mysticism*. Boston: Shambhala, 1997.

Bettenson, Henry, and Maunder, Chris, eds. *Documents of the Christian Church*. Oxford: Oxford University Press, 1999.

Borysenko, Joan, Ph.D. *A Woman's Journey to God: Finding the Feminine Path*. New York: Riverhead Trade, 2001.

Buber, Martin. Trans. by Esther Cameron. *Ecstatic Confessions: The Heart of Mysticism*. San Francisco: Harper & Row, 1985.

Bucke, Richard Maurice, M.D. *Cosmic Consciousness*. New York: Dutton, 1969.

Campbell, Joseph, ed. *Pagan and Christian Mysteries: Papers from the Eranos Yearbooks*. New York: Harper & Row, 1955.

Cohen, Abraham. *Everyman's Talmud: The Major Teachings of the Rabbinic Sages*. New York: Schocken, 1995.

Collinge, William, Ph.D. *Subtle Energy: Awakening to the Unseen Forces in Our Lives*. New York: Warner Books, 1998.

Come, Arnold B. *Human Spirit and Holy Spirit*. Philadelphia, PA: The Westminster Press, 1959.

Cooper, David A., Rabbi. *God Is a Verb: Kabbalah and the Practice of Mystical Judaism*. New York: Riverhead Books, 1997.

Crim, Keith, Bullard, Roger A., and Shinn Larry D., eds. *Abingdon Dictionary of Living Religions*. Nashville, TN: Abingdon, 1981.

Dewar, Lindsay. *The Holy Spirit and Modern Thought*. New York: Harper, 1959.

Douglas-Klotz, Neil. *Prayers of the Cosmos: Meditations on the Aramaic Words of Jesus*. San Francisco: Harper & Row, 1990.

———. *Desert Wisdom: Sacred Middle Eastern Writings from the Goddess Through the Sufis*. San Francisco: HarperSanFrancisco, 1995.

Doyle, Brendan. *Meditations with Julian of Norwich*. Santa Fe, NM: Bear and Company, Inc., 1983.

Drummond, Richard Henry, Ph.D. *A Broader Vision: Perspectives on the Buddha and the Christ*. Virginia Beach, VA: A.R.E. Press, 1995.

———. *Islam for the Western Mind: Understanding Muhammad and the Koran*. Charlottesville, VA: Hampton Roads, 2005.

Dupré, Louis, and Wiseman, James A., O.S.B., eds. *Light from Light: An Anthology of Christian Mysticism*. New York: Paulist Press, 1988.

Ehrman, Bart D. *Lost Christianities: The Battles for Scripture and the Faiths We Never Knew*. New York: Oxford University Press, 2003.

Einstein, Albert. *Ideas and Opinions*. New York: Three Rivers Press, 1995.

Eliade, Mircea, and Couliano, Joan P., eds. *The HarperCollins Concise Guide to World Religions*. New York: HarperCollins, 2000.

Feldman, Christina, and Kornfield, Jack, eds. *Stories of the Spirit, Stories of the Heart: Parables of the Spiritual Path from Around the World*. San Francisco: HarperSanFrancisco, 1991.

Fowler, James W. *Stages of Faith: The Psychology of Human Development and the Quest for Meaning*. San Francisco: Harper & Row, 1981.

Fox, Matthew. *Creation Spirituality: Liberating Gifts for the Peoples of the Earth*. San Francisco: HarperSanFrancisco, 1991.

———. *A New Reformation: Creation Spirituality and the Transformation of Christianity*. Rochester, VT: Inner Traditions, 2006.

———, ed. *Hildegard of Bingen's Book of Divine Works*. Santa Fe, NM: Bear & Co., 1987.

Gaskell, G. A. *Dictionary of All Scriptures and Myths*. New York: Avenel Books, 1981.

Gaster, Theodor H. *The Dead Sea Scriptures*. New York: Anchor Books, 1976.

Goswami, Amit. *The Self-Aware Universe: How Consciousness Creates the Material World*. New York: Putnam, 1995.

Griffiths, Bede. *Universal Wisdom: A Journey Through the Sacred Wisdom of the World*. San Francisco: HarperSanFrancisco, 1994.

Gyatso, Tenzin. *Ethics for the New Millennium*. New York: Riverhead, 2001.

Harvey, Andrew. *The Essential Mystics: The Soul's Journey into Truth*. San Francisco: HarperSanFrancisco, 1996.

———. *Teachings of Rumi*. Boston: Shambhala, 1999.

———. *Light Upon Light: Inspirations from Rumi*. Berkeley, CA: North Atlantic Books, 1996.

————, and Baring, Anne. *The Divine Feminine: Exploring the Feminine Face of God Around the World*. Berkeley, CA: Conari, 1996.

Helminski, Camille Adams, Helminski, Kabir. *Jewels of Remembrance: A Daybook of Spiritual Guidance Containing 365 Selections from the Wisdom of Mevlana Jalaluddin*. Shambhala, 2000.

Helminski, Kabir. *The Knowing Heart: A Sufi Path of Transformation*. Boston and London: Shambhala, 1999.

Helminski, Camille Adams. *Rumi Daylight: A Daybook of Spiritual Guidance*. Boston and London: Shambhala, 1999.

Holl, Adolf. Trans. by John Cullen. *The Left Hand of God: A Biography of the Holy Spirit*. New York: Doubleday, 1998.

————. *The Last Christian: A Biography of Francis of Assisi*. Garden City, NY: Doubleday, 1980.

Holtz, Barry W., ed. *Back to the Source: Reading the Classic Jewish Texts*. New York: Summit Books, 1984.

Horsley, Richard A., with Hanson, John S. *Bandits, Prophets, and Messiahs: Popular Movements at the Time of Jesus*. San Francisco: Harper & Row, 1973.

Isaacson, Sara. *Jewish Spirituality*. London: Thorsons, 1999.

James, William. *Varieties of Religious Experience*. New York: Modern Library, 1999.

Jung, C.G. *The Undiscovered Self*. Princeton, NJ: Bollingen (Princeton University Press), 1990.

Khan, Hazrat Inayat. *The Heart of Sufism: Essential Writings of Hazrat Inayat Khan*. Boston: Shambhala, 1999.

Kidd, Sue Monk. *The Dance of the Dissident Daughter: A Woman's Journey from Christian Tradition to the Sacred Feminine*. San Francisco: HarperSanFrancisco, 1996.

Küng, Hans. *Great Christian Thinkers*. New York: Continuum, 1995.

Lawrence, Brother. *The Practice of the Presence of God*. Translated by Sister Mary David, S.S.N.D. Westminster, MD: The Newman Book Shop, 1945.

Lawrence, Brother. *Conversations and Letters of Brother Lawrence*. Oxford, UK: One World Publications, 1993.

LeShan, Lawrence, Ph.D. *The Medium, the Mystic, and the Physicist*. New York: Penguin, 1974.

Lesser, Elizabeth. *The New American Spirituality: A Seeker's Guide*. New York: Random House, 1999.

Lipton, Bruce, Ph.D. *The Biology of Belief: Unleashing the Power of Consciousness, Matter, and Miracles*. Santa Rosa, CA: Mountain of Love/ Elite, 2005.

Marty, Martin E. *A Short History of Christianity*. Philadelphia: Fortress Press, 1987.

Meyer, Marvin, trans. *The Gospel of Thomas: The Hidden Sayings of Jesus*. San Francisco: HarperSanFrancisco, 1992.

Miller, John, and Kenedi, Aaron, eds. *God's Breath: Sacred Scriptures of the World*. New York: Marlowe, 2000.

Miller, Robert J., ed. *The Complete Gospels: Annotated Scholars Version*. San Francisco: HarperSanFrancisco, 1994.

Needleman, Jacob. *Lost Christianity: A Journey of Rediscovery to the Center of Christian Experience*. Garden City, NY: Doubleday, 1980.

O'Brien, Elmer. *Varieties of Mystic Experience*. New York: The New American Library, 1965.

Pagels, Elaine. *Adam, Eve, and the Serpent*. New York: Random House, 1988.

———. *The Gnostic Gospels*. New York: Vintage Books, 1981.

Perry, Whitall N. *A Treasury of Traditional Wisdom*. New York: Simon & Schuster, 1971.

Pink, Arthur W. *The Holy Spirit*. Grand Rapids, MI: Baker Book House, 1974.

Powers, John. *Introduction to Tibetan Buddhism*. Ithaca, NY: Snow Lion Publications, 1995.

Rose, Steven, ed. *From Brains to Consciousness? Essays on the New Sciences of the Mind*. Princeton, NJ: Princeton University Press, 1998.

Roth, Ron, Ph.D., with Occhiogrosso, Peter. *Holy Spirit: The Boundless Energy of God*. Carlsbad, CA: Hay House, 2000.

Saint Thérèse of Lisieux. *Story of a Soul: The Autobiography of St. Thérèse of Lisieux*. Washington, DC: ICS Publications, 1999.

Satchidananda, Sri Swami. *The Golden Present*. Buckingham, VA: Integral Yoga Publications, 1987.

———. *The Yoga Sutras of Patanjali*. Yogaville, VA: Integral Yoga Publications, 1990.

Schonfield, Hugh. *Essene Odyssey: The Mystery of the True Teacher and the Essene Impact on the Shaping of Human Destiny*. Rockport, MA: Element Books, 1993.

Smith, Huston, Ph.D. *The Religions of Man*. New York: Harper & Row, 1958.

Spearing, Elizabeth, et al., trans. *Medieval Writings on Female Spirituality*. New York: Penguin, 2002.

Tart, Charles T., Ph.D. *Body, Mind, Spirit: Exploring the Parapsychology of Spirituality*. Charlottesville, VA: Hampton Roads, 1997.

———. *Waking Up: Overcoming the Obstacles to Human Potential*. Boston: Shambhala, 1986.

Thurman, Howard. *The Creative Encounter*. New York: Harper & Brothers, 1954.

Van Dusen, Henry P. *Spirit, Son and Father: Christian Faith in the Light of the Holy Spirit*. New York: Scribner, 1958.

Wach, Joachim. *Types of Religious Experience, Christian and Non-Christian*. Chicago: University of Chicago Press, 1972.

Weatherhead, Leslie D. *The Christian Agnostic*. Nashville, TN: Abingdon Press, 1965.

Weiner, Herbert. *9 1/2 Mystics: The Kabbala Today*. New York: Macmillan, 1992.

Welburn, Andrew. *The Beginnings of Christianity: Essene Mystery, Gnostic Revelation, and the Christian Vision*. Edinburgh: Floris Books, 2004.

Wilber, Ken. *The Marriage of Sense and Soul: Integrating Science and Religion*. New York: Broadway Books, 1998.

———. *Quantum Questions: Mystical Writings of the World's Great Physicists*. Boston: Shambhala, 2001.

———. *The Eye of Spirit: An Integral Vision for a World Gone Slightly Mad*. Boston: Shambhala, 2001.

———. *The Essential Ken Wilber: An Introductory Reader*. Boston: Shambhala, 1998.

———. *A Sociable God: Toward a New Understanding of Religion*. Boston: Shambhala, 2001.

Wise, Michael, Abegg, Jr., Martin, and Cook, Edward, trans. *The Dead Sea Scrolls: A New Translation*. San Francisco: HarperSanFrancisco, 1996.

Wolf, Fred Alan, Ph.D. *The Spiritual Universe: How Quantum Physics Proves the Existence of the Soul*. New York: Simon & Schuster, 1996.

———. *Mind into Matter: A New Alchemy of Science and Spirit*. Portsmouth, NH: Moment Point Press, 2001.

Wolpe, David J. *Why Be Jewish?* New York: Henry Holt, 1995.

Zaleski, Philip, and Kaufman, Paul. *Gifts of the Spirit: Living the Wisdom of the Great Religious Traditions*. New York: HarperCollins, 1998.

Index